Recreation Handb
for Camp, Conference
and Community

Recreation Handbook for Camp, Conference and Community

Second Edition

ROGER E. BARROWS

McFarland & Company, Inc., Publishers
Jefferson, North Carolina, and London

LIBRARY OF CONGRESS CATALOGUING-IN-PUBLICATION DATA

Barrows, Roger E., 1955–
    Recreation handbook for camp, conference and community /
Roger E. Barrows. — 2nd ed.
        p.   cm.
    Includes bibliographical references and index.

    ISBN 978-0-7864-4280-5
    softcover : 50# alkaline paper ∞

    1. Group games.   2. Indoor games.   3. Youth — Recreation.
4. Recreation leadership.   I. Title.
GV1203.B32   2010
790.1'922 — dc22   2009049622

British Library cataloguing data are available

Front cover ©2010 Shutterstock

Manufactured in the United States of America

McFarland & Company, Inc., Publishers
    Box 611, Jefferson, North Carolina 28640
    www.mcfarlandpub.com

To my mother
and
in memory of my father

Contents

Preface

This book aims to help youth leaders engage young people in fun and wholesome recreation. It is intended for use by camp counselors, religious directors, scout and 4-H leaders, club advisors, parents, and others who work with youth between the approximate ages of 8 and 18.

Recreation is vital to good living. It not only refreshes body, mind, and spirit from the daily demands of life, it also draws us into the creation and "re-creation" of self. Play fosters confidence, courage, determination, fairness, mental and physical agility — and it enhances both a cooperative and a competitive spirit. The Duke of Wellington proclaimed that "the battle of Waterloo was won on the playing fields of Eton." In a loose paraphrase, the leaders of tomorrow are training on the playing fields of today.

Bearing these thoughts in mind, I have written this book with my chief aim simply to provide ideas of fun and fellowship. The role of the youth leader can be a demanding one, and — like parenthood — the position usually comes without any training, except the experiences of one's own youth. The college student employed as summer camp counselor, the parent-turned-scout leader, the youth center volunteer, and the church or temple youth advisor can benefit from ample ideas herein for games, rainy-day activities, campfires, meditations, skits, stories, and songs.

As a resource, this book offers a wealth of ideas; as a leader, you make the ideas come alive. Your energy and enthusiasm, your warmth and caring, and your sense of fair play and humor strongly influence the attitudes of the young people you lead. As you play, sing, and tell stories with them, you may have the pleasure of developing a rich rapport with your kids. Their interests and abilities will be your guide as you select, borrow, and adapt activities from this book. The kids will be further resources, each brimming with their own stories, songs, games, and things to do.

This book emerged from my personal experiences working with many hundreds of young people, to whom I am grateful for enriching my life. I owe tribute to my father for any number of reasons, including his sermons,

1

a well into which I dipped for the chapter on worship and devotion. I am indebted to Jim and Nancy Sandahl, from whom I learned the essentials of camp counseling and teaching, and to my family, for their eternal patience and encouragement. To Lisa and Alexis, thank you for granting me time away from our valuable recreation time to work on this second edition.

Roger E. Barrows
January 2010

Chapter 1

Icebreakers and Teambuilders

ICEBREAKERS AND MIXERS

Introductions

To relieve the anxiety commonly aroused when people are asked to introduce themselves in front of a group of total strangers, let them instead introduce someone sitting next to them. Seat the group in a circle, perhaps around a campfire, and allow them a few minutes to interview the person on their left. Then, as leader, you begin the introductions by presenting the person on your left; that person then introduces the person on his left, and so on around the circle until all introductions have been made.

For a sure-fire way to learn names, each person introduces himself by giving his name and describing his favorite place (or favorite movie or proudest accomplishment, etc.). Going around the circle, each person names all those already introduced and then introduces himself. This continues around the circle so that the last person has to repeat everyone's name before introducing himself. To avoid tedium, it's best to use this with small groups only. Variation: Players each choose an animal whose initial letter is the same as the initial letter of their first name and introduce themselves using both names (e.g., Buffalo Bill, Foxy Felicia, Tiger Ted, and Mary Mouse). Instead, they could choose an adjective that describes them (e.g., Crazy Cathy, Tough Tom, Petite Paula, and Generous George).

Bumpety-Bump-Bump-Bump

Younger kids will enjoy this lively way to learn new names. The leader points to someone and shouts, "Right (or left), bumpety-bump-bump-bump!" The player pointed to must give the name of the person seated at his right (or left, as the case may be) before the leader finishes speaking. If unsuccessful, he becomes the new leader.

Birthday Groups

Sociologists claim that getting people to work in teams is one of the best ways to develop a spirit of camaraderie. Get kids working together in game activities as soon as possible. One such team activity for younger kids begins with grouping them according to the month in which they were born; each group then plans and performs a simple presentation which illustrates a holiday or typical occurrence of their birth month. The rest of the groups try to guess what month is being represented.

Who Are You?

In a circle, participants answer questions about themselves by using the letters of their first name or nickname as the initial letters of their response. If the first question is, "How would you describe yourself?" Tess might answer, "I'm Tess, and I'm Talkative, Exciting, Smart, and Sassy." Ron might introduce himself by saying, "I'm Ron, and I'm a Really Obnoxious Nut." (Participants like Gwendolyn and Thaddeus will be thankful their names can be shortened.)

Answers are bound to become more creative and more amusing as each player takes a turn.

Continue around the circle more times by asking other questions, always using the same initials for the responses: What's your favorite activity? What are your career goals? What do you like to do on a date? What advice can you give us?

Who Am I?

Upon arriving, each participant is pinned on the back with the name of a famous person — names like Napoleon, Julia Roberts, Charlie Chaplin, Susan B. Anthony, Abraham Lincoln, Harriet Tubman, Neil Armstrong, and Joan of Arc. While participants mingle, they attempt to determine their identity by asking questions to the people they meet: Am I a political figure? Am I alive today? Am I a singer? Did I invent something?

Alternatively, participants offer each other hints about their identity: "You sure are a tall man." "Have you flown anywhere recently?" "I see you left today without your cane and black hat."

Variations: Assign animals instead of famous people, and players must try to guess what animal is taped on their back. Or ask each participant to list ten characteristics of a type of animal and tape the list to their back; they then mingle and attempt to identify the type of animal for each person in the group.

Find Your Other Half

Collect a number of famous quotes and cut them in half. Participants are to find the person who has the other half of their quotation. This activity forms partners in preparation for the next activity. Sample quotations: "Don't count your chickens before they hatch," "A penny saved is a penny earned," "Better to be safe than sorry," and "You can lead a horse to water, but you can't make him drink." Church groups could use Bible quotations.

Older participants could be provided historical or literary quotations: "Ask not what your country can do for you; ask what you can do for your country", "Whose woods these are, I think I know; his house is in the village though." Variations: one person has a joke and the other has the punchline; one person has the first half of a short poem and the other has the second half; each person has half of an object cut from construction paper (in the shape of a leaf, an animal, or some other nature shape) and searches for his other half without speaking; in a similar way, players match the shapes of animals to the tracks they make or authors to their books or athletes to their teams.

Nametag Search

Nametags are printed for each participant, but then are handed out randomly so that every person receives someone else's nametag. Everyone is to search for the person whose nametag they have and try to find their own nametag. When they do, they should introduce themselves. This mixer causes each person to meet at least two other people: the person to whom and from whom each nametag is given.

Five Card Draw

Everyone receives a playing card and is told to form groups of five people, whereupon they are to introduce themselves to the rest of their group.

After a few minutes, the group with the best poker hand wins a prize, perhaps a deck of cards for each of them. Now, groups have been formed in preparation for the next activity. Variation: Participants are to find and meet the owners of the three number or face cards which match theirs (kings, tens, aces, etc.). This arranges participants in groups of four.

Barnyard Sounds

This one's as fun for the leaders to watch as for the participants to do. Whisper the name of an animal to each participant. Without using words, participants are to find and join with the other members of their animal family — by making the sound of the animal. By the end of this activity, all cows will be together, as will all chickens, ducks, roosters, donkeys, pigs, etc. Participants are then grouped for the next activity.

Two Truths and a Lie

After everyone pairs up, partners tell each other three things about themselves: two truths and a lie. When the entire group gets back together, participants introduce their partners, mentioning the three things. The group must try to decide which is the lie. This may not be as easy as it seems, for fact is often stranger than fiction.

M & M Mixer

Pass a bag of M & M's around the circle, everyone taking three of different colors. Then, participants tell the group information about themselves, depending on which colors they selected. For example: green — favorite movie; blue — favorite TV show; yellow — favorite music; red — ideal person of the opposite sex; light brown — number of children they hope to have; dark brown — career goals.

There's Plenty for Everyone

Pass a bowl of candy (or a roll of toilet paper) around the circle, telling everyone, "There's plenty for everyone; take as much as you think you'll need."

No one knows yet what they might need it for, so some people may take little and others a lot. Then, go around the circle so that all participants tell as many things about themselves as pieces of candy (or sheets of toilet paper) they took.

Human Scavenger Hunt

Give each person a list like the one which follows and set the group free to mingle, getting signatures of individuals who fit the specified categories. The first player to fill his or her sheet with signatures is winner.

Find someone in the group who ...

wears contact lenses _____   has the same shoe size _____

is left-handed _____   has the same birth month _____

plays the guitar _____   is an only child _____

is wearing a watch _____   has the same zodiac sign _____

has freckles _____   wears a size 11 shoe _____

likes spinach _____   has a mom who's a teacher _____

is over six feet tall _____   can name Santa's 8 reindeer _____

has an unusual pet _____   can touch tongue to nose _____

wears braces _____   is wearing red socks _____

Consider creating a scavenger hunt specific to the focus of your organization and the interests of your participants. For a musical group, you could include "has perfect pitch," "knows what a demisemiquaver is," etc. For an outdoors group, consider "has held a snake," "has a pet that swims or flies," etc. For an athletic group, try "has the personalized signature of a famous athlete," "can name the team which won the 2000 World Series," etc.

Human Bingo

This is a variation of the previous game. Arrange the categories on a bingo-type grid of nine, sixteen, or twenty-five squares. Signatures are written in each box. When the signatures have been obtained, play bingo by pulling from a hat the names of the participants. When each name is called, players mark an X through that name if it appears on their card. The first player who has a row of X's — horizontally, vertically, or diagonally — wins a prize, perhaps several pieces of candy, some of which he or she must give to the players whose names appear on the row marked out. Remembering and matching each name with a face is a game in itself.

Map Hunt

People normally bond together when in pursuit of a common goal. A good way to establish these bonds while also becoming familiar with the new environment of campgrounds or conference center is to distribute maps with a list of questions which each team seeks to answer. For example,

1. How many steps lead up to the front porch of the dining hall?
2. What color is the banner on the head counselors' cabin?
3. What words are inscribed over the door of the infirmary?
4. What initials are etched into the tree at the top of the stairway leading to the beach?
5. What are the colors of the rings of the archery target from center outwards?

It is wise to set a time when all teams meet back at the starting point. The team with the most correct answers might win a prize.

Ten Fingers

Join everyone in a circle and ask them to hold up all ten fingers; then, tell them something about yourself. If you say, "I was born in the United States," all participants who were not born in the United States put one finger down; all those who, like you, were born in the U.S., keep their fingers up. The next person in the circle reveals something like "My favorite ice cream is strawberry" or "I have never traveled to Hawaii." Those who do not share the trait, put one finger down. Continue around the circle with participants telling a fact about themselves until someone has no fingers remaining up. The person with the most fingers up probably has a lot in common with members of the group.

Cross the Circle

This icebreaker is something like musical chairs, because it leaves someone standing. You stand in the center of the circle and say, "Cross the circle if you ___," filling in the blank with something which you yourself have done or can do. Immediately, all participants who could say the same thing about themselves get up and cross to the other side of the circle to claim a seat of someone else who has crossed the circle. In the meantime, you quickly grab a vacated seat, leaving someone standing. That person must then say, "Cross the circle if you ___," and then fill in the blank with something he or she has done or can do. For example, "Cross the circle if you have been to a live concert" or "Cross the circle if you can wiggle your ears." Participants who "cross the circle" may not return to the seat they just vacated, or to the seats on either side of their vacated seat. Variation: Instead of crossing the circle, participants who fit the description which the leader calls out simply stand if they are sitting or sit if they are standing.

Speed Meeting

Create an inner circle and an outer circle, each with the same number of participants, so that each individual on the inner circle is facing someone on the outer circle. Inspired by "speed dating" of the first decade of the twenty-first century, this activity rotates partners for a timed getting-acquainted period. Each pair has two minutes to get to know each other. When the time is up, rotate one of the circles so that each member faces a new partner. With each rotation, specify a different topic that each pair must discuss: What is your favorite book or movie? If you could meet one person from history, who would it be? What are you passionate about? If you could travel anywhere in the world, where would you go? Besides your parents, who has had the most influence on your life?

What's in Common?

Without explaining why, pick out certain individuals to stand up. Those you select should have something in common: they might all be wearing red shirts, or all sport a logo on their shirts, or all be wearing Nike footwear, or all be blondes. The group must try to figure out what they have in common.

Silent Interview

This icebreaker could follow an activity that divides the group into pairs. After the partners introduce each other, instruct them to remain silent as they each tell three things about themselves to their partner. They may not talk, so instead they must mime that they were #1 on their swim team or that they have a pet cocker spaniel. Once the silent introductions are over, each person introduces his partner to the rest of the group — using words.

TRUST ACTIVITIES

One aim of the youth leader is to develop camaraderie, team spirit, and trust among his or her group of young people. Trust activities aim to achieve this sense of mutual reliance and support, but it is important that the group has attained a level of comfort with each other before beginning these activities. Icebreakers, mixers, and time for gaining some familiarity will afford a basic sense of security which will serve as a foundation for developing the deeper trust which these activities aim to establish. Without a basic level of security in a group, individuals may refuse to participate in trust activities or may be very cautious of developing trust.

All trust activities require a level of maturity among the participants. Some young people are not ready to take seriously the trust which these activities can engender.

Trust Walk

This is the most basic of trust activities. The group pairs off, one partner being blindfolded and the other serving as guide. A course is established, perhaps on an open field with obstacles placed along the way, or in a wooded area that has been scouted out ahead of time and judged safe. Using only verbal instructions and without touching, the guide directs her blindfolded partner around, under, or over obstacles, carefully guarding him from stumps, branches, and gullies. She is responsible for his safety. After the course is completed, the partners switch roles.

It is a good idea to debrief after this activity: How did you feel while blindfolded? How did it feel to be the guide? What did you learn in each role?

Variation: Another type of trust walk obstacle course is a mine field, in which mines might be marked by masking tape located at various places on the floor or ground. Each time the blindfolded individual steps on tape, a pot might be struck with a ladle to indicate an explosion. The guide's role is to use verbal directions to keep her partner safe from "explosions."

Another variation: After half of the team is blindfolded, each of the sighted guides randomly chooses a partner. In this variation, only the blindfolded player may speak while holding onto the arm of the guide, who leads him. Before the blindfolds are removed, the guides move away so that they remain anonymous. After everyone has had a chance to be blindfolded, each person tries to guess who his guide was and explain why. This can lead to very positive observations about each guide's leadership style.

Car Ride

This is yet another variation of the trust walk. The blindfolded partner is the car, with bumpers (hands) projecting in front. The sighted partner is the driver, who holds onto the shoulders of the car and guides him through the traffic of other cars and drivers. The aim is to move throughout the designated area without hitting another car or driver. Drivers' instructions to the cars can include "yellow light," "stop sign ahead," "move into the right lane," etc.

Flying Carpet

One person stands erect with hands crossed over chest and eyes closed. The other members of the team lift him up over their heads and fly him around as though on a magic carpet before returning him gently to earth.

People Pass

Two rows of people lie down on the grass, head to head, with about one foot of grass between their heads. They use their hands raised above them to carry someone down the line, continuing until everyone has been passed down. A leader should be stationed at each end of the line to help each person get on and off the people pass.

Ambulance

One person functions as the "injured," while two others clasp their hands together and serve as the ambulance, carrying the injured through an obstacle course to the "hospital." The objective is for a sense of trust to develop among the teams of participants.

Blind Guide

One person is blindfolded and two ropes are tied around his waist, each rope held by a guide. Without talking, the guides use the ropes to move the blindfolded walker through an obstacle course.

Circle Fall

Everyone gets in a small, close circle, except for one individual who is in the center. That person stands erect, closes her eyes, and falls back, trusting the circle to catch her. They then push her to fall to the other side of the circle, and this continues until time is called for another person to enter the center. This can also be done with partners, each partner catching his falling companion.

Falling Circle

Everyone joins together in a circle and holds hands. Number off 1-2-1-2-etc. All of the 1's fall backward, while all of the 2's fall forward, never letting go of hands.

TEAMBUILDING ACTIVITIES:
INITIATIVE OR CHALLENGE GAMES

Initiative or Challenge Games are team activities which encourage participants to work cooperatively, creatively, and analytically to solve a problem. Each game is a challenge in which there is no single right answer; the fun lies in working together to find a solution. Initiative Games may be set up at different stations; when a team rotates to a new station, the leader manning it explains the challenge and the restrictions in solving it. The leader then offers no advice, allowing the team members to work together for a solution. Cooperation and initiative are the key elements in these games, though a competitive spirit may be introduced by comparing each team's time in completing a given task.

An excellent activity to follow any of these initiative or teambuilding games is a debriefing session in which team members discuss what happened and what they learned from the experience. How well did they communicate? How did they work as a team? What did they do especially well? What could they have done better? What did they learn about each other? How did they grow as a group?

Spider Web

Tie a web of ropes — some taut, some loose — between several trees. The entire team must cross the web without anyone touching the ground.

Composite Creature

Team members create a creature that, once formed, must move ten feet forward. Stipulations: all participants must become part of the creature; everyone must be touching someone else; one-third of the participants' legs and one-fourth of their hands may touch the ground. This may be done as a race between two or more creature-teams.

Radioactive Field

The entire team must cross a "radioactive field," stepping only on the five safe footpads (pieces of rubber, carpet, or wood) supplied to them. Variation: Several stumps one foot high and seven feet apart are set upright. Team is given two eight-foot boards. The team must cross the field without any person or board touching the ground. If anyone touches the ground, the entire team must begin again.

Touch the Top

Everyone must touch the top of a high pole set in the ground (e.g., football goal post), being supplied only with 20 feet of rope and an eight-foot board.

Cross the Swamp

A 50-foot length of the field is marked off as the swamp. The team is supplied with three eight-foot boards, which must be brought across the swamp with them, thereby not leaving a trail.

Electric Fence

An "electrified" rope is tied between two trees. The entire team must cross over the fence without touching the rope or the trees, using the only item provided: an eight-foot long pole.

Reach for the Sky

The team tries to make a mark, using chalk or tape, as high as possible on a wall or tree, without climbing it.

Barnyard Hunt

This is a teambuilding competition in which teams compete to collect the most items (small items like elbow macaroni or toothpicks work well). Each team selects a captain and is given the name of an animal. All members of the team hunt for the items, but only the captain may actually touch and collect them. Team members must communicate to their captain without using words; instead, they must make the sound of their team's animal.

Blindfolded Zoo

Whisper the name of an animal into each blindfolded player's ear. Using only the sounds of the animals, the players must line up from tallest to shortest. No words may be used.

Maze

Blindfold team members and lead them to the entrance of a maze made of rope. The entire team must find its way out. Talking *is* allowed.

Blind Hike

The team begins at a starting point where they are shown their destination — some landmark that is visible from the beginning of the course. They are given a few minutes to plan their strategy for a blind hike to the destination, and then they are blindfolded and set on their way. Youth leaders should assure that they do not run into anything or damage wildlife.

Build a Tent

All team members except one are blindfolded. The blindfolded players must build a tent following the instructions of the sighted player, who may have no physical contact with the tent or the players.

Group Directions

This activity works best with a small team of five to eight individuals. All of the team members stand behind a line, except for two individuals. One of these is blindfolded and stands some distance from the line; he is directed not to talk. The other is situated halfway between the blindfolded person and the rest of the team; she is the only person permitted to speak, but she must face the team during the entire game. Team members must communicate to her solely by miming (they may speak no words), and then she must instruct the blindfolded person by words — though she cannot see what he is doing behind her. The object is for everyone to work together to communicate and carry out the instructions. After everyone is in place, written instructions are given to the miming members and several items are set up near the blindfolded person. The instructions might be, "Walk to the chair, put on the wig that is lying on the seat, sit down, pour some water into the plastic cup, and drink it."

The Log

Everyone on the team at the same time balances on a log which is lying on the ground. Then, they are instructed to do several squats without falling off. Next, they should line up on the log by height or birth date without stepping off of the log.

The Rock

Get all team members on top of a large rock that is in the water (lake, river, or ocean). Alternatively, all members must try to fit on top of a blanket without any body parts touching the ground. To make this more complicated, once they are all on the blanket, tell them that the next instructions are pinned to the underside of the blanket. They must read and follow the directions without anyone getting off the blanket. The instructions may simply be the rules to the next challenge.

FURTHER RESOURCES

Bordessa, Kris. *Team Challenges: 170+ Group Activities to Build Cooperation, Communication, and Creativity.* Brookline, MA: Zephyr Press, 2005.

LeFevre, Dale N. *Best New Games: 77 Games and 7 Trust Activities for All Ages and Abilities.* Champaign, IL: Human Kinetics Publishers, 2001.

Chapter 2

Games and Activities

Games are fun.
Games draw people together.
Games give people a chance to know each other.
Games open lines of communication.
Games develop physical, psychological and social skills.
Games improve strategic thinking.
Games foster creativity.
Games allow children to experience some of the struggles
and vicissitudes of life in a fun way, without the very real
consequences of real life.
Games are fun.
Play on!

INDOOR, RAINY DAY, AND CAMPFIRE GAMES

In My Suitcase

This game is a lot of fun as long as those who catch on early keep the key to themselves. Start by saying, "I am going on a trip, and in my suitcase I am taking a(n) _____." Whatever word you use to fill in the blank should begin with the initial of your first name. Going around the circle, each per-

16

son repeats that statement, filling in the blank with a word. You, as leader, give permission to take that object if it begins with the same letter as the individual's initial; otherwise, you deny permission. The game may continue several times around the circle before most everyone has figured out "the catch" by careful listening to all the accepted items.

For greater difficulty, the catch could be the initials of both first and last names. If, for example, your initials are R. B., "roast beef," "red butterflies," and "razor blades" would be the types of items given.

There are several variations to "In My Suitcase." One is to start by saying "Billy Miller likes swimming, but he does not like diving" or "Billy Miller likes cheeseburgers, but he does not like hamburgers." Going around the circle, each person then guesses an item Billy Miller likes and one that he does not like. The catch here is that Billy Miller likes anything that has double letters and dislikes anything that does not. The name Molly Miller could be substituted for Billy Miller.

Another variation starts, "My mother doesn't like tea, but she likes *(coffee)*." The catch is that she doesn't like anything that has the letter T in it. A similar variation begins, "Name something to eat, but remember that the cook doesn't like peas." Here, the catch is that any word that has the letter p in it is rejected.

Buzz

Another good circle game is "Buzz," a simple counting game with a twist. The leader begins the counting by saying "1," the next person "2," the next "3," and so forth around the circle. The challenge is that every number that has a "7" in it or that is a multiple of 7 must be replaced by the word "buzz." Therefore, the counting would go like this: 1, 2, 3, 4, 5, 6, buzz, 8, 9, 10, 11, 12, 13, buzz, 15, 16, buzz, 18, etc. "77" would be "buzz-buzz." If a person says a number when he should say "buzz" or says "buzz" when he should say a number, that person is out. The game continues around the circle until only one or two players remain. Pick up the pace of the counting to make the game even more exciting.

Twenty Questions

Here's an old game that is still loads of fun. Someone who is "*it*" thinks of a familiar person, place, or thing. By asking questions which can be answered with only a "yes" or a "no," the rest of the group must try to discover what *it* is thinking of. Only twenty questions are permitted, which may be shouted at random or asked in order around the circle. The game is customarily played by having *it* state at the beginning whether his object is animal, plant, or mineral. Usually the group has only three chances to guess what the object is. Whoever correctly guesses then becomes *it*.

Try Twenty Questions "French-Style" (or so I'm told): what *it* is thinking of is "the person to your right."

Rhythm (or Slap-Clap-Snap)

This is yet another circle game, great for a rainy day or free-time activity. Players count off, each getting a number in consecutive order. In unison, following Player #1's lead, players slap their hands twice on their knees, then clap their hands together twice, and then snap their fingers twice (first the fingers of the left hand, then the fingers of the right). Assume that you are Player #1. As you snap the fingers of your left hand, you call out your number (1), and as you snap the fingers of your right hand, you call out someone else's number (say, 6). Without breaking the rhythm, everyone slaps their knees, claps their hands, and snaps; Player #6 must then call out his number during the first snap and another number during the second snap. This continues until a player breaks the rhythm or calls out a wrong number. The player who makes the mistake must then become the last person in the circle (say, 9), so that Player #9 becomes #8, 8 becomes 7, and 7 becomes 6. The game continues. If Player #1 makes a mistake, he becomes #9 and *everybody* moves up so that #2 now becomes #1, the new leader. This, of course, confuses matters because now everyone has a new number. The object of the game is to get the leader to move to the end of the circle, while each leader tries to stay in #1 position as long as possible. As the group gets better, try speeding up the rhythm. Even with a lot of concentration, it's easy to get messed up, and that's what makes this game so much fun.

Charades

One summer when I was counselor to a cabin of junior high boys, they wanted to play charades at every campfire. They liked the spotlight, as well as the imagination and guesswork involved. It's an activity enjoyed by all ages.

Charades involves communicating without words — using only gestures and actions. This rule must be strictly adhered to: no talking by the person who is *it*. *It* thinks of (or draws from a hat) the title of a book, movie, play, song, or television series, which he must try to convey to the group through gestures. The members of the audience, who are allowed to speak at will, try to figure out the title which the person who is *it* has in mind. *It* begins by letting the group know under which category his title fits. For the title of a book, hold open the palms of the hands as if holding a book; for a movie, portray a camera man running a moving picture camera; for a play, pose as an actor; for a song, pretend to sing, mouth open, while holding a songbook; for a TV series, draw a rectangle in the air (representing a TV screen).

It indicates the number of words in the title by raising that many fingers. Then he acts out or makes gestures to describe a certain word or syllable. While he is making gestures, the audience interprets the actions out loud, makes guesses, and asks questions. By putting two fingers behind his ear as if listening attentively, *it* can show that the word sounds like another word which he then acts out. By putting his index finger and thumb close together, he can show that a word is small. If someone guesses a word or syllable correctly, *it* points to that person to indicate that he or she is correct and then proceeds to another word or syllable. The first person who guesses the full title which *it* is thinking of then becomes *it*, taking center stage to act out his own title.

Pantomime

Charades are a form of pantomime in which the mime silently acts out the words or syllables of a title. Another form of pantomime involves acting or miming something in its entirety, such as a nursery rhyme, a parable, or a proverb. Consider "a bird in the hand is worth two in the bush." The mime might look into the sky as if searching for something. Then, glancing to the ground, he appears to spot what he was looking for, sneaks up on it, and catches it, smiling at his success. But then he notices something else with interest, displays two fingers to the audience, and allows what he has in his hand to escape. He sneaks up on his new discovery, but stops, looking disgusted, as his eyes move towards the sky.

Pantomime is an art which relies on exaggeration of expression and gesture. It draws upon one's imagination and powers of expression. Some well-known proverbs:

1. Don't cry over spilt milk.
2. The early bird catches the worm.
3. Beggars can't be choosers.
4. You can lead a horse to water, but you can't make him drink.
5. Practice makes perfect.

Mimic

One person who is *it* leaves the circle while a leader is chosen from the members of the circle. *It* returns to the circle where all the participants are doing an identical action such as clapping hands, bouncing a knee, and rubbing stomachs. The leader changes the action when *it* is not looking in his direction, and everyone else immediately performs the leader's action. *It* must determine who the leader is. It's not as easy as it may sound!

How, When, Where?

Here, one player is sent away while the other participants decide on something that is *it*. The player then returns and can ask anyone only three questions: "How do you like it?" "Where do you like it?" and "When do you like it?" These questions must be answered honestly so that the player can attempt to deduce what *it* is.

It

This is a fun circle game. One or more players are sent away, while the rest of the participants are informed that *it* is the person to the right. The other players return and have to guess what *it* is by going around the circle and asking questions that can be answered with only "yes" or "no." It gets real confusing until they finally realize (or are told) that *it* is the person to the right of whomever is being questioned!

Murder

Distribute one playing card (or stick or leaf with one of them marked) to each person in the circle. The person with the ace of spades or the marked stick is the "murderer." He "murders" someone in the circle by winking at that person when he thinks no one else is looking in his direction. The victim slumps down or announces that he or she has been killed and moves out of the circle. Game continues until someone "living" successfully detects the identity of the murderer.

Ghosts

The first player calls out a letter of the alphabet. The next player provides another letter, and so forth around the circle. Each player aims to add a letter that can spell a word comprised of more than three letters. The first person who cannot add a letter to those already named to spell an acceptable English word loses the round; that player is "branded" with the letter G. Once someone receives all the letters of the word ghosts, he or she is out. Play continues for several rounds until only one player — the winner — remains.

Challenges can be made. If someone adds a letter that cannot ultimately lead to spelling a word, the next player may challenge. If the challenged player cannot think of a word using the letters given, he or she receives a letter of Ghosts. If the challenged player can name a word using all the letters given thus far, the challenger receives a letter.

For example, player 1 calls out S. Player 2 calls out T. 3: R. 4: O. 5: H. This last letter is challenged, and because the player cannot think of a word beginning with the letters stroh, he receives a letter. If player 5 says N and is challenged, he can name the word strong, and the challenger is assigned a letter of Ghosts against him. If players 6, 7, and 8 give the letters G, E, and R, and player 9 cannot add a letter to form a word, player 9 is assigned a letter of Ghosts.

What's Your Problem?

In a circle, one person explains and demonstrates a certain problem or ailment that he pretends to have and everyone in the circle imitates it. He may say his knee bounces up and down, whereupon his knee does just that and everyone in the circle follows suit. The next person might say he is unable to lower his left eyebrow, whereupon everyone keeps his left eyebrow raised, while at the same time the knee continues to bounce. Keep going around the circle, adding another ailment with each person. It's bound to be hilarious (and will look exceedingly strange to passersby).

Mock Debate

Divide your group in half and run a regular debate over a silly resolution to bring about wild persuasive arguments. For example, Resolved: That henceforth dogs should be called "cats" and cats should be called "zebras." Or, Resolved: That work should be outlawed.

Silent Movies

At one campfire, my campers (ages 9–11) wanted to do nothing but this. In fact, they started it, teaching me that the best activities are often spontaneous and camper-initiated. One kid mans a flashlight, flickering it on others who move about in slow motion, creating a visual effect similar to that of old black and white movies. If they get hooked, they are apt to work out an entire story using everyone in the group. (They are also apt to continue after lights-out!)

Rhyme Guess

The leader tells the group, "I am thinking of a word that rhymes with *(book)*." The players must guess what the word is without saying the word. They might venture:
Is it something you catch fish with?
"No," the leader says, "it is not a *hook*."
Do you use your eyes to do this?
"No, it is not *look*."
Is it someone who robs banks?
"Yes, it is *crook*."
The player who guesses then becomes *it*.

Ha

Form a circle. Solemnly and seriously, one person says, "Ha." The person next to him says, "Ha, ha." The next, "Ha, ha, ha." Anyone who really laughs is out. Or simply go around the circle to see how long it takes before people start laughing. This can be even more fun when someone's head is resting on someone else's stomach.

Keep from Laughing

Like "Ha," the object here is to hold back laughter in a unique and humorous situation. One person begins by touching some part of her neighbor's head, perhaps rubbing her nose, tapping her forehead, scratching her chin, or pulling her ear. That person then does something similar to her neighbor's face and so on around the circle, everyone trying not to laugh. Makes an interesting coed activity.

If You Love Me

Everyone sits in a circle, and the person who is *it* sits on someone's lap (or kneels, staring in his/her eyes) and says, "Honey, if you love me, then please, please smile." The person in the circle must respond, "Honey, I do love you, but I just can't smile," reciting this without cracking a smile. If he is successful, *it* tries this routine on someone else. If the person seated in the circle smiles, she becomes *it*.

I Like Everybody

It stands in the middle of a circle of seated players. *It* says, "I like everybody, especially those who (have blonde hair, are wearing sandals, are chewing gum, etc.)." Anyone who fits *it*'s description must get up and find another seat while *it* tries to sit in a vacated seat. Whoever remains standing becomes *it*.

Circle Game

Chairs are arranged in a circle and players take seats, leaving one vacant. A person who is *it* stands in the center and yells either "move right" or "move left." If "move right," the player who has the vacant seat to his right moves into it and all other players likewise move right. As they move, *it* attempts to sit in a vacated seat before one of the seated players does. If *it* gets a seat, the player whose seat he took becomes *it*.

Seat Exchange

Everyone sits in a circle and numbers off from one to the highest number playing. *It* stands blindfolded in the center and calls out two numbers. The players whose numbers are called run across the circle to exchange seats, while *it* tries to tag one of them or to take one of their seats. If she is successful, the person tagged becomes *it*. All players must remain within the circle.

Wink

This coeducational circle game usually begins with the girls seated in chairs formed in a circle, each with a boy standing behind her. One seat is vacant, and the boy behind it winks at a girl, who gets up and moves to the vacant seat — unless the boy behind holds her down by the shoulders quickly enough so that she can't get up. The sly winker will eventually draw a girl to his seat, leaving the boy with the vacated seat as the winker. Switch places and have the boys seated with the girls behind.

Frozen

Young kids especially love this one. The leader tells everyone to "freeze," and everyone sits absolutely still. Who can remain frozen (unmoving) the longest? When the leader sees someone move, that person is out. She can assist the leader in spotting other people who move. Of course, movement due to the essential act of breathing is allowed.

Syllables

Have two or three people leave the group. While they are gone, the remaining participants choose a word of several syllables, such as *xylophone*. Divide the participants into groups equal to the number of syllables in the word (in this case, 3) and give each group one of the syllables. After the other players return, all of the groups shout the syllable in unison, leaving the returning players to figure out what the word is.

Group Sneeze

Divide the group into three sections, each section given a different sneezing sound: "Ka-hishi," "Ka-hashi," "Ka-hoshoo." At the given signal, everyone sneezes at once.

Rainstorm

In this activity, sound effects are created to imitate a passing storm. As leader, you begin each effect, which is then copied in turn around the circle. Start by rubbing your hands together (the wind); as more and more members of the circle do the same, the wind grows stronger. Then snap your fingers (raindrops), and, in turn, members of the circle do the same. Next comes patting the thighs (heavy rain) and stamping the feet (heavier rain). The rain subsides as you return to patting your thighs, then snapping your fingers, and finally rubbing your hands together until there is complete silence.

Common Thoughts

This amusing activity works well with younger kids. Explain to them, in a humorous way, that if they all think silently together, their thoughts will be similar. Tell the group that each member should think of some object and concentrate hard on it. Then have the person next to you tell what he was thinking of. He might say, for example, "My thought was an owl." You then tell what your thought was and explain why it is similar to the first thought. "I was thinking of a watch and it is similar to an owl because both have round faces." Each person in the circle tells his thought and how it was similar to the first. This often requires considerable imagination. "I was thinking of an apple and it's like an owl because an owl eats and an apple is eaten." "My thought was a pencil, and it's like your thought because a pencil is sometimes used to write the word *owl*."

See how similar the thoughts were?

Spell-Down

This game is also for younger kids. The person who is *it* goes to someone in the circle and gives him a word to spell. That person must spell the word, but without using any of the five vowels. For the letter *a*, he must raise his right hand. For the letter *e*, he raises his left hand. For *i*, he points to his eye. For *o*, he forms an *O* with his mouth. And for *u*, he points to the person who is *it*. If he makes a mistake by saying a vowel or spelling a word incorrectly, that person changes places with *it*.

Alphabet Game

Before this game is played, 75 to 100 index cards (4" × 6") are labeled on one side with a letter of the alphabet. In addition, a story is written, leaving blanks for campers to fill in the words.

Select a topic, such as animals, plants, fish, or people's names. The leader reads the story and stops at each blank to turn over a card. The first person to name an animal beginning with that letter wins the card for himself or his team. If the letter is R, for example, players might yell out raccoon, rabbit, robin, or rooster. Sample story:

Last Saturday, I went for a hike in the woods, hoping to spot a _____.
Before ten minutes had elapsed, I found myself face-to-face with a _____.
I slowly backed away, only to step on a _____. It was then that I bolted. I ran as fast as I could, jumping over _____, passing _____, and occasionally hearing the call of a _____. (And so on.)

Once an animal has been named, it cannot be used again. The individual or team with the most cards wins.

Musical Chairs

Line up a row of chairs so that alternate chairs face the opposite direction, one chair for each person playing. When the music starts, remove one of the chairs as players walk in a circle around the chairs. When the music stops, everyone scrambles to sit in a chair. The person who remains standing is out. Begin the music again and remove another chair, continuing to play until only one chair is left and only one player — the winner — seats herself after the music stops.

Musical Hat

This is a version of musical chairs without the chairs, suitable for a campfire setting. A paper hat is passed around the circle; each player must put the hat on his head before passing it to the next person. When the leader stops the music (or the clapping), the person in possession of the hat drops out. Variation: Instead of a hat, some other object (a ball, a bean bag, a stick) is passed around the circle. When the music stops, the leader names a category (animals, trees, countries, baseball players, etc.). The person in possession of the object then passes the object on, but must name four things which fit the category before the object goes around the circle and comes back to him again.

Chair Game

This is similar to Musical Chairs, though it requires no music. Everyone gets a chair and places it in a tight circle, each chair facing inward and touching the chairs on each side of it. The player who is *it* stands in the middle of the circle and attempts to sit in an empty seat, while all of the seated players continue to move into the vacant seat, making it difficult for *it* to get seated. This is a fast-paced game as the vacancy continues to shift from one seat to another. When *it* gets seated, someone else becomes *it*— the player who did not move fast enough to fill the vacant seat.

Human Anagrams

Depending on team size, each team member is given one, two, or three letters of the alphabet, each printed large with a marker on a paper plate. For each question which the emcee asks, the team that first spells out the correct answer by physically getting up and moving into place with the appropriate letters receives a point. Sample questions:

the largest mammal that swims in the ocean	(whale)
the planet farthest from the sun	(Pluto)
the alpine country whose capital is Bern	(Switzerland)
a container for arrows	(quiver)
the "Pine Tree" state	(Maine)
8 + 3 - 7 + 1 - 3	(two)
the sound a duck makes	(quack)
your zodiac sign if you were born on Sept. 8	(Virgo)
the square root of 3,600	(sixty)

This is great fun as bodies collide into each other while frantically arranging themselves in correct order.

Categories

For a fun pencil-and-paper game appropriate for individuals or teams of all ages, have everyone make a chart of 25 boxes, as shown. Select a five-letter word (perhaps related to camp or from the Bible) and write the letters across the top. Then, choose five categories (TV stars, book titles, sports, etc.) and write these down the left side. Give five minutes for everyone to try to fill in every category with words beginning with the letters provided. Keep score by giving one point for each box correctly filled in.

	B	E	A	C	H
FOOD	blueberry	egg	apple	cheesecake	hamburger
ANIMAL	baboon	elephant	antelope	canary	horse
MOVIE	Bambi	Elephant Man	Apollo 13	Cinderella	Home Alone
COUNTRY	Bulgaria	England	Australia	Canada	Honduras
CAR	Buick	Eclipse	Allegro	Chevrolet	Honda

Verbal Fun (Word Game)

Either cooperatively or competitively (in teams), players attempt to determine the common expression or title indicated by each phrase:

carhouse bargain	*expression*	garage sale
unravel the rouge rug	*expression*	roll out the red carpet
coal-colored hocus pocus	*expression*	Black Magic
a monkey fruit division	*object*	banana split
mimicking feline	*expression*	copy cat
stenographer of Ohio or Utah	*person*	secretary of state
scrub and put on	*phrase*	wash and wear
a bunny's twelve inches	*object*	a rabbit's foot
continue grinning	*expression*	keep smiling
go pilot a stringed toy	*expression*	go fly a kite
do not squander, do not desire	*expression*	waste not, want not
a sugar molar	*expression*	a sweet tooth
the tranquility apple center	*name*	the Peace Corps
a keg of baboons	*expression*	a barrel of monkeys
paid athletes and crooks	*phrase*	pros & cons

in the swelter of the darkness	*phrase*	in the heat of the night
Eden Misplaced	*title*	*Paradise Lost*

Riddles and Conundrums

An evening of riddles and mindbenders can be lots of fun, especially for younger kids. Participants can try to top each other with their riddles and mind games. An old-time favorite asks:

WHAT IS IT?

Luke had it before.
Paul had it behind.
Matthew never had it at all.
All girls have it once.
Boys cannot have it.
Old Mrs. Mulligan had it twice in succession.
Dr. Lowell had it before and behind too.
He had it twice as much behind as before.
    (The answer is L.)

WHAT AM I?

I am in the morning and evening, but not in the noon.
I am in the universe, but not in the sun, the stars, or the planets.
I am in pain and suffering, but not in sorrow.
What am I?
    (The letter I.)

Indoor Football

Use a large piece of paper (or a chalkboard, if one is available) and mark off the yardage of a football field. Place a mark or a button (to function as the football) midfield at the 50 yard line, where play begins. Divide participants into two teams. Two players compete at a time, one from each team. Ask a question to these two players. Whichever player answers the question correctly first gains ten yards towards his team's goal line. The object, as in ordinary football, is to score a touchdown. Then the next player on each of the two lines is given a question, and whoever answers it scores ten points for his team, moving the ball on the field ten yards towards his goal line.

For example, after one team has answered the first two questions correctly, the ball is on the 30 yard line nearest their goal. If the third question is then answered correctly by the opposing team, the ball moves back to the 40 yard line. If this team also answers the fourth question, the ball returns to midfield.

Team names can be chosen. Additional yardage can be given for tough questions. You can devise similar games for most any sport. Questions should be gathered ahead of time and can concern nature, trivia, and whatever participants might be learning about. What kind of tree has white bark? (birch) Which planet is closest to the sun? (Mercury) What does the term *love* signify in tennis? (zero) How many counselors work at this camp? What is the name of the last book in the Christian Bible? (Revelation)

This game can also be played like baseball, where questions are valued as singles, doubles, or triples, depending on difficulty.

Norwegian Football

Sometimes the best games are played with the simplest equipment. Two mops, a towel, and masking tape comprise the equipment you need for Norwegian Football. Mark off goal lines on the floor with masking tape, and tape an X halfway between, whereupon the referee places the towel. Two teams of players count off, each team sitting on opposite sides of the playing field. The referee calls out a number, and the team member on each side with that number grabs the team's mop and attempts to push the towel over their goal line. Mops must remain touching the floor at all times. Each team scores a point when it pushes the towel over the goal line.

Group Ping-Pong

If you have a ping-pong table and a group of kids interested in playing, you can get them all involved in a single game. Line up half of the participants at each end of the table. When one person hits the ball, he passes the paddle to the next person on line, who then hits the ball when it returns. After each person has hit the ball, he moves out of the way and to the end of the line. This makes for an exciting, fast-moving game.

Another method of rotation involves having each person play until he loses a point for his team, at which time the next person on line takes over.

"Mad Libs"

Beginning way back in the late 1950s, Roger Price and Leonard Stern put out a series of party games known as Mad Libs. Decades later, they are still ready-made fun, ideal for campfires and rainy days. First, you ask the group to give you a word or title for each item requested in brackets; then the zaniness begins when you read the passage filled in with their choices. You can even make up your own passage, as I did:

> You probably do not know this, but _____ [name of person in the group] once played a role in the movie _____ [title of a recent movie] and became known as The Kid. It all began like this. _____ [name of a movie star] spotted The Kid walking along a _____ [location] and became deeply attracted to The Kid's _____ [adjective], _____ [color] _____ [noun]. The star shouted out, _____ [exclamation], Kid! Where have you been all my life? You are absolutely _____ [adjective]. I would _____ [adverb] _____ [verb] for you if you would come to Hollywood to star in a new movie. You're just the sort of _____ [noun] we need." The Kid said, _____ [exclamation]! Of course I will!" What role did The Kid play, you wonder? If you watch it closely, you'll see The Kid playing the part of the dog's _____ [body part].

Minute Mysteries

A number of books have been published containing short "minute mysteries" or "mini-mysteries," in which clues are provided that may lead the reader to the solution of a fictional crime. These are both fun and challenging to the deductive powers of young minds. You can even make up your own mysteries, as I have done here:

"MURDER!" SHE SAID

Inspector Kluliss has made it a habit to take you along with him to crime scenes due to your uncanny knack at solving mysteries. He thinks that you are clairvoyant or psychic, but you simply have developed powerful skills of observation and deduction. In fact, it's pretty certain that, without you, the Inspector would be filing reports or sweeping floors—anything but detective work. You don't mind, because these excursions are right up your alley, and because the Inspector is a genial and good-natured person whose company you come to enjoy.

The Inspector and you step into the palatial home of Rita Rankin, who is teary-eyed and distraught.

"Murder!" she says. "I can't believe that my poor, sick husband would be murdered! Inspector, I want you to make a speedy arrest!"

"All right, Mrs. Rankin, calm down," the Inspector responds. "Please, have a seat and tell me what happened. Who discovered the murder?"

"I did!" she exclaims, seating herself on the plush sofa, surrounded by expensive vases and valuable sculptures. "Oh, the blood and that butcher knife! It's all too horrible! It's got to be the money. Poor, bedridden Albert! I know that beady-eyed gardener did it for the money. He —"

The Inspector interrupts her. "What makes you think the gardener did it?" he asks.

"I saw him!" Mrs. Rankin proclaims. "And he would have killed me if I hadn't screamed."

"Tell me exactly what you saw, ma'am," the Inspector says calmly.

"Yes, Inspector. I had just stepped out of a long, hot shower — that's the way I pamper myself after tending to Albert's demands. I shut out the whole world. I close the bathroom window and the door, and I simply enjoy myself without any interruptions. But just as I stepped out of the tub and wrapped the towel around myself, the bathroom door swung open. I was so startled, I let out a bloodcurdling scream — loud enough to wake the dead, and surely loud enough to alert one of the household help. And the gardener fled. It was then that I went into the bedroom to discover my husband's dead body covered in blood and a butcher's knife on the floor."

The Inspector interrupts. "So you saw the gardener at the door?" he asks.

"Not face-to-face. I was looking in the mirror, and there I saw the reflection of his beady eyes and his pock-marked face. There was blood on his shirt. Oh, I'm sure he's disposed of it by now. But he's your man, I tell you."

"Well, I guess I'd better find the gardener and arrest him," the Inspector concludes.

"Not so fast," you say. You then suggest that he arrest Mrs. Rankin instead. How do you know that she is not telling the truth?

[Answer: Mrs. Rankin claims she saw the reflection of the beady eyes, the pock-marked face, and the blood in the mirror, but the bathroom was all closed up and she had taken a long, hot shower. The mirror would have been too steamed-up to see details.]

THE STOLEN JEWELS

"I was sitting in my bedroom reading an edifying book, as I do every evening after dinner," Mr. Billings explains as he recounts the event. "Then, the electricity went out. Being out in the woods, this house gets really dark when the lights go out. Nevertheless, I felt my way out to the hallway and saw the light of a flashlight bouncing against the wall as the thief ran off. I keep little of value in the house, but my wife's jewels just happened to be in the safe. We usually keep them in a safe-deposit box at the bank, but we had gone to a swanky party two nights ago, so we stored them in the safe for the weekend. Anyway, I fumbled into the next room where the safe is, turned the combination lock, and then felt around inside the safe to find it completely empty. Thank goodness I had those jewels insured. As soon as I found a flashlight, I made my way to the power switch, turned on the lights, and called you immediately. Thanks for being so prompt in coming, Inspector."

"We'll get the fingerprints and check the police files for safecrackers recently released from prison," the Inspector assures Mr. Billings.

But you tell the Inspector there's no need to search any further. There's something wrong in Mr. Billings' story. What is it?

[Answer: Mr. Billings says he turned the combination to open the locked safe, but the room was still dark, so he would not have been able to read the dial.]

THE MAID'S STORY

"I suspect foul play," the maid says as she brings you and the Inspector into her bedroom, "and I believe the children's nanny, Henrietta, killed the Mrs." She sobs. "I know the Mrs. can be difficult to work for, but Henrietta is no darling either. I should know; we room together."

"What makes you think Henrietta killed your employer?" the Inspector asks.

"The blood on her dress," the maid answers. "Look at it right there on her pile of dirty clothes. Henrietta just flings her clothes in a heap when she takes them off at night. Just leaves them there until morning when she finally puts them in the laundry hamper. I have to step over them every night and every morning."

"Where is Henrietta now?" the Inspector asks the maid.

"After I found the body, I called you. Then, I immediately came in here to wake Henrietta. She threw on a bathrobe and went upstairs to wake the children. After she left, I noticed the blood on her dress. My guess is, if you analyze the blood, you'll find it's from the Mrs. How cold-blooded! To kill the Mrs., get into a nightgown, and go to bed. No remorse!"

"Have you touched anything in here since Henrietta left to be with the children?" the Inspector asks.

"Not a thing," says the maid. "I didn't want to tamper with the evidence."

"That was smart," the Inspector states. Then, looking at the dress on top of the clothespile, he adds, "We'll have the blood on this dress tested, as you suggest."

"The poor Mrs.," the maid sobs. "She didn't deserve this. She was no saint, but neither was Henrietta."

"Is that why you killed your employer and have tried to pin the crime on Henrietta?" you ask.

How do you know the maid's story is not completely true?

[Answer: The dress would not have been lying on top of the clothes heap since Henrietta would have taken off her dress before her underclothes.]

ACTIVE OUTDOOR GAMES

Dodge Ball

A large circle is formed enclosing a small group of players. Using a ball that is soft, the players forming the circle try to hit the players within the circle until only one remains. Those within the circle try to dodge the ball and stay in as long as possible. If a player is hit, he is eliminated from within the circle and joins the circle itself, trying to get others out.

Battle of the Knights

This is very similar to chicken fights, but safer since players ride piggyback instead of on each other's shoulders. The object is for the knights, who are on the horses' backs, to knock other knights off their horses. This can be done as a free-for-all or in two teams, the winning team being that which still has knights riding on horses. This activity can also be run as a contest, in which the battle takes place between two knights at a time. (Arms and hands are used instead of lances, of course!)

Battle of One-Legged People

Each player must hold one leg up with one hand at all times throughout the "battle." Each person hops around on the other leg trying to knock people over. Any player falling to the ground or allowing both feet to touch the ground is out. The winner is the last person remaining on one leg.

Human Croquet

This is played like regular croquet but involves no objects except people. Instead of croquet balls, blindfolded players move from wicket to wicket. Two people — or two stakes placed parallel to each other — are used as the wickets (arches). Each player points his "ball" in the direction he wants it to go and tells it how many steps to take. No other information can be given. It's an interesting twist to the original game.

A similar type of contest might be developed called "human archery."

Spud

Everybody gets in a circle and counts off. Player #1 throws the ball (volleyball or rubber ball) straight up in the air while at the same time yelling out someone else's number. As he does this, everyone scatters while the person whose number is called tries to catch the ball. If he succeeds, he then throws it up and calls another number. The person with that number must run back to get the ball. The first player called who fails to catch the ball yells "Spud" the moment he gets hold of it. All the other players freeze where they are. The player with the ball then takes three giant steps toward any player and tries to hit that person with the ball. If he succeeds, the person who was hit gets the letter "S"; if he does not succeed, he himself gets the letter "S." Everyone then gets back in a circle, and the player who has just received the letter throws up the ball, while calling off a number. The first person to acquire the letters S-P-U-D is the loser. When we played as kids, the loser had to pass through a spanking machine.

Steal the Bacon

This is an old-time favorite. Divide your group into two equal teams which line up facing each other about 20 feet apart. Each team counts off so that player #1 on each team is facing the last number of the other team. In other words, the counting off is done in opposite directions for each team.

1 2 3 4 5 6 7 8 9

"bacon"

9 8 7 6 5 4 3 2 1

In the center of the playing area between the two lines of players, place a rag or stick (the "bacon"). You, as referee and scorekeeper, call off a number. The two people with that number run out to grab the bacon, each trying to bring it back to his team line. The person who grabs the bacon must bring it back to his team line *without being tagged by the other player*. This is the catch. The player who succeeds in getting the bacon back to his line without being tagged earns a point for his team. However, if he is tagged, the other team gets the point. More than one number can be called at a time to make the game more exciting and challenging. The team with the most points wins.

Treasure Hunt

This can be played with just a few people or with more than a hundred, divided into teams. Some treasure (a box of leaves for nature study, a book, a certificate to an ice cream party, etc.) is hidden. Each team is given a clue which leads them to another clue, leading them to another clue, and so on until they find the treasure. The first team finding the treasure gets to keep it. Clues might be like this:

> A wise philosopher once wrote,
> "Row, row, row your boat."
> If your team doesn't want to lose,
> Be sure to check out the canoes.

> The first word is not very neat;
> The second is not too petite.
> If you can't digest this clue now
> See the place where they dish out the chow. (mess hall)

> A place when you're dirty,
> A place when you're hot.
> The girls all know this one;
> Some guys might not. (girls' showers)

Variation: Each team with one counselor is given its own destination in scrambled letters (e.g.: glpefola = flagpole; aunter ancib = nature cabin). Teams run to their destination to find their next clue. Other clues may be maps, riddles, and puzzles. Each team is given a rope which every member must hold onto throughout the hunt. The counselor's role is to enforce this rule; if anyone lets go, everyone must freeze until all are once again holding the rope. This builds teamwork and cooperation. (A variation of this hunt is to supply a list of scrambled sites to each team, each site having hidden a painted stone. The team that returns with the most stones wins, or stones can be turned in for prizes.)

Another treasure hunt could use maps and give experience in map-reading or using a compass.

Newcomb

For younger players. Newcomb is played with the same rules as volleyball except that the ball is caught and thrown instead of hit.

Scavenger Hunt

Each team is given a pillowcase or bag and a list of items to find, collect, and bring back by a given time. The team which brings back the most items on the list wins.

Sample list for an outdoor hunt: acorn, frog, oak leaf, grasshopper, pine cone, fern, bottle cap, sandstone, caterpillar, 10 pieces of litter, bird's feather, piece of string, etc. The list of items need not be so specific; e.g.: something red, something dry, something damp, something light, something which smells bad, something that can float through the air, something furry, something that tastes sweet, something that is edible, etc.

An alphabetical scavenger hunt consists of teams making up their own list of items, each beginning with a different letter of the alphabet, and then finding items such as acorn, beetle, cattail plant, etc.

A variation of the scavenger hunt is a "Dutch Auction." (Why it's been given this name, I've never learned.) Each team is sent to gather objects in a single pillowcase or bag. At a given time (say, in twenty minutes), they return to a central location and empty the contents of their pillowcase. The auctioneer then names items from a predetermined list, and any team that has that item receives the number of points allotted the item. A Dutch Auction at camp might include sunglasses, jackknife, an insect, a pine cone, mint-flavored toothpaste, a 2002 penny, a T-shirt, clothespins, etc. "Going once, going twice, gone!"

Another variation: the leader calls out items that can be found on the players' bodies (a yellow ribbon, a silver ring, a Casio watch, a belt with an initialed buckle, the person with the most freckles, etc.). If the players are made aware of this event beforehand, they may come wearing some pretty outlandish objects that they think might be called.

Carnivals

Hold a camp or council carnival. Each cabin, unit, or group plans and runs a booth. The sponge throw is always popular, especially when staff members become the target. Booths might include mini-golf, Frisbee throw, Western Union (which relays "telegrams"), a fortune teller, a massage parlor, a spook house, a firing range (squirt guns used to douse a candle flame), a "computer" dating service, an M & M count, a tennis ball toss into coffee cans, a "shave the balloon" contest, and an argument booth (stop at the booth and argue with the grump on duty). Add to the carnival atmosphere by providing cotton candy and ice cream. A watermelon seed-spitting contest is especially fun on a hot summer carnival day. Half of the fun comes in planning and preparing for the carnival.

Tickets can be given out at the beginning of the carnival to "pay" for each event, and more tickets can be acquired by winning at contests and entries.

Carnivals make a terrific summer evening event if you string lights along the carnival area.

Water carnivals are also great fun, with events ranging from a 100-yard crawl to a sand castle contest. Humorous events can include the goofiest dive contest, the biggest splash event, the lighted candle relay (the candle must stay lit or you start over again), the disrobing relay (each swimmer, wearing pajamas or other clothes, swims to opposite dock and removes clothes for the next swimmer to don), the swimming singing relay (swimmers must sing at the top of their lungs while swimming the relay), and the carrot relay (couples eat from separate ends of a carrot while swimming to the goal line). End the event with a free swim.

Staff Hunt

Teams search for hidden staff members. When a staff member is found, he or she records the team's name and stays in place for other teams to find. At a pre-set time, everyone meets to tally points. Some staff members have been prescribed many points (25), some negative points (-10), and some no points at all! There is nothing so hilarious as finding a staff member thirty feet up in a tree posing as a member of the owl family!

Variation: African safari — each counselor wears a sign naming an animal and its point value. The counselor-animals take to the woods with teams of players released minutes later in hot pursuit. Each team tries to capture as many animals as they can and return them to the "pen." Like a real safari, animals may show themselves and then run off. The winning team is the one that collects the most points.

Obstacle Course

This ends as a friendly joke on an unassuming player. Choose one person (or two for a race) who passes through a short obstacle course consisting of varying-sized objects placed on the ground. Then the player is blindfolded to see if he can go through the course a second time without stepping on anything, this time being aided by the spectators' directions. He may wonder what is so funny until he discovers he has been stepping over obstacles which were removed after he was blindfolded.

Blind Monkeys

This is another game enjoyed more by the spectators than the players. Couples are blindfolded; one participant shells and feeds peanuts to his partner.

Blind Fetch

Divide players into two teams, each behind a line of the playing area. One player from each team is blindfolded and stands in the center of the playing area. When a ball is thrown in, the blindfolded players compete to obtain the ball and bring it back to their respective team's line, based entirely on directions shouted out from their team members. Carrying the ball across the team line earns 2 points; however, if the player who picks up the ball to carry across his team's line gets tagged by the other blindfolded player, the tagging team earns 1 point.

Prisoner's Base

The aim of this game is to capture all members of your rival team by tagging them and putting them in prison. Divide the playing field into two equal sides, with a square prison marked off at the opposing corner of each side. Players may cross into enemy territory to capture prisoners, but if they are tagged, they are placed in their opponent's prison. The only way they may be freed is by being tagged by one of their free teammates. However, rival team members may tag and send to prison both the prisoner and his savior as they attempt to make their way back to their team's territory. Game is won when one side captures all members of the other side, or when a free man from one side enters the enemy prison when none of his teammates are prisoners.

Capture the Flag

This perennial favorite is usually played by a large number of participants on a huge field, and can last well over an hour without becoming boring, though it may end after only fifteen minutes. It's an exciting game of teamwork, strategy, and lots of exercise.

Two teams are formed, each given half the field for their home territory. A center line is demarcated in some way. Each team wears an identifying color (or light shirts vs. dark shirts) and is given a flag (handkerchief, bandana, or cloth). The object of the game is to capture the opposing team's flag and bring it across to home territory while protecting your team's flag from being captured.

These are the typical rules:

1. Players begin in their home territory. When they cross into opponent territory and are tagged by an opponent, they go to "jail," an area marked off on each team's side. Capturers accompany each captive to jail while placing a hand on the prisoner's shoulder.
2. Prisoners escape from jail after (a) being tagged by a free player on his team or (b) tagging the jailer, who usually stands out of reach of the prisoners. Lifelines may be formed by prisoners by holding hands so that if one is set free, all who form the lifeline are freed. They are then allowed free passage back to home territory.
3. Clear boundaries are established before the game. Anyone who goes out of bounds while being chased automatically becomes captive.
4. The flag must be openly displayed by each team, usually deep in home territory.
5. People guarding the flag must stay at least six feet (two yards) away from it. The flag must not be physically impossible to capture.
6. If an opponent is tagged while running to her home territory with the flag, the flag is returned to its position.

Teams usually develop defensive and offensive strategies, decoys, planned passes of the flag from one capturer to another, etc. For really large teams and a more exciting game, try two flags per team.

War

Two teams are formed, each designated by color. Members of each team tie a strip of cloth of their team's color around their upper arm. Each team's headquarters is a tent or small cabin at some distance from each other. Thirty flour bombs (made of ½ cup of flour tied up in a stocking or paper towel) and 10 sticks of dynamite (foot-long broom handles) are given to each team. Teams are also given two armbands of the enemy team's color, to be worn by spies, who hide their own armbands under their shirts.

Teams try to bomb enemy headquarters and eliminate enemy team members by pulling off the armbands, thus disqualifying them from further play. Points are scored as follows:

Pulling off enemy armband	1 point
Bombing enemy headquarters (dynamite must hit headquarters)	5 points
Throwing dynamite into enemy headquarters	10 points
Capturing enemy spy	15 points

Referees are needed to keep score and ensure safety and fair play. Set an ending time, usually an hour after play begins.

Balloon Games

Balloon Burst

Each player blows up a balloon and ties it to his ankle or waist (leader decides). The objective is to pop as many balloons as possible while protecting yours from being popped. Last player with an unpopped balloon wins.

Balloon Blow-Up

Contestants inflate balloons of equal size. Use a tape measure to determine whose balloon is inflated the largest without breaking it.

Balloon Kick

Contestants race to be the first to kick their balloon into a basket.

Balloon Relay

Each team lines up behind the starting line. Using a broom, the first player in each team sweeps the team's balloon to the finishing line and back again, each player doing the same until one team is first to finish. Variations: Instead of sweeping the balloon, it can be kicked, butted with head, or hit with hand (the leader decides which). Another alternative is for each player to run to the finish line, blow up a balloon until it pops, and run back to start for the next player to go.

Balloon Basketball

Apply the rules of basketball, substituting a balloon for a basketball. Two people hold out their arms in the form of a circle for the baskets.

Balloon Baseball

Instead of using a bat when the balloon is pitched, the "batter" hits the balloon with his fist. Once hit, the opposing team attempts to blow the balloon to the ground before the batter can make it around to home base. When each member of the team has been up to "bat," the opposing team is up.

Balloon Volleyball

Two people hold a string, which serves as the net, between two teams of players seated on the floor. Players follow normal volleyball rules, except that they hit a balloon while remaining seated on the floor. A more challenging variation is to blow the balloon instead of hitting it, hands not being allowed to touch the balloon.

Balloon Volley

Arrange two sets of chairs facing each other. Players are told they must remain seated at all times. The object of the game is to hit the balloon over the heads of the opposing team members to land on the floor behind them. The opposing team may reach up to catch the balloon or hit it back. If a player forgets and rises up out of her chair, she is removed from play, making it more difficult for the team to keep the balloon from landing behind them. Make sure the two teams' chairs are close enough together so that it is physically possible for the balloon to be hit behind the opponents' chairs.

Balloon Shave

See which team can be the first to use a razor, long needle, or plastic knife to shave shaving cream off a balloon without popping it.

BEAN BAG GAMES

Hot Potato

This is a fun game for young children. Everyone stands in a circle and imagines the bean bag to be a hot potato which will burn your hands if you hold it too long. Children pass the bean bag around as quickly as possible. This is a good activity for developing dexterity and coordination.

Bean Bag Toss

Everyone stands in a circle around the person who is *it*. *It* throws the bean bag to someone in the circle who must catch it. If the throw is good, above the ankles and below the head, and the intended recipient does not catch it, that person then becomes *it*. If the bean bag is caught, it is thrown back to *it*, who then tosses it to someone else. The game becomes exciting when *it* starts to use deception by looking at one person and throwing to another, or throwing behind him, etc.

Beast, Bird, or Fish

A circle is formed and a person who is *it* stands in the center. He throws the bean bag to one of the members of the circle and shouts, "Beast, bird, or fish — *bird*!" The player to whom the bag is thrown must quickly think of an appropriate animal (such as "robin") to fit the category *it* named (here, bird), and yell out his choice as he throws the bean bag back. He must give his response before the leader counts aloud to 10. If he can't, he becomes *it*.

200 or Bust

Divide players into two teams, each team forming a separate circle and receiving a separate bean bag. In the center of each team's circle is a target worth 25 points. The inside "doughnut" is worth 10 points, and the outside ring worth 5. Each player in a team gets three consecutive tosses, going around the circle until the score of 200 is reached. If a team goes over 200, it must start again. First team to get a perfect 200 wins.

Poison

This is like musical chairs. A bean bag is passed around a circle until the leader blows a whistle. The person who is holding or passing the beanbag is eliminated until only one or two players remain. For a large group, use more than one beanbag.

TAG GAMES

There must be over a hundred variations of the game of tag. Here are some of the best:

Tag

A playing area is set off and goal lines are designated. *It* is situated in the center of the field, while all other players stand behind one goal line. At a given signal, players try to race across to the opposite line without being tagged by *it*. Any person tagged also becomes *it*, and the game continues until only one or two players are left untagged.

Twin Tag

This is like regular tag, except that players pair up and hold hands. To be tagged, only one member of a couple needs to be touched by one member of the couple that is *it*. There need be no goal lines to run towards, but a demarcated playing area must be designated.

Chain Tag (Net Tag)

This is like regular tag, except that all players once tagged hold hands to form a human chain, and only those players at the end of the chain can do the tagging.

Elbow Tag

Players join into pairs and hook elbows with their partner. Their free hand should rest on their hip, allowing someone else to hook onto the free elbow.

A pair of players is separated so that one player is designated as the "chaser" and the other as the "flee-er." The chaser pursues the flee-er, who can dodge in and around the pairs and can hook her elbow with one of the pairs. The member of the pair that she doesn't hook onto must then separate from his former partner and become the flee-er. If a flee-er gets tagged, he becomes the chaser.

This tag game gets exciting the more confusing it gets, as chaser and flee-er roles continually change. Try having more than one chaser and flee-er.

Freeze Tag

When the person who is *it* tags a player, that player must freeze in position. Another player can touch the frozen person, thereby allowing him back into play again. *It* tries to freeze all players.

Keep-Away Tag

A bean bag or ball is used. Here, there are no goal lines to run to, but there is a designated playing area. The players try to keep the ball away from the person who is *it*, who tries to intercept the ball or touch the person holding the ball (in which case the thrower or tagged individual becomes *it*). When the ball is thrown to a player, he must count aloud to five before throwing it to someone else.

Runaway Tag

Base lines are established at each end of a playing field, creating a large center field. Players stand behind either line until *it* yells, "Run-Run-Runaway, anyway to get away." All players try to run across center field to safety behind the opposite base line without getting tagged. Players who are tagged join *it*; the game continues until everyone has been tagged. The last person tagged becomes *it* in the next game.

Blind Tag

All players but one wear blindfolds. The sighted player wears or holds a bell which rings whenever he is moving. The blindfolded players attempt to tag the player who is ringing the bell. Whoever tags him gets the bell and switches places with him.

Double Tag

It names only one person whom he must attempt to tag. When the chase begins, however, the person named can tag another player, who must now become *it*'s object of pursuit. Play continues until *it* tags whatever player he is supposed to be chasing at the time. That person then becomes *it*.

Crows and Cranes

Divide your group into two teams, one the "Crows," the other, "Cranes." Both teams meet at the center of the playing field. The youth leader yells the name of one of the teams; that team must run to their goal line for safety while the other team chases them. Any members tagged by the chasers join that team.

The team name called could be decided by the toss of a coin.

Safety Tag

There are many variations of safety tags in which a player is safe from being tagged if he is kneeling, or squatting, is touching wood, is standing frozen, etc.

RELAY RACES

The fun and excitement of relay races lead to laughter and camaraderie. Generally, two or more teams compete to be the first to complete the race, which is often made more complicated (and hilarious) by the specific rules of the race.

Sack Race

Teams of equal size are established. Each team lines up behind a starting line. The first person on line steps into a burlap sack and jumps to a designated point, then back to the starting line. When he reaches the line, he steps out of the sack, and the next person climbs into it and races. The first team to cross all players back to the starting line is the winner.

Leap Frog Relay

Players begin in a crouched position. The last person in the column leaps over the back of each player in front of him and then runs to the turning line. He runs back and takes his place at the head of the column. (The column has moved back to give him room to crouch at the starting line.) The next person at the back of the column then leapfrogs over each of his team members until everyone has participated.

Paper Plate Race

In this race, participants must walk on paper plates. The first participant is given two paper plates. At the given signal, she places a plate on the ground and steps on it, then places the other plate in front of her and steps on that, continuing until she reaches the turning line. She then picks up both plates and runs back to pass them to the next person in line. On some surfaces, it may be possible to slide the plates along the floor without lifting them up.

Somersault Race

Players are permitted to progress to the finishing line only by doing somersaults.

Apple Race

Participants in this race run with an apple on their heads. If the apple falls off, they must return to the starting line and begin again.

Spoon Race

Players race with a potato, egg, or similar object on a spoon. Like the apple race, if the object falls off the spoon, the player must return to the starting line and begin again. For a more challenging race, try peas on a knife.

Cottonball Race

Each player is given a straw. Each team is given a cottonball. One at a time, each player carries the cottonball by sucking on the straw so that it attaches to the open end.

Water Race

Each team member is given a paper cup. At the beginning of each team line is a milk jug filled with water; at the end is an empty milk jug. When a signal is given, the player at the front of the line fills his paper cup with water, then pours from his paper cup to the cup of the person in line behind him. Each player pours water in similar manner, from cup to cup, until the last player pours the water into the empty jug. This continues until all the water in the original jug has been poured into the jug at the end of the line. The winning team is not only the one that finished first, but that also got the most water into the jug.

Sponge Race

The first person in the line dips a large sponge into a bucket of water and then passes it over her head to the next person, who passes it over his head to the next, and so forth. The last person squeezes the water out into a second bucket at the end of the line and then passes the sponge back down the line. Again, the first person dips the sponge into the bucket of water and passes it down the line overhead. Two sponges can be used per team at the same time. After five minutes, whichever team has the most water in the second bucket is the winner. This can be a lot of fun to watch, as well as a lot of fun to play on hot days.

Variation: Each player runs from the starting line to a bucket, loads up the sponge, and then runs back to the starting line and squeezes the water into a second bucket before passing the sponge to the next person in line.

Whistle Race

Each player runs to a designated spot, eats a cracker, and then must whistle before he can return to the starting line.

Needle and Thread Race

Players race to a designated point and thread a needle while sitting on a bottle before returning to the starting line.

Balloon Race

Have plenty of balloons already filled with air. Each player runs to a chair and sits on a balloon until it pops, then runs back to the starting line, where the next player takes off towards the chair and sits on the next balloon to pop it. The team which first pops all of its balloons is the winner.

Tire Race

The first player on each team rolls an old car tire to the mark and then back to the next player, who rolls the tire, and so on, until the all members of the team have participated. The first team to have all runners complete the race is the winner.

Shoe Race

Each team is given a pair of old, large shoes, which players, in turn, put on and run in.

Another type of shoe race is to put everyone's shoes in a pile. At a given signal, everyone races to the pile to find and put on their shoes. The winner is the first person to return to the starting line wearing both of his own shoes. This can be complicated by tying together pairs of shoes, being sure that no shoe is tied to its mate.

Suitcase Race

Each participant races with a suitcase to a designated point, where he opens the suitcase and puts on all of the funny clothes placed therein. He then runs back to the starting line, takes off the clothes, and returns them to the suitcase before handing it to the next participant.

Everyone's Different Race

The difference with this race is that each person must reach the finish line in a completely different way. The first person might run, the second might somersault, the third might crawl, the fourth might waddle like a duck, the fifth might boogie, etc.

Three-Legged Race

Before the race, each team pairs off. One player ties his right leg to his partner's left. At a given signal, the first pair in each team runs to a designated point and then back to the starting line. Once they have crossed the line, the next pair does the same until a team wins by being the first to have all pairs race and cross their team line.

Wheelbarrow Race

This race is also done in pairs. One player holds the ankles of her partner, who must walk on her hands. In this wheelbarrow manner, each pair in a team runs to a designated point, switches position (the walker becomes the wheelbarrow), and then returns to the starting line. The next pair can then begin. An easier variation is to have players run piggy-back, switching positions before returning to the starting line.

Backward Race

Each person runs backwards to the turning line and then forward to return to the starting line. Once he has reached the starting line, the next player begins.

Over and Under Race

The first player passes a ball over her head to a second player, who passes the ball between his legs to a third player, alternating in this manner to see which team gets the ball passed to the end of the line most quickly.

Hop Race

Players must place a volleyball or soccer ball between their knees and hop to the end of the line, passing the ball to the next player without using hands.

Crab Race

Team members again divide into pairs, each pair back-to-back, interlocking arms. They must race sideways like a crab. This can be an individual race if contestants are instructed to race sideways on their hands and feet, with their belly (not their back) facing the sky.

Jello Race

One partner gets a spoon and a bowl of jello, which she feeds to her partner, who wears a bib. The pair that finishes the jello first wins.

Present Race

Each pair runs to a designated point and wraps a present. The challenge is that one player is only allowed to use her right hand while the other may only use his left. The other hand should be held behind each player's back.

Orange Race

This race is especially enjoyed by coed groups, who often arrange themselves boy-girl-boy-girl. Participants must pass an orange along the line until it reaches the last member. However, the orange may not be touched by the hands, but must be passed by clinching it between the chin and the neck.

Variation: Kids run to the goal line and back with an orange squeezed between their knees.

Marshmallow Race

This is also a good coed event. Thread a string through the center of a marshmallow so that the candy is in the middle of the string. At each end, the boy or girl sucks the string like eating spaghetti to see which contestant is first to reach and eat the coveted marshmallow.

Rock-Bridge-Tree

Three individuals for each team position themselves some distance from the starting line, the first crouched down on knees to be a rock, the second standing with legs apart to be a bridge, and the third standing with arms and legs stretched to be a tree. Each runner leaves the starting line, jumps over the rock, under the bridge, around the tree, back under the bridge, over the rock, and back to start, when the next runner begins. The team which finishes first is the winner.

Pyramid Relay

Groups of ten compete to be the first to form a human pyramid.

COOPERATIVE GAMES

It started one evening after dinner in the large field as soon as a counselor pulled out an old parachute from the rec shed and a number of kids gathered around to see what was happening. Whatever it was, they decided to become a part of it, taking hold of the parachute, causing it to rise in the air, inventing things to do as the parachute ballooned and fell gently to the ground. More people joined in. A little later, they left the parachute and formed a human caterpillar, laughing and joking as they slowly made their way across the field. More people joined in. By the time the evening ended, seventy or more kids and adults had become part of the spontaneous play, having fun and making friends.

That's when it started for me. Actually, it all developed in the 1970s. They called it "New Games," and it was a movement of bringing people outdoors for creative and cooperative play. There are no fixed or established "new games." Any game you invent is a new game and any new game that has been invented can be changed or altered to fit the needs and desires of the players, so long as everyone agrees to the rules. The New Games motto is "Play Hard ... Play Fair ... Nobody Hurt."

Now better known as "Cooperative Games," these activities are based on the concept of play aimed at everyone having fun. Everyone who plays is a winner because everyone has fun playing. In Cooperative Games, there are no star athletes, no fierce competitive loyalties or antagonisms, no age or sex barriers, no one on your back if you lose.

Some of the cooperative games that have been invented and played successfully are discussed below. Many of these games are competitive, but the emphasis is on the challenge and the fun, not the winning. I think you'll see what I mean if you try some.

Stand-Up

Take a partner, sit on the grass back-to-back, and lock arms. Try standing up together. Now try it with a circle of people all linked as a single unit.

Hunker Hawser

This game is designed for two people who each crouch on a tree stump or block of wood a few inches high and separated by approximately 6 feet of land. Each player takes hold of one end of a 15-foot rope to attempt to cause the other to fall off the pedestal.

Stand-Off

This game for two requires no special apparatus. Face your partner at an arm-length's distance, each of you with your feet together. Join your palms with those of your partner and see who can get the other off-balance. Make up a way to score, if you want.

Flying Dutchman

The rest of these games are for groups. This one is reminiscent of a ship looking for port. Everyone joins hands in a circle except for two who, hand-in-hand, are the ship looking for port. These two players make their way around the outside of the circle and break open a port somewhere. They then run (hop or skip, however your rules go) around the circle back to port while the couple whose hands have been broken join again and run around the circle in the opposite direction. The pair which returns first to close the circle is home and the other pair then becomes the Flying Dutchman looking for a place to dock.

Catch the Dragon's Tail

Form a line, clasping your hands on the waist of the person in front of you. The person on the end of the line hangs a piece of rope or a handkerchief from a rear pocket or belt to be the tail. The object is for the head of the dragon, the person in the front of the line, to get a hold of the tail. Or try two or more dragons attempting to catch each other's tail.

Anatomy

An outer and an inner circle are formed, each with the same number of people. One circle walks clockwise, the other counter-clockwise. Like Musical Chairs, the leader plays music or claps hands, but when the music stops, the leader shouts out two parts of the anatomy, such as "elbow-shoulder." Both circles stop walking, and each pair of adjacent members of the inner and outer circles must connect those parts of the anatomy. The last pair that makes the connection is removed from the circle, and the music begins again until it stops and two more anatomical parts are announced: knee-nose, rear-rear, head-foot, chin-toe, etc.

Mingle

Another variation on musical chairs, this time everyone mingles until the leader calls out a number. Participants scramble to form groups with that number of people. Individuals left out of groups — or the last group to form — is eliminated.

Fox and Squirrel

Here is a fast-moving game played in a circle. You need three balls: two to represent the foxes and a smaller one to represent the squirrel. The squirrel has the advantage of being able to leap by being thrown across the circle from one player to the other, while the foxes have the advantage of being two in number, but they can only be passed from one person to the next around the circle, in either direction, the passer calling out the name of the animal as it is passed. The object of the game is for the squirrel to be caught, which is done when a player with a fox ball tags the holder of the squirrel ball.

Knots

Imagine being tied up as part of a giant human knot. That's what this game is all about. To begin, everyone becomes part of a tight circle and puts both hands toward the center. Each person then grasps two other hands that do not belong to the same person or to either neighbor. Then they try to get out of the knot just created without releasing hands. It's a challenge!

Hula Hoop Pass

Everyone joins hands in a circle, one person with a hula hoop resting on his or her shoulder. The fun comes in passing the hula hoop around the entire circle without breaking hands.

Around the World

Players hold hands to form a circle. A hula-hoop is placed on one player's wrist before holding hands. The object of the game is to move the hula-hoop all the way around the circle without letting go of each other's hands. Two circles may race to see which can get the hoop "around the world" fastest.

Egg Toss

Here's a great game which I've used as part of a camp tournament. A dozen eggs or water balloons are the only materials you need. Form two long lines of players who face each other and who are three feet apart. Each person stands opposite his partner. One line of players is given eggs. Each person tosses an egg to his partner. If it breaks, those two partners are out. If it is caught without breaking, the game becomes more challenging as everyone remaining in both lines takes one step backward. Then each egg is thrown back, and play continues like this, everyone taking one step backwards after a successful, non-splatter toss. The winning team is the last pair with an unbroken egg.

British Bulldog

This tag game is for a significantly large group. About one-tenth of the players are the catchers and play in the center of the field. The remaining players divide up and position themselves at the two ends of the field, the "end zones." When the catchers call out "British Bulldog 1-2-3," all the other players run to the opposite end zone while the catchers try to capture as many runners as they can. This is done by lifting a runner off the ground long enough to yell "British Bulldog 1-2-3." Sometimes it takes a group effort by the catchers to hold onto and lift a person long enough to do this, but once done, the captured runner then joins the efforts of the catchers. The game continues in this manner until all runners are captured.

Blob

This is a form of tag which is lots of fun with a large group. Establish boundary lines within which to play. One person begins as the tagger, but what makes this special is that each person tagged holds hands with the tagger, gradually forming a line known as the "Blob." The Blob roams the field, narrowing in and tagging other players, who then also join the line. Only members at the ends of the line can tag others, but it is permissible for the Blob to split into smaller lines and go in different directions or surround an untagged player. The last player tagged can become the initial tagger of the next game.

Rock-Paper-Scissors

Here's another tag game, this one beginning with the old contest of Rock-Paper-Scissors, in which each player simultaneously presents a hand signal: a fist signifies a rock; two fingers signify scissors; and a flat, open hand signifies paper. Rock wins over scissors, scissors over paper, and paper over rock. (Rocks can break scissors, scissors can cut paper, and paper can hold up a rock.)

In this game, the field is divided into three parts: a safety zone for each of the two teams and a central zone for deliberations. Each team determines which hand signal it will use and meets together in the central zone with the other team. Both teams simultaneously display their chosen signal. The team that wins the throw then chases the other team in an attempt to tag members before they reach their safety zone. Anyone tagged joins ranks with the tagging team. Both teams then meet in the central zone for another throw and chase, continuing until everyone becomes part of a single team.

Sometimes after a throw it takes a few moments before realizing whether to chase opposing players or run to safety. In addition, the constant changing of who's on what team adds to the confusion — as well as the excitement — in this game.

Caterpillar (or People Roll)

Everyone lies stomach-down in a line on the ground, bodies squeezed side-by-side. Then, the person at one end rolls over the backs of the bodies to eventually end stomach-down at the other end. After the first person starts rolling along, the next person follows right after, and each person after that, causing the caterpillar to crawl from one end of the field to the other. You'll have the players laughing and other kids wanting to become part of the fun.

To make this a competitive game, have two (or more) human caterpillars engage in a race across the field.

Vampire

Here, all players keep their eyes closed as they roam around the playing field. Without letting other players know, designate one player to be the vampire. When this vampire runs into another roaming player, he holds on and gives a terrible scream (instead of biting his victim!). This player then becomes a vampire as well, roaming around to prey upon other players. If two vampires should meet to prey upon each other, they then become ordinary mortal players. There's no saying, then, whether the game will end with all mortals or all vampires. (It's a good idea for the counselor-referee to keep players from running into anything not human.)

Hagoo

This game is bound to have even your quietest kids in stitches. It's a game that originated in Alaska by the Tlingit Indians whose word *hagoo* means "come here." Form two lines of players and elect or invite a spirited member to walk between the lines perfectly straight-faced while members of the lines try, without any touching, to make the walker break his frozen stare into a smile or into complete laughter.

Try making teams, each line being a team and each team supplying a member who becomes a straight-faced walker. That person stands on one end and his or her opponent on the other. The two walk between the lines, pass each other, and reach the other end while team members try to make the opposing player laugh (or just smile). Any player who can travel completely straight-faced between the two laugh-tempting lines, from one end to the other, is a person of terrific self-control.

Amoeba Race

Here's a race that requires a unified effort by team members. Gather together plenty of people. Have a good number of them stand close together in a clump (the protoplasm) and then have others (the cell wall) link arms around this group. Now you have your amoeba. Form a second (and third...) and instruct the amoebae to race to a designated finish line. They'll have a singular good time!

The Lap Game

Everyone stands close together in a circle, then turns to the right so that every person is facing another player's back. Players then sit on the lap of the person behind them so that everyone in the circle is sitting on another's lap. The fun is finding out a good way to get everyone seated and then to determine what to do after that feat has been accomplished. (Try breaking the record for the most number of people involved in a single sitting of this game.)

Infinity Volleyball

This is played with the regular rules of volleyball, except that any number can be on a team and the objective is to keep the ball in the air — without hitting the ground — for as long as possible. Like regular volleyball, each side may hit the ball only three times before it must cross the net to the other team. Instead of competing against each other, both teams work together to

see how many times they can volley the ball without it hitting the ground ...
50? 75? 100?

Where Is Susie?

This is a terrific activity for camps and conferences because it usually continues for several days. At announcements, the leader makes a big deal about one individual who is so unfriendly, so untidy, and so undesirable that no one wants anything to do with her. After a big build-up, he introduces "Susie," a poker chip painted with a face, which he pulls out of his pocket.

The objective of the game is to slip Susie into someone else's pocket without that person knowing it. If she catches you putting the chip into her pocket, you must take it back. If, however, she later discovers it, she tries to slip it into someone else's possession.

At the next announcement time, everyone sings, "Where Is Susie?" (to the tune of "Way Down Yonder in the Paw-Paw Patch"):

> Where, oh where, oh where is Susie?
> Where, oh where, oh where is Susie?
> Where, oh where, oh where is Susie?
> Way down yonder in the Paw-Paw Patch.
>
> Come on, gang, let's go find her.
> Come on, gang, let's go find her.
> Come on, gang, let's go find her.
> Way down yonder in the Paw-Paw Patch.

The person who had Susie at the last announcement time tells who he gave it to, and that person tells who she gave it to, and so forth, until the unsuspecting possessor of the chip is called and discovers Susie in his pocket. He must then come forward and lead everyone in a song. He must also try to rid himself of the chip by planting it on someone else before next announcement time.

SPORTS

There's no need to neglect the traditional sports:

baseball	boating	archery	soccer
basketball	cycling	croquet	tennis
football	kite flying	four-square	tether ball

kickball	bocce ball	hockey	wiffle ball
softball	swimming	horseshoes	badminton
volleyball	fishing	ping-pong	riflery
boating			

FRISBEE GAMES

An amazing thing, the Frisbee. That a plastic disc capable of gliding through the air can provide so much fun and a wide variety of games is credit to the human imagination. I've watched kids invent or play Frisbee football, golf, tag, baseball, volleyball, and other games that weren't even given a name. No recreation program should be without one.

FURTHER RESOURCES

Fluegelman, Andrew. *More New Games!* New York: Doubleday, 1981.
_____. *The New Games Book.* New York: Doubleday, 1976.
Harbin, E. O. *The Fun Encyclopedia.* New York: Abingdon Press, 1940.
_____. *The New Fun Encyclopedia.* rev. Bob Sessoms. 5 volumes. Nashville: Abingdon Press, 1984.
LeFevre, Dale N. *Best New Games: 77 Games and 7 Trust Activities for All Ages and Abilities.* Champaign, IL: Human Kinetics Publishers, 2001.
_____. *The Spirit of Play: Cooperative Games for All Ages, Sizes, and Abilities.* Rev. ed. Scotland: Findhorn Press, 2007.
Luvmour, Josette & Sambhava. *Everyone Wins!: Cooperative Games and Activities.* Canada: New Society Publishers, 2007.
Orlick, Terry. *Cooperative Games & Sports: Joyful Activities for Everyone.* 2d ed. Champaign, IL: Human Kinetics Publishers, 2006.

Chapter 3

Nature Activities and Games

If I had influence with the good fairy who is supposed to preside over the christening of all children, I should ask that her gift to each child in the world be a sense of wonder so indestructible that it would last throughout life.

— Rachel Carson

Among the greatest gifts we can offer young people are opportunities which develop their sense of wonder and instill a love of the natural world. Positive experiences in the outdoors are essential to children's physical, mental, and spiritual well-being.

Outdoor activity not only improves children's physical health, it also enhances mental stamina and agility. Children who spend time outdoors are less frequently depressed and lonely than those confined to four walls; they are more prone to having strong immune systems and vivid imaginations. Outdoor activity has also been found to reduce stress and attention-deficit disorder among children.

"Nature-deficit disorder" is the term Richard Louv applies to children who lack sufficient exposure to the out-of-doors. Author of *Last Child in the Woods: Saving Our Children from Nature-Deficit Disorder*, Louv asserts that youthful experience with nature has a profound impact on children: it awakens their sense of adventure, wonder, and awe; it provides rich sensory stimulation in which they have primary and physical contact with the real world; it makes them active and independent participants who develop a sense of well-being and self-assurance. Equally important, young people who connect with nature become adults more likely to serve as stewards of our planet.

American youth sit staring at a flat screen for an average of 44 hours a week, more hours than the typical adult spends at work. They spend only about eight minutes outdoors each day. While these statistics are alarming, the solution is as nearby as the schoolyard or the local park. The allure of the three-dimensional green world of fun and adventure can captivate even the most habituated flat-screen addicts — as long as they are exposed to it in large-enough doses.

Best of all, outdoor activities are fun. It is not difficult to entice young people outside, especially if you appeal to their sense of adventure, action, and self-reliance. Experiences that connect young people to the natural world inevitably lead to the development of joy, appreciation, and respect that will last a lifetime.

NATURE HIKES:
HIKING TIPS AND HIKING TRIPS

A nature hike can occur anywhere there is nature: in a city park, in a field, in the woods, in a garden, along a sidewalk, or at the beach. It can take ten minutes or two hours. The following suggestions will help you make the most of the opportunity to guide young people to enjoy the natural world we inhabit.

1. **Be amazed.** You do not have to be a nature expert to lead a hike; you must simply possess wonder, appreciation, and an ability to express your feelings about the natural world. The world is filled with so much amazement: that a mighty oak can grow from a tiny acorn, that it draws its nutrients through a root system as vast as its span of branches, that it serves as a habitat for a variety of living things, that each of these living things is equally remarkable. When young people hear you speak with wonder and reverence towards the natural world, it inspires them to look carefully and to respond genuinely. Your own genuine enthusiasm about the natural wonder you encounter is enough to make any hiker's experience a meaningful one.

2. **Have fun.** An enjoyable hike can be a nature lesson, but it need not be. Simply trekking through the woods or fields will develop mem-

orable experiences with the natural world. Telling tales or jokes, singing songs, and enjoying each other's company along the way can enliven and unify the hikers. Adventure hikes and hunts, like those below, can also bring great pleasure. General goals for all hikes should be fun, camaraderie, and vigorous exercise.

3. **Explore wildlife.** Young people like to explore, and the natural world offers an endless array of adventures and learning opportunities. Hikes with a specific purpose can be both fun and educational, whether to learn about wild animals or plants, to bird-watch, to study the effects of erosion, or to photograph the beauties of the mountainside. If you are not already trained in the study of wildlife, it is a good idea to take the hike ahead of time, along with a trusty nature handbook, and learn some interesting facts and concepts to point out. Don't worry about not knowing the answers to every question a hiker might ask; instead, share in the hikers' sense of wonder, join them in hypothesizing an answer, and then research the subject upon your return. Better yet, take a guide book along with you and join the hikers in a search for the answer. Remember, though, that more important than knowing the names of things is understanding and appreciating what you are seeing.

4. **Keep together.** Hikes can help to unify a group. If you are guiding a large number of hikers, at least two leaders should accompany the group, one to serve as "leader" and the other to serve as "sweeper," sweeping up the hikers who lag behind and encouraging them to keep up with the rest of the group. If the leader and the sweeper each have a whistle handy, they can easily signal each other if the group gets separated.

5. **Be prepared.** Dress in comfortable shoes and wear appropriate hiking clothes, including a hat. Don't forget to bring sufficient water for hydration, and for longer hikes, carry trail mix, granola bars, or some other convenient foods that restore energy. Also consider taking a basic first aid kit, insect repellent, sunscreen, camera, nature guide book, and binoculars.

Alphabet Hike

Hikers take along a sketchbook to illustrate a natural object for each letter of the alphabet. They need not find items in alphabetical order. See how many letters of the alphabet they can illustrate. Alternatively, provide a list of items hikers try to find and sketch: acorn, bird, chipmunk, dandelion, evergreen, fuel (something that can be used as fuel or energy, such as a stick to fuel a campfire), etc. Instead of sketching, checking off the item or photographing it with a digital camera would work. A further option is to bring along a nature guidebook, and for each item they find, they use the book to learn something new, which they can later share at a campfire or group session. This activity adheres to the credo "Take only pictures; leave only footprints."

Nature Scavenger Hunt

Hikers walk along a hiking trail and work together to spot as many items on a list as possible, or — instead of having them check the items off — they could be provided with a digital camera to photograph each item they find. Points could be given to each item (3 points for an oak tree, 2 points for moss, 5 points for a deer), and teams could work competitively to obtain the most points. A variation is to distribute egg cartons, in which participants collect one item for each category, but nothing living: something smooth, something hard, something white, something with various colors, something wildlife might eat, something from an animal, etc.

Mystery Hike

This hike provides hikers with clues along the way, each clue leading to the next and ultimately to a campfire and food, or to a swimming area, or to some other fun conclusion to the hike. This hike can be done in teams, where each team is given different routes, all of which eventually lead to the same location. Clues can be written on paper and strategically hidden along the way, using directions and natural landmarks to guide the group along.

Tall Tale Hike

Teams start hiking in the afternoon and rendezvous in the evening at a designated place and time, where they gather around a campfire for dinner and then the telling of tall tales. The one stipulation is that the tales be based on things that occurred while on the hike. Tale-tellers, one from each team, may freely use their imaginations and a strong dose of hyperbole, as long as their stories are rooted in actual sights and incidents. For example, the sight of a leaping squirrel could become a lunging mountain lion, and a bee that got smashed after landing on a hiker might become a kamikaze pilot. Hikers or leaders can vote on the best story; the team with the best story gets released from clean-up duty after the campfire is over.

Photography Hike

The convenience of digital cameras allows hikers to hunt for beautiful images on their hike, while it simultaneously focuses their attention on the sights around them. Any pictures that do not turn out well can be easily deleted, while those that the photographer likes can later be printed. A single disposable camera can be brought along, each hiker permitted only one or two shots with the camera. After the pictures are printed, they can be displayed in a Hikers' Gallery. If awards are given for the most artistic or most beautiful photograph, consider also giving awards to the best poem or sketch created on the hike.

Flashlight Hike

Each hiker is armed with a flashlight as the "night owl walk" progresses on paths with which the leader is well-familiar. The sights and sounds of nocturnal animals will enchant the hikers and bring them to an awareness of a world they might not have imagined to exist while they were sleeping. They may be more alert than usual as they rely less on sight and more on their other senses.

Trailing Hike (Hare and Hound Hunt)

Divide hikers into two groups, one being the hares, the other being the hounds. Give the hares a 5- or 10-minute head-start, and then set the hounds on their way to try to trail and capture (tag) one of the hares. Hounds must sharpen their senses to detect the trail of the hares. Set a time at which everyone should be back at the starting point. Alternatively and more cooperatively, the hares could leave a trail behind them — perhaps rice or sugar cubes — to be picked up by the hounds as they track the hares.

Bike Hike

Although a bike hike goes at a faster pace than one on foot, it is still possible to keep attuned to the natural world through which you are passing — and at a higher vantage point. Notice the plants along the way, look up at the telephone poles for resting birds, and keep your eyes open for other wildlife. Stop periodically to lie in the grass, smell a crushed spicebush twig, or taste the honeysuckle.

Find a Critter Hike

Take a hike in which the team tries to find ten or fifteen different creatures, which includes not only animal sightings, but evidence of their presence, such as footprints, scat, and feathers.

Hiking Songs

Telling tales or singing songs along the way can enliven and unify a group of hikers. Any rousing song is appropriate on a hike, but these lively and cadenced songs are especially suitable for hiking: *The Happy Wanderer; The Whistling Gypsy; Waltzing Matilda; Kookaburra; Marching to Pretoria; The Caissons Go Rolling Along; Tramp, Tramp, Tramp (The Boys are Marching); When the Saints Go Marching In;* and *Tale of a Bear (The Other Day I Met a Bear)*. Songs that have one part of the group echoing the other part, like these last two, are especially fun on a hike. Hikers in the back can echo the ones in the front.

ACTIVITIES AND GAMES

Blindfold Walk

Kids pair off, one member tying a blindfold over the eyes of the other. The seeing partner becomes the eyes for both of them as he carefully guides the blindfolded one along a path to touch, hear, and smell the world of nature. Without sight, these other senses become more acute, and the hiker is more likely to sharpen awareness of his environment. The guide leads his partner around obstacles, steers his hands to interesting tactile objects, and directs him to notice specific sounds and smells of wildlife. Then, the kids switch roles.

Hug a Tree

In pairs, one participant is blindfolded and led to a tree, which she hugs, smells, touches, and explores. She is then led back to where the pair started and, with the blindfold removed, attempts to find the tree with which she became so familiar. The kids then switch roles. This can be such a powerful experience, that participants will return later and talk about "my tree." Any blindfolding activity requires a large measure of trust, so it is important that these activities be done with mature participants to whom the objectives and procedures have been fully explained and perhaps demonstrated.

Make a Terrarium

Create a mini-ecosystem inside a large glass jar or clear plastic container. Wide-mouth gallon pickle jars from the camp kitchen and Mason jars work well. Start by putting a layer of pebbles in the bottom for drainage, then add soil about two inches thick, followed by moss, plants, and interesting stones which can be collected during a hike in the woods. Strive for an interesting arrangement that is pleasing to view. For beginners, make an open terrarium, in which the jar is not covered. Encourage the kids to keep the soil slightly moist as they observe the development of the terrarium each day.

Explore a Microworld

Each participant chooses a 3 feet × 3 feet plot of land in which to sit and explore for an entire hour the vast world of life and activity contained in that small patch of nature. Instruct participants to focus only on the terrain they have plotted, and they will become amazed at the huge world of nature on a small scale.

Look Closely

Along a short trail, or within a designated area, strategically place a couple dozen man-made objects that can be seen without moving anything. Items like a ribbon, a rubber band, a pen, a paper receipt, a piece of wiring, and a hand mirror work well. Some can be hung or placed on branches or in bushes, and others positioned on the forest floor. It might be a good idea to write down what you placed and where, so that you don't miss retrieving each object after the activity is completed.

Explain to participants that there is a veritable abundance of life and activity in nature that we often miss seeing. Some of what we don't notice is due to the camouflage of creatures that want to blend in so that they are not observed by other creatures looking for supper. Some of what we miss is due to our not really looking. This activity will encourage kids to look carefully as they walk along the trail.

Instruct participants to walk silently along the trail and look for as many man-made objects as they can find. They are not to touch or move anything. After everyone has reassembled, ask how many man-made objects each person discovered, and see if they can name them.

Listen Carefully

Find a pleasant spot in a meadow or woods and ask participants to find a comfortable place to sit. With their eyes closed, instruct them to listen carefully to the sounds of birds, and each time they hear a different bird song or call, they should raise a finger. This activity encourages careful listening to the sounds of nature.

Alternatively, they could listen for any nature sound at all to discover the symphony of nature. Another option is to listen for man-made sounds to discover how pronounced the human impact on nature has been. It is difficult to sit for longer than five or ten minutes, even in a remote spot, without hearing an airplane, automobile, lawnmower, or other man-made sound.

Sit Quietly

This activity is hardly active, except for the active awareness that develops for those who participate. Everyone chooses a spot in nature simply to sit and think for half an hour. There is no need to draw, to write poetry, or to meditate in any formal way, though these would be good methods to respond to nature. You might be surprised how even the most energetic youngster will sit quietly to let the energies of the mind take over. Kids have actually asked to do this again and again, and they have developed a kinship with a particular place that they consider their own. They often discover a sense of peace and refreshment.

If it is nighttime, they can do the same activity while lying under the stars, taking in the vastness of the galaxy.

Nature Symphony

Each player hunts for an item from nature that can be used as a musical instrument. This may be grass or a hollow bone that can be blown, rocks that are rubbed together, or any of a variety of percussive instruments. Encourage them to use their imaginations, and they may surprise you. After each player demonstrates his instrument, conduct the orchestra in playing familiar melodies.

The Stalking Game

One-fourth of the players are given locations where they are to stand blindfolded, with a stone or stick lying on the ground between their outspread legs. The rest of the players attempt to move very quietly to obtain the stone without being caught. When the blindfolded player thinks he hears a stalker, he should point in her direction; if he catches someone, the two players switch roles. If she successfully acquires his stone, the blindfolded person is out of the game. The object of the game is to see who collects the most stones. This game requires the intent listening skills of potential prey in the wilderness, as well as the cautious stalking skills of hunter-animals.

Camouflage

Participants are taken along a short hiking trail and given four or five minutes to hide no more than 20 feet from the trail. Their objective is to camouflage themselves so that they cannot be seen. One player then walks along the trail trying to spot as many people as possible. When he has reached the end, he calls the names of the people he spotted and where, and if he is accurate, they emerge. Then, all of the other players are asked to surface and describe how they camouflaged themselves.

Food Chain Lap Sit (or Pyramid)

Give everyone an index card on which is written a living creature that is a member of a food chain or web. Each person should find the animal above or below her on the food chain and hold hands with them until a circle is formed. Everyone then turns to the right, tightens the circle, and sits on the lap of the person behind. To show the interdependence of all creatures on the web of life, ask one person to try to leave the circle without disturbing the rest of the chain. A variation is to build a human pyramid, in which the primates, highest on the food chain, are situated at the top of the pyramid. After the pyramid is erected, see what happens when one "species" at the bottom or middle of the pyramid becomes extinct.

Nature Says

While the games "Mother, May I?" and "Simon Says" work best with young children, combine the two together and the new game becomes challenging and fun for older kids as well. Ask players to select and then announce their favorite animal, which they will "be" in this game. They then all stand behind a line facing you, about fifteen feet way. Like "Mother, May I?," you give instructions which players must follow, and their aim is to be the first to reach you. Like "Simon Says," players should only obey your instructions if you precede them with the phrase, "Nature says..."; players who fail at this task are removed from the game.

For example, "Nature says, all birds hop forward one giant step," "all animals that hibernate, step back three small steps," "Nature says, all reptiles lie on the ground and crawl forward the length of your body," "all mammals take two giant steps forward," "Nature says, a drought hits the area; everyone moves back one giant step — except animals that live in the sea," "Nature says, all fish wiggle forward five small steps," "Nature says, poachers kill all animals that have ivory tusks," etc. When you feel it is time for the game to end, you can announce to those who remain in the playing field, "Survival of the fittest rules: Nature says, whoever runs up and taps my left shoulder first is the winner."

I Am a Camera

Participants pair off, and one puts on a blindfold or simply closes his eyes while the other guides him around seeking scenes of natural beauty. When the sighted "photographer" discovers something of beauty or interest, he moves his blindfolded "camera" into position for a five-second exposure to the natural beauty and then taps the "camera" on the shoulder, who then removes his blindfold and views the scene for that duration. Remind participants that close-ups of moss at the base of a tree or ants scurrying on a log can be as awe-provoking as vast mountain scenes or placid lakes. This activity allows participants to share beauty, as well as to look intently.

Noah's Ark

Whisper into each person's ear the name of an animal, making sure that every animal you name is given to two different people. This becomes a riotously fun game as the players begin to imitate their animal's sounds and movements in search of their mate — the other person given the same species. No talking allowed as the frogs, snakes, seagulls, ducks, horses, bears, and wolves strut and parade in the timeless game of attraction.

Blind Nature Walk

This is a cooperative activity in which a destination is pointed out to a group of participants, who then take a few minutes to discuss how they will reach the point when blindfolded. Once blindfolded, they all hold onto a rope and help each other to reach the destination. A youth leader should walk silently alongside them to assure that no one gets hurt.

Nature Scatter Hunt

This is a fast and fun variation of a scavenger hunt. Instead of giving out a list of items to find, you call out an item and allow the kids three minutes to scatter and then return, each bringing back the information you requested. This regrouping gives everyone an opportunity to describe and discuss what they discovered before you call out the second item on your list, and so forth. Samples of things to find: a pine cone with seeds in it (and count the seeds); moss (describe where you found it); a crawling insect; something furry; something extremely tiny; the tallest thing you can find; something shiny; something left by an animal; something beautiful; something multicolored; something with a geometric pattern; something that makes you happy; something that makes you sad; something that has a pleasant smell; something that has a bad odor; something that doesn't belong where it is.

Nature Meditation 1

This meditation has led to such relaxation and communion with nature that participants have asked to have it repeated again and again. Everyone sits on the ground within easy hearing of your voice as you read or recite, at a relaxed pace and tone, the following meditation.

Start by getting yourself in a comfortable position. It's easier to stay alert if you sit upright, with your back erect and your hands resting loosely on your knees, but you can lean against a tree or lie on your back, if you prefer. Close your eyes if you feel comfortable doing so. This meditation will begin by trying to empty your mind of the thoughts and distractions of our busy lives, to make you relax right where you are, and then to focus your full attention to the world of nature surrounding you.

Let's begin by asking you to feel your breathing. Feel the oxygen pass through your nostrils and fill up your lungs. Just focus on that sensation, and then feel your lungs empty as you exhale. That's the only sensation you should notice. Your chest and stomach rise, and then your chest and stomach fall. Rising ... and falling. Rising ... and falling. Just like that. That's the only sensation. You may find that thoughts and distractions enter into your mind. That's normal; simply notice the thought or distraction and then gently dismiss it. You can come back to it later, after the meditation. Each time you notice being distracted, simply let the distraction go and return your attention to your breathing. Return your focus to the rising and falling of your chest and stomach. Rising ... and falling. What you'll begin to notice is that your breathing slows down, becomes smoother, becomes deeper. Slower ... smoother ... deeper. You're calm and relaxed.

Now we're going to start with the top of your head and work our way down to the bottom of your feet and become completely relaxed as we go. Notice how cool and relaxed your scalp is, how your forehead loosens as all the tension drains from your body. Your eyebrows level, not pointing upwards or downwards, and any little wrinkles or worry lines smooth out. Let your eyelids be comfortably closed, not tight, just comfortably closed. Notice how your jaw muscles loosen and go slack; your chin may drop and your lips part a little. Your teeth are unclenched, and your jaw is loose. Your whole head feels easy and loose ... easy and loose.

Now feel the muscles of your neck and shoulders relax and loosen. Your head may bob a little, and your shoulders may lean forward. Your neck and shoulders are calm and relaxed ... calm and relaxed. Now feel the muscles down your back loosening and relaxing. Feel the muscles along the spine loosening from your neck all the way down to your hips. Your back is loose and relaxed ... loose and relaxed. Notice that your stomach is rising and falling as you're breathing, just as your chest is rising and falling. You're breathing as naturally as a young child. Your stomach is soft and relaxed ... soft and relaxed.

Notice your arms, how they feel heavy and completely relaxed, supported by your body or the ground with no effort from you. Notice how they bend at the elbow, how your hands are limp, how your fingers are curled. Your arms are completely relaxed ... completely relaxed. Let yourself be aware of the weight and the ease of your legs. Your legs are supported by the ground with no effort from you. They're bent at the knees, with your toes pointing slightly away from your body. Your leg is relaxed from your hip all the way to the tip of your toes. Your legs are heavy and relaxed ... your arms are loose and comfortable ... your breathing is deep and slow ... your heartbeat is soft and regular ... your whole body feels heavy and warm. You're completely tranquil and undisturbed.

You feel no tension, no stress. Your body is comfortable and relaxed. You are a child of the universe, a part of the entire flow of life. You are completely attuned to the world around you. Using each of your senses, become more aware of the world of which you are a part. Listen, and hear the sounds of nature calling to you. Notice each sound individually and pay complete attention to it. Then, feel the sunlight or the shade; feel the breeze or the stillness in the air; feel the solid earth beneath you. Now, as you breathe in, smell the freshness of the air; notice the scents of the natural world; try to distinguish each scent individually. Slowly open your eyes and observe the sights around you. Notice the swaying of the trees and the grass, the colors of the sky and the ground. Now focus on one blade of grass or one stone or one other natural object near you. Don't touch it; just look at it and see it completely.

And now, to feel fully awake in the world, count forward in your mind from 1 to 5, and when we reach 5 together, feel fully alert, calm, and at ease in the natural world. 1 ... counting up ... 2 ... 3 ... counting up ... 4 ... 5. Now stretch your arms, your back, your legs, and get up when you're ready.

Nature Meditation 2 — Visualization

This nature meditation requires visualizing — totally picturing a scene in the mind to the extent that it almost seems real. To remain alert, participants are usually asked to sit in the lotus position, with legs crossed; however, this particular cloud visualization tends to be more effective when begun in a reclining position, with eyes closed. The tree visualization which follows is best done standing.

Cloud visualization: Lie quietly for a few moments, breathing deeply, and letting thoughts and cares slip away. Now, picture a cloud — a big, soft cloud — in a bright, sunny sky. It is drifting without trouble, passing over a green landscape as it moves through the crisp blue sky. Now, imagine that *you* are that cloud; you are floating free through the sky; you are floating without a worry or a care. You have the ability to look down on earth and see everything with clarity as you slowly drift by. You are passing over a calm lake; it is as still as a mirror, and you can see your image, as well as the shadow you are casting on a portion of the lake. Birds are flying beneath you, and a slight breeze moves the treetops as though they are in a slow, rhythmic dance. You move on, following a brook or river, and you spot fish jumping and even a bear catching its dinner. You are now passing over a forest; you look down into a clearing, where you can see squirrels playfully scamper and run up and down a tree. You are just floating in a sea of blue sky, and as you pass over a green meadow, you spot cows chewing their grass. You are gliding along, light and carefree, wafting through the summer sky. You are peaceful and happy; everything is in harmony, and everything is good. Hold this feeling for as long as you can; you are relaxed, peaceful, and serene, just like the summer day.

Tree visualization: Stand firmly on the ground while you try to visualize a tree. Picture its trunk, its branches reaching outwards and upwards, its leaves of green. Now picture yourself as that tree. You are a tree, strongly rooted in the soil, your roots spread as wide as your arms will reach, and extended as deep as you are tall, into the rich earth, the loose dirt which you reveled to play in as a child. You can feel a sense of strength as your roots draw upon the earth for nutrients, extracting everything you need to live in fullness and health. Your branches reach toward the sun, as you draw energy from the source of all energy. Try to feel the sun providing you comfort and warmth. It radiates through you, passing through your leaves, your branches, your trunk, and deep to your roots. You are mighty and strong, a proud monument of nature, but you are also resilient, yielding to the winds so that you do not break. You can withstand powerful forces of nature; you can live for a hundred years; you can provide shade and comfort; you are the home to animals of the land and birds of the sky. Hold this image for as long as you can; you are strong, mighty, and significant.

Nature Meditation 3 — A Quiet Place

Give each participant an index card with a quotation and related questions to focus their thoughts as they meditate upon nature. Then, direct each person to find his or her own quiet place to sit and reflect, returning in a half hour. This meditation has been so effective that some kids return to their quiet place again and again, or think back upon the experience after returning to the routines of their daily lives. Sample quotations are provided below.

*   *   *

*The best remedy for those who are afraid, lonely or unhappy is
to go outside, somewhere where they can be quiet, alone with the
heavens, nature and God. Because only then does one feel that
all is as it should be and that God wishes to see people happy,
amidst the simple beauty of nature.*

— Anne Frank

Do you feel happy now, in the midst of nature? If so, why do you think "the simple beauty of nature" brings happiness? If not, do you think a different location would bring more satisfaction? Why do you think Anne Frank recommends sitting someplace quiet for those who are "afraid, lonely or unhappy"?

*   *   *

To me a lush carpet of pine needles or spongy grass is more welcome than the most luxurious Persian rug.

— Helen Keller

Do you agree that sometimes the comforts of civilization are not as pleasing as raw nature? Try to think of several aspects of nature that you find more appealing than the pleasures of our "civilized" world.

*   *   *

A weed is no more than a flower in disguise.

— James Russell Lowell

Look around you to see if you can find something that would be considered a weed or an undesirable plant. Look at it closely to try to find aspects of beauty in it. Are you able to discover "a flower in disguise"? In what ways can this quotation apply to people as well?

*   *   *

Climb the mountains and get their good tidings. Nature's peace will flow into you as sunshine flows into trees. The winds will blow their own freshness into you, and storms their energy, while cares will drop off like autumn leaves.

— John Muir

Whether you are in the mountains, on a beach, in a field or forest, sit quietly and take in your surroundings. It may be only minutes before "nature's peace" flows into you. Then, try to think back on an experience where your cares and troubles dropped off when you had an experience with nature.

*   *   *

It is a wholesome and necessary thing for us to turn again to the earth and in the contemplation of her beauties to know of wonder and humility.

— Rachel Carson

Look around at the beauties that surround you. List some things that arouse a sense of wonder. These could be questions you have or simply an attitude of amazement. Why do you think the beauties of the earth lead most people to feel humble?

*   *   *

I believe a leaf of grass is no less than the journey-work of the stars.

— Walt Whitman

Pick a single blade of grass, or if you are sitting where there is no grass, find a grain of sand, a leaf, or some other small item from nature. Look at it closely, examining its shape, its texture, its color(s), and its lines. Everyone seems to be captivated by the night stars, by their vastness and beauty. Find as many things about this leaf of grass that are also captivating.

*   *   *

I would feel more optimistic about a bright future for man if he spent less time proving that he can outwit Nature and more time tasting her sweetness and respecting her seniority.

— E. B. White

Think of several ways in which humans attempt to "outwit Nature"— ways in which our species uses, damages, or alters the natural world. Next, think of several ways in which nature reveals "sweetness." Finally, think of ways in which nature shows her seniority and power (such as tree roots causing cracks in sidewalks).

* * *

Adapt or perish, now as ever, is nature's inexorable imperative.
— H. G. Wells

According to this quotation, the laws of nature command that all living things either adjust to changes or fail to survive. The dinosaurs are thought to have become extinct because they could not adapt. Trees bend with the wind and survive fierce winds and hurricanes; some lizards change color so as not to be seen by predators. Look around you and find ways in which living organisms have adapted so that they can survive.

* * *

The goal of life is living in agreement with nature.
— Zeno

The author, who lived around 300 B.C., wrote these words over 2000 years ago, and many people today believe them. Think of ways in which you live in agreement with nature. Then, think of more ways in which you could live in agreement with nature.

* * *

I love to think of nature as an unlimited broadcasting station, through which God speaks to us every hour, if we will only tune in.

— George Washington Carver

Many people have believed that God speaks to us through nature. Listen carefully as you sit amidst the natural world. What do you hear? What can nature teach us? What messages might God be sending to you?

* * *

Who looks upon a river in a meditative hour, and is not reminded of the flux of all things?

— Ralph Waldo Emerson

All of nature is in flow and flux — in continual change — which you can see even if you are not by a river. Things are born, they mature, they diminish in power, and they pass on. The continual flow of life in and near a river reveals this clearly; so does a forest of trees, some young and some decaying.

Think about the flux of life. In what ways can you learn about your own life from the changes seen in nature?

* * *

I thank you God for this most amazing day, for the leaping greenly spirits of trees, and for the blue dream of sky and for everything which is natural, which is infinite, which is yes.

— e. e. cummings

The poem from which this comes is more of a prayer of thanks for "everything which is natural"; it is a poem that exclaims a positive "yes!" to the experiences nature has to offer us. Look around and make a prayer (or list) of thanks for what you appreciate.

* * *

Nature does not hurry, yet everything is accomplished.

— Lao Tzu

The Chinese philosopher Lao Tzu spent the last years of his life in nature. This sentence represents one of his discoveries about the natural world. Our lives tend to be rushed and hurried, but notice that nature is not; things grow and develop in their own time, and everything works out. What do you see that supports Lao Tzu's statement? How can this be applied to your own life?

* * *

I go to nature to be soothed and healed, and to have my senses put in order.

—John Burroughs

Sometimes our lives are troubled by demands and disappointments, but nature has the power to soothe and heal. By going to nature, we can put things into perspective. Simply sit in silence for a few minutes, taking in what you see and hear, and try to forget about things that may be troubling. Let nature work its powers on you, and simply be.

FURTHER RESOURCES

Cornell, Joseph. *Sharing the Joy of Nature: Nature Activities for All Ages*. Nevada City, CA: DAWN Publications, 1989.

_____. *Sharing Nature with Children.* 2d ed. Nevada City, CA: DAWN Publications, 1998.

Louv, Richard. *Last Child in the Woods: Saving Our Children from Nature-Deficit Disorder.* Chapel Hill, NC: Algonquin Books, 2008.

_____. Resource Guide. http://richardlouv.com/children-nature-resources.

McKinney, John. *The Joy of Hiking: Hiking the Trailmaster Way.* Berkeley, CA: Wilderness Press, 2008. Contains a chapter on hiking with kids.

Milord, Susan. *The Kids' Nature Book: 365 Indoor/Outdoor Activities and Experiences.* Rev. ed. Charlotte, VT: Williamson Publishing Company, 1996.

Sawyer, Susan. *Hands-On Nature: Information and Activities for Exploring the Environment with Children.* Quechee: Vermont Institute of Natural Science, 2000.

Nature Book Series

Peterson Field Guides, including *Wildflowers, Reptiles and Amphibians, Birds of North America, Bird Songs, Birding by Ear, Animal Tracks, Insects, Stars and Planets, Atlantic Seashore,* and *Eastern Forests.* Boston: Houghton Mifflin.

Peterson First Guides, including *Astronomy, Butterflies and Moths, Insects of North America, Caterpillars of North America, Reptiles and Amphibians, Trees, Birds of North America, Clouds and Weather,* and *Rocks and Minerals.* Boston: Houghton Mifflin.

Take a Walk Series, including *Take a Backyard Bird Walk, Take a Tree Walk, Take a Beach Walk, Take a City Nature Walk,* and *Take a Walk with Butterflies and Dragonflies.* Windsor, CO: Stillwater Publishing.

Take-Along Guides, including *Trees, Leaves and Bark; Caterpillars, Bugs and Butterflies; Rabbits, Squirrels and Chipmunks; Berries, Nuts and Seeds; Frogs, Toads and Turtles; Tracks, Scats and Signs; Birds, Nests and Eggs; Planets, Moons and Stars; Seashells, Crabs and Seastars; Rocks, Fossils and Arrowheads; Snakes, Salamanders and Lizards; Wildflowers, Blooms and Blossoms; Fun with Nature;* and *More Fun with Nature.* Bel Air, CA: Northword Books for Young Readers.

Chapter 4

Theme Days

These all-day events are both eagerly anticipated and long-remembered well into adulthood. Packed with excitement and fun, they promote a united and buoyant spirit: one entire day of continuous joy.

ALL-DAY OLYMPICS

Especially during summers when international Olympic events are underway, consider holding an all-day Olympics. After serving a "breakfast of champions," teams design their own flags, choose their own colors, and designate their own contestants for each event. Ceremonies begin with the lighting of the Olympic torch, which remains lit throughout the events. This is followed by an opening parade, in which the flags are displayed, and a brief speech recounting the history of the games, the value of physical strength and endurance, and the importance of sportsmanship.

Events may include: the 50-yard dash, shot put, broad jump, high jump, canoe race, discus throw (using a Frisbee or a toilet seat), swimming races, and softball throw. Team games, involving everyone, develop team spirit and enthusiasm: tug-of-war, softball, kickball, volleyball, and an all-teams relay race.

Each event is given a point value, and team points are tallied throughout the day.

Dinner may be a gala meal or cookout, followed by an awards ceremony. An evening campfire or dance may conclude the day.

A variation is Wacky or Goofy Olympics, in which the events are as crazy as the name implies.

PIRATE DAY

Shiver me timbers, matey — it's Pirate Day. Early in the day, each team chooses a name (like the "Jolly Rogers," "Bluebeard's Bandits" or the "Pie Rats") and designs an insignia (like the skull and crossbones) by which it will be identified. Everyone dresses in pirate attire (eye patches, scarves, hooks, etc.) and wears its team's insignia throughout the day. Then, using a cardboard box or a crate, each team decorates its treasure chest and decides upon its contents. After hiding the chest, they make a map utilizing compass points. The hunt is then ready to get underway.

Photocopy and distribute a map and a compass to each team, along with a few fake maps which lead to nothing. To make things even more interesting, you might rip one or two maps in half, requiring that the teams find the other half before they can find the treasure.

At a given time or signal, everyone gathers at the beach for pirate races in canoes or rowboats. Other water contests can be held, including a relay in which a pirate's scarf is relayed back and forth by the swimmers and a walk-the-plank contest to see who can make the largest splash off the dock. Non-swimmers might hunt for golden doubloons (gold-painted stones) in the shallow water.

After a special pirate dinner, prizes can be awarded for the day's events, as well as for best costume, meanest pirate laugh, ugliest pirate, etc. A viewing of *Peter Pan* or *Pirates of the Caribbean* could end the day. Yo-ho, yo-ho, a pirate's life for me!

PAUL BUNYAN DAY

The night before, tales of Paul Bunyan may be read in anticipation of this special day. Everything on Paul Bunyan Day is done big and rugged, so counselors make a rousing wake-up call, and everyone dresses in rugged clothes before heading to a breakfast of super-large pancakes. The morning activities include friendly competitions between logging teams:

1. Log-sawing contest. Each team is supplied with a saw and a log approximately four inches in diameter. Contestants try to be the first to saw through their log.
2. Log-splitting contest. Contestants trained to use axes split logs of equal size to see who finishes first.
3. King of the Log contest. A log is nailed upon two posts two or three feet above the ground. Two contestants try to knock each other off.
4. Log-heaving contest. A log of appropriate length and weight is heaved by various members of each team, aiming for greatest distance.
5. Nail-driving contest. The winner is the first to fully drive three long nails into a log.
6. Whittling contest. This is a creative event, in which the winner is the person who whittles the most original item or toy from a piece of wood.
7. Tree-climbing contest. With a stopwatch, time contestants as they climb a tree to strike a bell you have placed there.
8. Tobacco spit contest. Each contestant is given a chew of licorice to see who can spit the farthest.
9. Shaving contest. Contestants use a razor to shave shaving cream off of a balloon. Who does the cleanest job without breaking the balloon?
10. Logger tug-of-war.

After lunch or rest period, teams can create their own Paul Bunyan tale (how he formed the Grand Canyon or the camp's lake) which will be told or performed at the evening's campfire. An afternoon swim before dinner should be a refreshing end to the afternoon.

Dinner should be a hearty logger's meal, perhaps ending with the cream puffs which delighted loggers at the Black Duck Dinner in James Stevens' Paul Bunyan story.

End the day with a campfire of tall tales. Prizes may be awarded to the best storyteller.

AMERICAN INDIAN DAY

Research the indigenous or First Nations people that once inhabited your local region, learning about traditional food, dwellings, apparel, customs, games, legends, beliefs, and their relationship to the land. Devote American Indian Day to learning about and honoring the culture of the tribe or nation. This would be a good opportunity to discredit stereotypes that may surround these peoples, as well as to highlight their traditionally close connection to nature. The day's activities might include

- preparing meals similar to traditional cuisine and methods
- building a dwelling fashioned after traditional residences
- creating and dressing in clothes that resemble traditional attire
- playing traditional games
- learning crafts and skills
- learning legends and lore
- discussing and practicing nature conservation of the tribe or nation
- telling traditional tales around the campfire

HAWAIIAN DAY

Aloha! Welcome everyone as they arrive dressed in bright summer clothing and garlanded with leis for a day of Hawaiian fun. Leis can be purchased ahead of time at party supply stores, or simply made by stringing colored construction paper cut into flower shapes — or even popcorn — into long necklaces. Activities throughout the day include making tiki masks, learning hula dancing, and decorating dinner tables with a Hawaiian theme. Enjoy a lu'au (the Hawaiian word for "feast), complete with contests in doing the limbo, hula hooping, and strumming the ukulele. Serve fresh pineapple and macadamia nuts. Play ulu maika, sometimes known as Hawaiian bowling: players traditionally tried to roll a disk-like rock between two sticks hammered into the ground. The game could be played just as well with a tennis ball and two soda bottles, placed six inches apart, 15 or 20 feet from the starting line. The player first to roll the ball through five times wins.

AMERICA DAY

This day is especially appropriate for July 4th, but could be held any day of the year. Fly American flags. Dress up like Uncle Sam. Consider holding a costume contest in which everyone poses as a famous American — historical or fictional — like George Washington, Abraham Lincoln, Susan B. Anthony, Yankee Doodle, Paul Bunyan, and Becky Thatcher. Play a game of baseball or whiffle ball and sing "Take Me Out to the Ball Game." Prepare a typically American barbeque of hot dogs and hamburgers, with apple pie and ice cream for dessert. Hold a watermelon seed-spitting contest. Run relay races. Have an afternoon snack of popcorn and cotton candy. Tell American tales around the campfire and sing American songs.

INDIANA JONES DAY

Compete for the title of "Indiana Jones" in adventure games and challenges set in the wild outdoors. Give a prize to the winner in an Indiana Jones look-alike contest. Hold a Snake Toss to see who can throw a rubber snake the farthest distance. Use the rubber snake instead of a ball in other games and competitions. Play Initiative Games from Chapter 1.

FIELD DAY

This is a traditional American event devoted to an entire day of fun and activity in a large field. Set up a dozen or more stations and divide kids into teams which rotate through the stations, 15 to 30 minutes per station. Each station is a different field activity; traditionally, relay races (see Chapter 2) are part of the fun, as well as numerous other activities which may include field sports, croquet, initiative or challenge games, goofy games, obstacle courses, scavenger hunts, and treasure hunts. One station could be a huge table of lunch foods (perhaps hot dogs and hamburgers on the grill) for the noontime hour. A watermelon break in the afternoon could include a seed-spitting contest. Consider an R&R (rest and relaxation) station or break in the afternoon, where puzzles are set up on a table, blankets are scattered, and bubble-blowing toys are available. A good finale to the day is an all-out tug-of-war.

Instead of establishing teams that stay the same throughout the day, let kids participate in the activities that appeal to them, encouraging participation by giving a ticket to each person after completing an activity. He or she writes his name on the ticket, which is placed in a box for a drawing at the end of the day. The more activities in which you participate, the better your chances of winning a prize in the drawing. (No tickets are distributed for participating in lunch or R&R!)

HOLIDAY DAY

Halloween in June, Christmas in July, and Chinese New Year in August ... or celebrate all holidays in a single day. It's a new day as you awake, so celebrate New Year's in the morning with sparkling grape juice, a healthy breakfast, and a new year's (or new day's) resolution. Happy New Day to all! After breakfast, dress up like Abraham Lincoln and George Washington. Give thanks and eat Thanksgiving turkey for lunch, either an open-faced hot turkey sandwich with gravy, or a sandwich spread with cranberry sauce and loaded with turkey and hot dressing. For dessert, eat candied apples and give awards for the scariest, most original, and most artistic Halloween masks. Give out candy treats only to those who perform a crazy trick for one of the leaders (singing a song while hopping on one leg, for example). Throughout the afternoon, hold a Fourth of July field day and enjoy an American barbeque for supper. End the day with a celebration of Hanukkah and/or Christmas, give gifts made earlier to a secret pal, and sing holiday songs and carols.

BACKWARDS DAY

Today, do everything backwards. Dress and walk backwards. Say "good night" in the morning and "good morning" at night. Begin the day with supper and end it with breakfast; eat dessert before the main course. Run to third base instead of first base. Reverse the day's schedule.

DISNEY DAY

Everyone dresses up and acts like a favorite Disney character. Hold a Mad Hatter's tea party in the afternoon. End the day with a *High School Musical*–style dance.

INTERNATIONAL DAY

This day celebrates cultures from around the world, enjoying multicultural crafts, songs, dances, plays, cuisines, and games. Here are some traditional and folk games and activities from various parts of the world:

- Tinikling (Philippines): Two participants kneel on the ground, each holding the ends of two long bamboo poles (any long poles will do). In an even rhythm, set to lively music, they first bang the poles on the ground and then clap the poles together, creating a strong percussive beat. Meanwhile, one or two dancers step in and out of the clapping poles, being sure not to get their feet caught. As the dance continues, the movement of the poles increases, making this a lively and exciting activity to watch, as well as to attempt.
- Jianzi (China): If you think hacky-sack is a modern game, look at Jianzi to see that the basic idea has been around for centuries, dating back to the Han Dynasty in China. This game uses a shuttlecock, and the aim is to keep the shuttlecock in the air as long as possible. Each player uses only his feet, usually the inner foot or the ankle, and earns a point for each time he kicks the shuttlecock, keeping it in the air. If the shuttlecock lands on the ground, he relinquishes it to the next player. The player with the most points wins. This game is called Chapteh in southeast Asia and Dacau in Vietnam. A similar game called Chegi is played in Korea.
- Mancala (Africa): Mancala boards can be purchased in most toy stores, or you can just as effectively use an egg carton and two bowls, one per player, each bowl positioned at opposite ends of the carton. To begin, three stones are placed in each hole of the egg carton. The objective of the game is to end with more stones in your bowl than your opponent has in his. Player One begins by taking all of the stones in any one hole on his side and, moving counter-clockwise, placing one stone in each of the three successive holes. Even though the end bowls begin

empty, if Player One's end bowl is one of the three successive holes, it also receives a stone. Player Two takes all of the stones in any one hole on his side and, moving in the same direction, places one stone in each of the successive holes until his hand is empty. Players never place stones into their opponent's end bowl. If the last stone placed is in the player's end bowl, he gets a free turn. If the last stone placed is in an empty hole on the player's side, the player takes that stone and any stones in the hole opposite it and deposits them into his end bowl. The game ends when all six holes on one side are empty. When that occurs, the player who still has stones on his side collects them and places them in his end bowl. The player who ends with the most stones wins.

- Stool ball (England): This game, perhaps the ancestor of cricket and baseball, began in the 14th century in southern England. Each player sits on a flat stone or cushion placed in a large circle, each some distance from the next. *It* stands in the center of the circle and throws a tennis ball into the air, whereupon each player runs clockwise to the next stone. When *It* catches the ball, she attempts to throw it at a player before she reaches the next stone. If the ball hits her, that player then becomes *It*.

- Gul tara (India): *Gul tara* means "tossing to the stars." Using a soft rubber ball, one player throws the ball into the air, whereupon other players try to catch it. The player who catches it throws it up again, and this continues until someone misses, and the ball hits the ground. When this happens, everyone scatters except for the person who threw the ball, who runs to pick it up and then throws it to hit one of the scattering players. If he succeeds, the person hit starts a new round by becoming the thrower. If he does not succeed, he remains the thrower for another round. This game is similar to SPUD (see chapter 2).

- Chigora danda (Zimbabwe, with earlier origins in India): Two strong pieces of wood about 6 inches high are placed upright about 4 feet apart, and a third pole, about 5 feet long, is placed upon the two upright poles. One player sits at each end of the cross pole, while a third stands next to it. In slow rhythm, the two players holding the cross pole raise it and tap it down atop the uprights, as the onlookers clap the rhythm. The third player hops on and off the pole. As the rhythm of the playing speeds up, the third player must speed up; when the speed becomes too fast for him, three other players take their turn.

- Fukuwarai (Japan): This game is similar to Pin the Tail on the Donkey, except that it uses a picture of a human face, with the eyes, eyebrows, nose, and mouth removed. These are pinned on the face by blindfolded players, with very amusing results.

- Jan ken pon (Japan): This is the Japanese name for rock-paper-scissors, known to most young people around the world. The fist represents rock, the open hand represents paper, and two fingers extended represents scissors. Two players say, "Jan-ken-pon," and then display either rock, paper, or scissors. (Or they count, "One-two-three-shoot," and on "shoot," they throw rock, paper, or scissors.) Rock conquers scissors, because a rock can break scissors. Scissors conquer paper, because scissors can cut paper. Paper conquers rock, because paper can hold a rock.
- Sambunot (the Philippines): This game is similar to Steal the Bacon (see Chapter 2). Two teams each stand behind their own line, facing each other, with a neutral line halfway between. Place a coconut husk on that neutral line (though any object will do). At a given signal, all players rush to grab the husk and bring it back behind their team's line. When someone does capture the husk, members of the rival team try to steal it from him, while members of his own team try to protect him. The team that brings the husk across its line wins a point; game ends when a team reaches five points.
- Many inexpensive games which originated in other countries can be purchased in toy stores. For example, Parcheesi is a board game from India, and Mille Bornes is a card game from France. While Chinese checkers did not originate in China, its origins in Germany make it a suitable game for International Day. Ping pong originated in England.

EARTH DAY

Why not devote an entire day to the planet which sustains us? Hone outdoor survival skills, enhance respect for the environment, and learn about our natural world — all while having fun. See Chapter 3 for nature activities and games appropriate to Earth Day. Discuss the "footprint" we leave on this planet, and make every effort to leave a very limited footprint on this day. Prepare and eat a meal outdoors, using no artificial or chemical ingredients. Alternatively, eat a meal of rice and beans to bring awareness of the staple of a large percentage of the earth's population. Explain that, while the United Nations recommends a diet of 2350 calories per day, people in most low income countries consume approximately 2100 calories today, and many eat far fewer; most people in developed countries like ours eat approximately 3700 calories per day, and many eat far more.

GOLD RUSH

Return to 1849 in search of fortune and adventure as you aim to strike it rich in your gold rush town in Californy or Alasky.

Teams begin by devising a name for their "town" in the fashion of actual gold rush towns, which were given such colorful names as Angels Camp, Flea Valley, Skunk Gulch, and Rattlesnake Diggings. The town which then invents and tells the most colorful story to explain its name wins the first of several awards which will be presented throughout the day: gold candy coins or a gold nugget (gold-painted rock) that can be exchanged for prizes at the end of the day.

For many prospectors, the Gold Rush was a race to be the first to stake a claim or discover gold, so relay races are in order (see Chapter 2):

- A wheelbarrow race would be especially appropriate, as would a spoon race using a ping-pong ball spray-painted gold (or a gold candy coin).
- Hold a donkey race in which one participant carries his partner on his back toward the goal line, where the two switch positions and run back to the start; the pair which first reaches the starting line wins.
- In another competition, each town selects one member to guard its claim (a balloon sitting inside a circle), while all of the other members of the town try to burst the balloons of rival towns without being tagged by the guard; tagged players are "jailed" (pulled off the field), and the winning town is the one with their balloon still intact.
- Set up an obstacle course which requires miners to climb (a mountain), leap (a creek), and crawl (into a cave).
- See which miner or town can pan the most gold (gold-sprayed gravel) buried in sand or at the edge of the shore.
- Each town receives a treasure map to compete in a race to find the gold mine, loaded with chocolate gold-covered coins.

Take the afternoon off from mining to attend a town carnival (see Chapter 2), make country crafts, bake sourdough bread, or dip candles.

End the day with a square dance, campfire, or stage show for all of the forty-niners. At the campfire, read Mark Twain's "The Celebrated Jumping

Frog of Calaveras County" and sing western songs like "Clementine," "Red River Valley," and "Sweet Betsy from Pike" (who reached California with her husband, Ike). Tell corny jokes ("What did the gold miner say when he staked his claim?— Be mine." "What tool should you take if you are a gold miner?— Take your pick.") The stage show and the campfire can both include entertainment and skits.

The Gold Rush is a long-time camp favorite that never loses its luster; your efforts to make this pan out will not be in vain.

Probably the best theme days are those devised from the imaginations of a group of leaders and/or kids, who brainstorm activities based on well-known subjects: Harry Potter Day, Narnia Day, Wacky Day, Outer Space Day, All-Day Rodeo, etc. Half of the fun comes in the planning.

FURTHER RESOURCES

California Gold Rush. http://www.usscouts.org/macscouter/CubScouts/PowWow 99/SCCC/Oct99.pdf. October 1999. This Cub Scout site provides excellent details for Gold Rush Day.

Chapter 5

Rainy Day Activities

Rainy days can dampen spirits and extinguish enthusiasm, or they can be exciting, creative, and educational. It all depends on what you do with them.

1. Take a hike! Go on a rainy day hike and hunt for worms, frog eggs, and rainbows that might otherwise be hard or impossible to find.
2. Challenge kids to a series of contests: how many states can you think of that end with the letter A? how many crackers (or marshmallows) can you fit in your mouth and clearly say, "Fluffy Bunny?" etc.
3. Play musical chairs. Hum, sing, or drum on a cardboard box if a musical instrument is not available.
4. Throw an unbirthday party (a party celebrating everyone's birthday, even if it's no one's birthday). Decorate the room. Play pin-the-tail-on-the-donkey, bob for apples, eat ice cream and cake. Divide kids into groups based on the month (or season) of their birth to create and perform skits or songs pertinent to that month.
5. Have a Noah's Ark Day. Read animal stories, sing animal songs, make animal sounds, eat animal crackers, drink bug juice, do activities in pairs.
6. Hold a sing-in. (This could be a competition. For example, you provide a theme like "days of the week," "colors," or "weather," and each group must think up and sing a song which contains words fitting the category.)
7. Tell stories.
8. Hold an indoor "campfire" around a battery-powered lantern.
9. Have an arts and crafts day.

10. Perform improvisations, pantomimes, or skits.
11. Go fishing.
12. Clean the cabin.
13. Put on rain gear and go on a treasure hunt or scavenger hunt.
14. Hold an indoor decathlon (discus throw using paper plate, javelin toss using a straw or uncooked spaghetti, shot put using a balloon, 20-feet hop instead of 100-yard dash, thumb wrestling, etc.). Use your imagination!
15. Have a board games day or a Las Vegas evening.
16. Do theatrical improvisations. (For example, each group is given a prop or bag of props which they use in creating and performing a scene.)
17. Write a letter home.
18. Do magic tricks.
19. Plan the next campfire, party, evening activity, or worship service.
20. Try a teach-in. Everyone teaches the group something that he or she is knowledgeable about. (You will be surprised by the hidden knowledge your young people have.)
21. Pop some popcorn and hold a movie marathon.
22. Make your own movies by darkening the room and rapidly waving a flashlight on actors, creating an effect reminiscent of old-time silent films.
23. Play charades.
24. Tell jokes, riddles and tall tales.
25. F.O.B.—feet on bunk, flat on back. (Take a nap or read silently.)
26. Construct boats from paper and float them on a puddle.
27. Develop an original story beginning with the line, "It was a dark and stormy afternoon."
28. Make puppets out of socks or paper bags and put on a puppet show.
29. Hold a dart-throwing contest.
30. Listen to a recording of Prokofiev's "Peter and the Wolf."
31. Have a Pickle Party. Elect a Pickle King and Queen. Pass out pickles and straight peppermint candy sticks, cut off the end of the pickle, and shove the stick through its center; then, suck on the end of the pickle. While enjoying the peppermint-sweetened pickle juice, make up songs and poems about pickles. Recite or sing them ("I'm Dreaming of a Green Pickle" or "If I Had a Pickle").
32. Read a story.
33. Write a story.
34. Have a "group write": as a group, create and write a tall tale.
35. Draw, color, or paint.

36. Make a piñata from balloons, newspaper, and papier-mâché. Plan a Mexican fiesta.
37. Invent something.
38. Tell each other's fortune by peering into a crystal ball, reading palms, or analyzing placement of playing cards.
39. Write and illustrate a newspaper, magazine, or story book.
40. Hold indoor relay races.
41. Put together a talent show.
42. Hold a balloon party (see Chapter 2 for balloon games).
43. Arm wrestle and Indian wrestle.
44. Communicate by human telephone. Pass a message by having each person whisper the message to the next person in line. When the message reaches the end of the line, find out how much it changed from the original message.
45. Play hangman, battleship, and other paper-and-pencil games.
46. Hold an indoor carnival with multiple booths: ring toss on legs of an upright chair, marble shoot into a tin can, clothespin drop into a bottle, bean bag toss into a wastebasket, Ping-pong ball hits into an egg carton, beans-in-a-jar count, etc.
47. Learn about weather — thunder, lightning, rain — and keep track of the day's rainfall.
48. Learn and practice different types of knots.
49. Learn how to build a campfire and cook in the rain.
50. Hold a rap session.
51. Make origami animals.
52. Collect and identify rocks, shells, seeds, or plants.
53. Have a backward day. Dress and walk backward. Say "good night" in the morning and "good morning" at night. Begin the day with supper and end it with breakfast.
54. Put on an indoor circus, complete with sideshows and three-ring performances.
55. Make face masks from paper bags, papier-mâché, or plaster.
56. Play chess or checkers. These classic strategy games are good for the mind.
57. Do mind-bending puzzles. For example, draw four straight lines without lifting your pencil or retracing any lines, being sure to pass through all nine dots, arranged in three columns and three rows. For another example, add one line to the left of the equal sign to make this equation accurate: $5 + 5 + 5 = 550$ (solution: $545 + 5 = 550$).
58. Play bean bag games (see Chapter 2).

59. Learn how to make paper, and then make some.
60. Make potato prints. Cut a raw potato in half, cut a design into the sliced end, ink it, and press it against sheets of paper.
61. Make collages out of old magazines or newspapers.
62. Design postcards on heavy paper, 4" × 6", write a message on the backs, and mail them home.
63. Hold a trivia contest. Use a trivia book or almanac for questions and see who can answer the most.
64. Go on a rainy day shoot. Wrap cameras securely in clear plastic bags and take pictures in the rain.
65. Play "Win, Lose, or Draw." Each team tries to guess the title of a movie, book, song, etc., as one member of the team draws clues to the title. No words may be spoken or written by the team member drawing the clues. It's like charades on paper. Let each team provide the opposing team with the titles they must use. Instead of titles, try familiar expressions or topics relating to church, temple, or camp.
66. Make cat's cradles.
67. If a kitchen is available, bake cookies or a cake.
68. Meditate.
69. Play card games. A single pack of cards can provide hours of fun and variety.
70. Go swimming (as long as there is no lightning). Why not? You're going to get wet anyway. Or get into bathing suits and hold a "beach party" on the lawn, even if you're miles from a beach.
71. Use a strong flashlight and make hand shadows on the wall.
72. Whittle. Use a jackknife to carve something out of a piece of wood.
73. Put on a fashion show. Try a crazy costume show, with awards going to the zaniest and most original costumes.
74. Blind Guess: See how many kids can guess the individual flavors of various gourmet jelly beans or baby foods while blindfolded.
75. Test the group's collective memory by seeing how many U.S. presidents, states, or capitals they can recall.
76. Play with Legos. Legos are not only for young children, as can be seen by the vast array of robots and Legolands adults have created over the years. Give each group an equal number of Lego pieces and time to construct an original creation, or a replica of a famous building or monument. This may be a competition by having a panel of judges rate the handiwork on beauty, originality, and structural soundness.
77. Play crab soccer or volleyball indoors, using a beach ball. Players start in a seated position and move around on all fours, with their

backs towards the floor and their bellies towards the ceiling. They may use either hands or feet to contact the ball. A string tied across the room a few feet from the floor can serve as the volleyball net.

78. Be a clown: each group chooses from a pile of old clothes and makeup to dress a member to be the zaniest clown. They can then prepare and present a short mimed skit — for example, falling in love, getting caught in a thunderstorm, or learning to ride a bicycle.

79. Blanket identification: two people hold up a blanket and a few kids line up right behind it, with only their feet showing; participants try to name the identities of each individual behind the blanket, merely by seeing their feet. This works best as a co-ed activity, with girls and guys on different sides.

80. Play Black Jack, a lively card game in which players slap the black jack when it appears.

81. Dead Horse: One person lies face-up on the floor, with her eyes closed, while everyone else attempts to make her laugh, without touching. Use a timer and take turns to see who can hold out the longest.

82. Make 'em smile: Create two lines on the floor 15 or 20 feet apart. Divide players into two teams, each team standing on its own line and facing the opposing team. One team is given a ball or some other object to pass down its line, but before each player passes the object on to the next teammate, he must call someone over from the other team. That person walks across the gap while maintaining steady eye contact with the player who called him; if she can make it across without smiling, her team gets the ball and attempts to pass it down their line, from the beginning. The object is to make the person on the opposing team smile so that the ball will not pass to the other team. The team that successfully passes the ball all the way to the end of its line wins.

83. Extreme Makeover: The kids will have a lot of fun dressing up their adult leader. Awards can be given for the team which creates the funniest hairstyle, the craziest apparel, and the overall zaniest makeover.

84. Set up a bowling alley using empty soda or milk containers. For the bowling ball, anything from a tennis ball to a soccer ball will work. Make the game more challenging by playing Bounce Bowling, where the ball must first bounce against the wall before knocking down "pins." Pins knocked down by a direct hit of the ball, without first hitting the wall, subtract points from your team, while pins knocked down after first bouncing off the wall add points.

85. Play Broom Hockey, imitating usual hockey rules, but using a broom for the stick and a box for the goal.
86. The stupidest thing I ever did: go around the room and have everyone tell or dramatize the stupidest thing he or she ever did.
87. Reader's Theatre: Keep on hand some plays or scenes that are appropriate to your kids' ages, and have students read or act the parts.
88. Play games from Chapter 2.
89. Make a list of ten more things to do on a rainy day, and then do some of them.

One summer, after it had rained for days on end with no let-up in sight, we decided it was high time to raise the spirits of the campers by proclaiming the next day "Sun Day," whether it was sunny or not:

SUN DAY PROCLAMATION

Be it known that tomorrow, Tuesday, the ninth day of August in the year of our Lord _____, is hereby proclaimed as Sun Day at sunny Northeast Music Camp in sunny downtown Hardwick, upon Ware, in the sunny Commonwealth of Massachusetts, beginning at sunrise.

Also be it known that festivities for Sun Day will include shiny faces, warm hellos, bright spirits, and radiant sounds of music.

Also be it known that the lustrous celebration of Sun Day will climax at sunset with a sunny "hay seed" sun dance in sunny Hardwick Hall, where spirits will be bright and sunny — fun for all the sunbeams.

Also be it known that Sun Mayors for the day will be the Honorable Artsun and Ellensun, camp directors. Sun Day activities will be coordinated by Jim and Nancy Sundial, Suntan Susan, and Radiant Roger.

Also be it known that the sunny staff will assist in making Sun Day bright and sunny. The entire camp family is encouraged to wear bright, cheery clothing and sunglasses in celebration of Sun Day.

Chapter 6

Dramatics, Skits and Stunts

Dramatics, skits and stunts are great fun, whether they be performed on a raised platform or in front of a campfire. Performing can build confidence, develop imagination, and strengthen group unity. If you keep in mind the following considerations, you'll have a maximum of fun and a minimum of complications:

1. Be sure no one is uncomfortable or embarrassed. Do not force anyone to perform; allow shy individuals to play their role as members of the audience. Reluctant but willing performers can be given small roles.
2. Be involved in the planning of skits and stunts, assuring good taste. In stunts requiring an unsuspecting "victim," make sure it is someone who will not be hurt by the joke. Stunt Nights are hilarious and high-spirited events only when a congenial and cooperative atmosphere is set from the start. If everyone is made aware that the evening is all in good fun and that no one person will be singled out to be the focus of all the stunts, then participants will more likely enter into the stunts good-humoredly. It also helps when staff members become the object of a stunt or two early in the evening.
3. Work out logistics ahead of time for maximum visibility and audibility of the actors. All equipment and details, including who will be called on for stunts, should be prepared in advance.
4. Strive for fun more than award-winning performances.

Impromptus

Impromptus are off-the-cuff mini-performances based on a given prompt. While the spontaneity of impromptus may at first sound difficult and intimidating, kids rarely feel threatened since it is so like the play they participated in as younger children. Often the shyest, most apprehensive individuals give more convincing performances than those students who always seek the spotlight.

Small teams of two to three work best. Each team is given a situation which they will be asked to role-play. Examples:

- police officer & driver: driver tries to convince officer not to issue ticket.
- boyfriend & girlfriend: one has seen the other with another girl/boy.
- husband & wife: husband forgets his wedding anniversary.
- two guys & a girl: two guys fight over a girl.

Teams should be given a minute or two to decide who will play each role and determine a starting point for their scene. They then assume the personality of the characters they are playing and act out the situation. It is not necessary for the conflict to end in a resolution. In fact, if either actor feels lost for something to say, he is permitted to conclude simply by stating, "That's it; we're through."

Impromptu situations can be either funny or serious. Many variations exist:

1. Silent impromptu: No dialogue is permitted; actors perform situation strictly by gestures, facial expressions, and body movements. Examples: a man passes a bag lady, then feels guilty; a guy and a girl working in the library begin to show interest in each other.
2. Prop impromptu: A scarf, hat, cane, ruler, or other item is used as a major element in each impromptu. As acting teams successively take the stage, the same prop or costume can be used, but each time in a totally different way, determined by the imaginations of the players. Example: a scarf can be worn variously to suggest a cowboy, a bandit, a cleaning woman, or a smart-looking, well-dressed lady. Consider keeping a bag of props, from which an actor for each scene pulls an object which will be the focus for the performance.
3. "Freeze/Justify": Four or five performers begin by spontaneously play-acting. At a point when the movements and gestures seem particularly expressive, tell the actors to "freeze" and replace one of them with a member of the audience, who "justifies" the poses of the frozen actors by starting a new scene with a new storyline suggested by the frozen positions. Once the new performer speaks, the actors are freed from their frozen positions to take on a new role. Example: an actor

might be crouched to hike an imaginary football to a quarterback; you freeze the action and remove the quarterback. The crouched posture might cause the new actor to begin the next scene by asking, "Did you lose your contact lens? I'll help you find it." At this point, the actors come back to life and spontaneously play out this new situation until you again freeze them at an appropriate spot and replace one of the performers.

MIMING

In miming (or pantomiming), the performer acts out a situation without using words. Many different guessing games can grow out of miming:

Each performer picks a job and portrays it silently for the audience to guess. For example, a pizza cook kneads the dough and tosses it into the air several times, then spreads the sauce and lays on other ingredients.

Try miming songs (like "The Bear Went Over the Mountain" or "Michael, Row the Boat Ashore").

Mime famous sayings (like "A bird in the hand is worth two in the bush" or "Early to bed, early to rise, makes a man healthy, wealthy, and wise") and see who can identify the saying.

MIMING A STORY OR POEM

While a short story or poem is being read, performers pantomime the actions in an exaggerated manner. "Casey at the Bat" is an old favorite. Consider, also, Lord Tennyson's "Lady Clare," which requires three performers:

Lady Clare
by Alfred, Lord Tennyson

Gestures:

It was the time when lilies blow
  And clouds are highest up in the air,
Lord Ronald bought a lily white doe   *Ronald & Clare enter, hand in hand.*
  To give his cousin, Lady Clare.

I trow they did not part in scorn;   *They part lingeringly.*
  Lovers long betrothed were they;
They two will wed the morrow morn —
  God's blessing on the day!   *She waves goodbye...*

"He does not love me for my birth,   *...and fondly thinks of him,*
  Nor for my lands so broad and fair;   *stretches out her arms,*
He loves me for my own true worth,   *folds them across her chest,*
  And that is well," said Lady Clare.   *and smiles.*

In there came old Alice the nurse,   *Alice enters*
  Said, "Who was this that went from thee?"   *and mimes her question.*
"It was my cousin," said Lady Clare;   *Clare responds delighted.*
  "Tomorrow he weds with me."

"O God be thanked!" said Alice the nurse,   *Alice expresses great joy,*
  "That all comes around so just and fair!   *clasps her hands together,*
Lord Ronald is heir of all your lands,   *then spreads them out, and*
  And you are not the Lady Clare."   *finally points matter-of-factly at Clare.*

"Are ye out of your mind, my nurse,   *Clare mimes amazement*
  Said Lady Clare, "that ye speak so wild?"
"As God's above," said Alice the nurse,   *and Alice shakes her head and points*
  I speak the truth; you are my child.   *to herself.*

"The old Earl's daughter died at my breast,   *Alice mimes holding a baby*
  I speak the truth, as I live by bread!
I buried her like my own sweet child,   *and drops her head.*
  And put my child in her stead."

"Falsely, falsely have ye done,   *Clare shakes her finger at Alice.*
  O Mother," she said, "if this be true,
To keep the best man under the sun
  So many years from his due."

"Nay now, my child," said Alice the nurse.   *Alice puts her arm around Clare's*
  "But keep the secret for your life,   *shoulders, consoling her.*
And all you have will be Lord Ronald's
  When you are man and wife."

"If I'm a beggar born," she said,   *Clare pulls away from Alice and*
  "I will speak out, for I dare not lie.
Pull off, pull off, the brooch of gold,   *strips off her jewelry,*
  And fling the diamond necklace by."   *flinging it to the ground.*

"Nay now, my child," said Alice the nurse,
  "But keep the secret all you can."
She said, "Not so; but I will know
  If there be any faith in man."

Alice quickly snatches up the
jewelry and tries to return it to Clare,
who refuses it.

"Nay now, what faith?" said Alice the nurse;
  "The man will cleave unto his right."
"And he shall have it," the lady replied,
  "Tho' I should die to-night."

Alice opens her hands, questioningly,

and Clare responds with determination.

"Yet give one kiss to your mother dear!
  Alas, my child, I sinned for thee!"
"O Mother, Mother, Mother," she said,
  "So strange it seems to me.

Alice points to her cheek.

"Yet here's a kiss for my mother dear,
  My mother dear, if this be so,
And lay your hand upon my head,
  And bless me, Mother, ere I go."

Clare kisses her,

and Alice fondly places her hand
on Clare's head in blessing.

She clad herself in a russet gown,
  She was no longer Lady Clare;
She went by dale, and she went by down,
  With a single rose in her hair.

Alice removes her outer robe,
and walks in plain clothes,

placing a rose in her hair.

Down stept Lord Ronald from his tower;
  "O Lady Clare, you shame your worth!
Why come you drest like a village maid,
  That are the flower of the earth?"

Ronald enters,
bewildered.

"If I come drest like a village maid,
  I am but as my fortunes are;
I am a beggar born," she said,
  "And not the Lady Clare."

She points to her clothes

and drops her head.

"Play me no tricks," said Lord Ronald,
  "For I am yours in word and in deed.
Play me no tricks," said Lord Ronald,
  "Your riddle is hard to read."

Disturbed, he gestures rejection
of her words.

O, and proudly stood she up!
  Her ears within her did not fail;
She looked into Lord Ronald's eyes,
  And told him all her nurse's tale.

Head up, she looks him straight in
the eyes as she opens her hands in
explanation.

He laughed, a laugh of merry scorn;   *He laughs, kisses her...*
  He turned, and kissed her where she stood;
"If you are not the heiress born,
  And I," said he, "the next in blood —

"If you are not the heiress born,   *and puts his arm around her as*
  And I," said he, "the lawful heir,   *they exit.*
We two will wed to-morrow morn,
  And you shall be Lady Clare."

Talent/Variety Show

It never fails that the young people in your charge come with remarkable talents of their own. Why not stage a talent or variety show utilizing their abilities? Such a show could revolve around a theme, such as:

1. Old King Cole: One boy and one girl dress as king and queen. Minstrels, jesters, musicians, and other performers keep the royal couple (and everyone else) entertained.
2. Home on the Range: Around a campfire, sing cowboy songs, tell tall tales, perform stunts, and allow participants to show off western-style skills.
3. Camp Night: Campers stage spoofs of camp life, sing camp songs with their own original lyrics, and perform stunts for everyone's entertainment.
4. Komedy Klub: For an evening of jests and buffoonery, participants tell jokes, imitate famous comedians, and perform comic skits and stunts.
5. Coffeehouse: Set up the dining hall with tables, low lighting, and candles. Provide refreshments while performers entertain.

The Rent

I could recite this perennial skit in my sleep, after having heard it over and over by campers who couldn't keep it from running through their heads.

This is appropriate for younger kids, who enjoy playing with the sounds of their voices as they assume different roles. The leader recites the short and simple skit, then leads the group in unison performance, using the following voices and gestures, and aiming for drama and rhythm:

The Landlord—a deep, gruff, and demanding voice; when he speaks, everyone puts index finger horizontally under nose to represent a mustache.

The Damsel—a high, innocent, and helpless voice; when she speaks, put back of hand to forehead in an expression of helplessness.

The Hero—a strong, assuring voice; when he speaks, assume a position of swaggering self-confidence, hands in fists.

THE LANDLORD: I've come for the rent! I've come for the rent!
THE DAMSEL: But I can't pay the rent! I can't pay the rent!
THE LANDLORD: You must pay the rent! You must pay the rent!
THE DAMSEL: Who will pay the rent? Who will pay the rent?
THE HERO: I'll pay the rent! I'll pay the rent!
THE DAMSEL: My hero! My hero!
THE LANDLORD: Curses! Curses!

SHADOW SHOW

Hang a white sheet tautly in front of the performing area and direct a strong light at the sheet from behind. Then, act out scenes, nursery rhymes, and other shows between the light and the sheet, creating shadows for the audience. For example, perform a medical operation and pull out of the body amusing parts, such as a tennis racket or old shoe. Ketchup might spray out over the top of the sheet. Corny puns make it all the more amusing: "I just can't stomach this" or "Have a heart!" Try an Old West fistfight, a murder mystery story, or a strip tease (stripping down to a bathing suit).

MISS OR MR. UGLY PAGEANT

Each cabin, team, or group chooses a contestant to represent them in this ugliest person pageant. As in the Miss America Pageant, contestants compete in three categories: evening gown, bathing suit, and talent. Teams use their imaginations to dress their contestant in the most outlandish attire and make-up, and to name her or him appropriately (such as Fat Flora, Betty Butts, Sexy Celia, or Cuddly Kitty). The talent contest is really a no-talent contest. Contestants sing off-key or trip while dancing or recite "To be or not to be" abominably. A funny and spontaneous emcee should be prepared to introduce each event, and teams can perform skits between entries. Staff members or selected youngsters serve as judges.

It should come as no surprise that this pageant becomes outrageously funny when males dress as females. It can be equally as funny when girls dress, grunt, and spit like certain stereotypical guys in a "macho contest."

RADIO PLAY

Producing a radio play can be creative, fun, and dramatic. Begin by challenging kids to invent and create different sound effects. They are likely to be highly imaginative and will come up with a lot more than the following standard effects:

battle sounds or thunder:	shake a piece of heavy foil, plastic, or cardboard
punches:	hit a pillow
anchor:	rattle a chain; drop object into a jug of water:
fire:	crumble paper
hoof beats:	slap coconut shells together; or open mouth and clap hand on cheek
telephone ring:	ring alarm clock

Once they've listed a variety of sound effects they can produce, have the kids create a radio drama which uses their sound effects. They can dramatize a familiar fairy tale or story, or they can invent their own from the effects they are able to produce. Then, at a campfire or skit night, some members can take parts and read their play while others produce the sound effects. Use a microphone for the sound effects, if one is available. Or tape the story with sound effects ahead of time and play it at a campfire or skit night; in this case, music may even be introduced to set the mood.

THE WIDOW'S GRIEF

A doctor tends to a dying man, while family and friends sit around the bed, sorrowful. The doctor pulls the sheet over the man and informs his wife that she is now a widow. She weeps uncontrollably. The will is then read at the bedside, the widow still weeping. The husband then sits up in bed, having been in a coma. The wife then scolds and beats her husband for the trauma he's put her through; his no-good, lazy ways; his ignorance; etc.

IS IT TIME YET?

Five or six actors stand side-by-side, facing the audience. Their right arm is crossed over their left arm and their right ankle over their left ankle. The first person asks, "It is time yet?" and everyone going down the line repeats the question, after which the last person in line says, "No." The word "no" is transmitted along the line back to the first person. A few moments later, this process is repeated, and then again for a third time. A fourth time, "Is it time yet?" is transmitted down the line. This time, the last person in line says, "Yes, it's time," and everyone switches position by crossing their left arm over their right arm and their left ankle over their right ankle.

TOMMY HILFIGER

One actor stands on stage; another enters, carrying a shirt and crossing the stage.

FIRST ACTOR: "Hey, that's a cool shirt you've got. Where'd you get that from?"

SECOND ACTOR: "Tommy Hilfiger." He passes offstage.

A third actor enters, carrying a pair of pants.

FIRST ACTOR: "Hey, man, where'd you get the new pants?"

THIRD ACTOR: "Tommy Hilfiger." He passes off.

A fourth actor enters, carrying a new pair of shoes.

FIRST ACTOR: "I like your new shoes. Where'd you get those?"
FOURTH ACTOR: "Tommy Hilfiger." He exits.

A fifth actor enters, wearing only underwear.

FIRST ACTOR: "Hey, don't come out here dressed like that. Who do you think you are?"
FIFTH ACTOR: "I'm Tommy Hilfiger!"

THE LOST RING

This skit is performed close to the campfire or, if on stage, under a flashlight held by someone standing on a chair, posing as a lamppost.

One actor starts searching near the light for something. Another enters and asks what he's looking for. "I lost my ring," he says. Actor Two helps him look for it. Others enter, one at a time, ask what is missing, and assist. Finally, someone enters, asks what's missing, and then, "Where did you lose it?" The first actor points some distance away and says, "Over there." The last actor asks, "Well, if you lost it over there, why are you looking for it over here?" The first actor responds, "Because it's dark over there. I can see better here."

DEAD BODY

A body is lying on the ground. An actor enters, sees the body, feels its pulse, gasps, and then goes to a nearby pay telephone to call the police.

"Police, I've just discovered a dead body on the sidewalk.... Where?... I'll check the street sign.... Okay, I'm on the corner of Wheedlemeyer Avenue and Christensen Lane.... Spell it for you?... Okay, it's Wied — no, Weedm — no, Whiedl — oh, forget it! I'll drag the body over to the corner of Elm and Maple!"

SOUP BOWL

Scene: cafeteria or dining hall. Three actors are spooning soup to their mouths from a big bucket. Each one makes high praise of the soup. "This is the best soup I've ever eaten." "Hard to believe our cook could make something this good." "Yeah, it's the best food we've had since we got here." And so on.

The cook enters, carrying a mop, and yells, "Hey, what are you doing? Get out of my mop water!"

LUNCHTIME

An announcer explains that the setting is a construction site. The lunch whistle blows, and two construction workers sit down next to each other to eat.

One worker opens his lunch pail, looks at his sandwich, makes a face, and then groans, "Not a cheese sandwich again! I'm sick and tired of cheese sandwiches!"

The announcer says that it is 24 hours later. The two workers again sit down for lunch. The worker again opens his pail, looks at his sandwich, and exclaims, "I've got it again! Another cheese sandwich! I can't stand cheese sandwiches!"

This is repeated for a third day. Finally, the second worker says, "Well, if you don't like cheese sandwiches, why don't you ask your wife to make you something else?"

The first worker responds, "I don't have a wife. I make my own sandwiches."

THE CARDBOARD BOX

Two or three people are congregated outside of a store, conversing. Along comes someone carrying a cardboard box. He tells them that today is his child's birthday, that he needs to go into the store for some balloons, and he asks one of the people to hold the box for him while he's inside. While he's in the store, each person wonders what's in the box. "It must be a birthday cake," one guesses. "Could be," says another. "Something's leaking out. Maybe it's the frosting. It is hot today." One rubs a finger along the bottom and licks his finger. "Mmm. Tastes lemony." Another tries the same thing: "It tastes more like chicken soup to me." The father comes out from the store and looks inside the box. "Bad puppy! You wet the box!"

ST. PETER

St. Peter stands at the pearly gates of heaven as each of three souls asks to be allowed in. St. Peter asks each, in turn, what suffering he or she has endured to deserve admittance.

FIRST SOUL: I've eaten camp food for an entire week.

ST. PETER: That's not enough suffering. I can't admit you. Next! [To next soul:] Why do you think you should be admitted?

SECOND SOUL: I've hiked for miles, straightened up the cabin, and even cleaned the latrine.

ST. PETER: That's a lot, but it's not enough suffering. I can't admit you either. Next! [To next soul]: What suffering have you endured, my child?

THIRD SOUL: I've had to live in _____'s cabin for an entire week!

ST. PETER: That's suffering enough. Come on in!

DOCTOR'S OFFICE

One patient enters and sits in the doctor's waiting room, continually scratching himself. He picks up a magazine to read, but can't get through an article because he is interrupted by his scratching. A second patient enters, constantly twitching his arm. After a few moments, each patient adds the other patient's affliction to his own. A third patient enters, his body jerking spasmodically. Soon, all three patients have all three symptoms. Finally, a pregnant woman enters. Immediately, all three male patients jump up and run out of the room.

Variation: Three patients enter the waiting room, one at a time, and sit down. Each has an obvious affliction, as above. One patient is called into the doctor's office and leaves soon after, the affliction gone. The second one does the same, leaving totally cured. The same happens with the third patient. Finally, the doctor leaves his office, passing through the waiting room with all three symptoms.

THE BRIEFCASE

One stand-up comic attempts to tell jokes or a funny story. She is continually interrupted by another performer who walks across the stage in front of her, saying and doing the following:

FIRST TIME *[carrying a briefcase]*: I'm taking my case to court.

SECOND TIME *[carrying briefcase and ladder]*: I'm taking my case to a higher court.

THIRD TIME *[putting the comic's hands out in front of her and resting the briefcase on her open hands]*: I rest my case.

FOURTH TIME *[entering empty-handed]*: I lost my case.

BUS STOP

This performance is done as a mime. One player stands at a bus stop, obviously chewing gum. He gets tired of the gum and sticks it on the wall behind him, and then exits. Another player comes to the bus stop and leans his arm against the wall. He comically wrestles with the gum: he finds himself sticking to the wall, so he uses his hand to remove the gum; now, the gum sticks to his hand; he uses his foot to get it off his hand; now, his foot sticks to the ground; he scrapes the sole of his shoe against the wall to remove the gum. He exits.

The first player returns, sees his gum on the wall, takes it off and puts it back in his mouth, and walks off.

Firing Squad

A firing squad lines up in front of a prisoner. The captain calls, "Ready ... aim..." and the prisoner yells, "Earthquake!" Everyone in the firing line scatters and runs for protection while the prisoner escapes. A second prisoner is brought out. The captain calls, "Ready ... aim..." and this prisoner yells, "Tornado!" Again, the firing line scatters as the prisoner escapes. A third prisoner is brought out. This prisoner yells, "Landslide" at the appropriate time, and he escapes. Finally, a fourth prisoner is brought out. The captain calls, "Ready ... aim..." and the prisoner yells, "Fire!" The firing squad shoots him down.

Spitfire

"The Amazing Spitfire" is introduced, the world's most proficient spitter. He enters with great pomp and self-importance. An assistant stands some distance from him, holding a plastic bucket. Every time Spitfire spits, the assistant raps the bottom of the bucket, making the audience think spit has hit the bottom of the bucket. Spitfire announces each of his amazing spits and then demonstrates them:

- The Short Shot: Spitfire spits and it lands immediately in the bucket.
- The Long Shot: Spitfire spits in the air, watches it as it rises high and descends, finally landing in the bucket.
- The Ricochet Shot: Spitfire spits against a tree or wall and watches as it ricochets off of several objects before hearing it land in the bucket.
- The Around-the-World Shot: Spitfire spits into the air, waits a long time, tells a few jokes, and finally, it lands in the bucket.
- The Master Shot: Spitfire takes time and effort to gather plenty of spit in his mouth. He builds to a climax. When he spits, a person planted in the front of the audience yells, "Yuccckkkkk!!" and stands up, wiping water off his face.

News Reporter

A player enters to see a dejected news reporter at the end of the stage or playing area, poised to jump, counting "One ... two..." The first player yells,

"Hey, what are you doing?" The reporters answers, "I'm going to jump off this bridge. Don't try to stop me! My life is a mess. I can't get any good stories. My editor thinks I'm a failure." And so on. The first player tries to cheer the reporter up, but ends getting depressed himself: "Your life can't be all that bad. Look at me. My husband (or wife) left me. My kids hate me. I lost my position as vice-president, and now the best I can find is a job mopping floors.... You know, I think I'll jump with you." The two count together, "One ... two..." when a third player enters. "Hey, wait! What are you two doing?" They each explain their story. The third player commiserates and decides to join them. All three prepare to jump, count, "One ... two ... three ... jump!" At the last minute, the reporter stops himself from jumping, while the other two actually jump off. "Hey!" the reporter says. "What a remarkable story this could be: two strangers jump off bridge together! What a break!" He runs off excitedly.

EMERGENCY WARD

A patient in great agony enters the emergency ward with an arrow in his abdomen. "Nurse, nurse! One of the campers missed the target and hit me! Can you help me?" The nurse is sitting in from of a mirror, primping and putting on make-up. She gradually stops and says. "Okay, but first I have to get some information." She gets her clipboard and asks for name, address, insurance company, etc., while the patient painfully asks her if she could hold off on the questions to take care of the problem. She says, "First things first." The telephone rings and she sits down to flirt or gossip over the phone. Meanwhile, the patient falls in agony on the floor. A hospital orderly, mop in hand, walks by and pulls out the arrow. The patient hops up, thanks the orderly, and exits the hospital.

PICKPOCKETS

"Magic Fingers" and "Slippery Sam" run into each other unexpectedly. They shake hands, pat each other's arms, punch each other gently as they tell where they've been the last few years. Both have been in various prisons for pickpocketing, we learn. When they are ready to part, one of them pulls out a watch and says, "By the way, you might want this. I just picked it off of you." The other takes it and pulls out a wallet, saying, "Well, I just got this from you." This continues with several items, until the last person pulls out a pair of underwear. The other person looks into his pants, gasps, grabs the underwear and runs off stage.

THE PIE-IN-THE-FACE ROUTINE

You can't have a collection of skits without one of them being a pie-in-the-face routine! In this routine, three players come out wearing plastic garbage bags, and an announcer introduces them as the demonstrators. Several aluminum pie tins filled with whipped cream are brought on a tray, and the announcer explains that several different types of pie-in-the-face shots will be demonstrated. The announcer briefly explains each shot, which the demonstrators then illustrate. However, it is always the middle demonstrator who ends up with the pie in the face. Even when this middle person switches positions with one of his colleagues, he still gets the pie. Ham it up and make it a comic scene!

Different pie-in-the-face shots: (1) pie directly in the face; (2) pie on top of the head; (3) pie on the side of the head; (4) two pies in the face at once; and (5) the swing-duck-down-miss-but-hit-someone-else shot. Perhaps the routine ends with the announcer — or even a leader in the audience — getting hit.

NATURE HIKE

CAMP COUNSELOR: Did you see it, Patty? Did you see it?
PATTY: No, what?
COUNSELOR: The yellow-breasted warbler. Oh, it was a beauty. You don't see many of those around. You have to keep your eyes open.
PATTY: Okay.
COUNSELOR: Oh! Oh! Did you see that? Did you see that, Patty?
PATTY [looking around]: I didn't see a thing. What are you talking about?

COUNSELOR: You missed the most remarkable raccoon. It had the most amazing mask and moved with a regal gait. I wish you'd pay more attention.

PATTY: All right. I'll try. *[To the audience:]* The next time I'm going to pretend I saw it so I won't get yelled at.

COUNSELOR: Patty, did you see it? Did you see it?

PATTY: Yes, I did see that.

COUNSELOR *[looking down]*: Then, why did you step in it?

BRUSH YOUR TEETH

An announcer tells how important it is to brush your teeth each day. If you're out camping, say, and have a shortage of water, this is what you can do. A line of four or five people are on-stage. The first one drinks some water, brushes his teeth with his finger, swishes the water around, and then leans his head toward the person next to him, who tilts his head to touch the first person's. His cheeks swell up as the first person's shrink. Then, the second person brushes his teeth with his finger, swishes the water around, and leans his head to the third person in line. This continues down the line until the last person (who drank some water before the skit began and has been storing it in his mouth) swishes the water around in his mouth and spits it out into a cup.

THE VIPER IS COMING!

An employee bursts into his boss's office and announces, "The viper is coming! The viper is coming!" The boss becomes clearly agitated. "The viper is coming? Oh, no. What do I do? Where do I go?" And so on. Other employees enter, equally upset, wondering what to do. Finally, someone enters with a sponge and bucket, saying, "I'm the vindow viper. I've come to vash the vindows. Hey, vat are you all looking so vorried about?"

GUM TO CANDY

A magician enters and announces that she can change a stick of gum into candy. She takes a fresh stick of gum and fingers it, squishing it and reshaping it, while she talks to the audience. She explains that throughout history, magicians have attempted to change the forms of things. In the Middle Ages, sorcerers attempted to change lead into gold. But this is even more miraculous, changing gum into candy. She drops the gum. "Did you see it? Did you see the gum drop?"

BRAINS FOR SALE

A few large cans or boxes are set up on a table, each marked with a dollar amount in ten-thousand-dollar increments. One is marked "$100,000." A customer enters and tells the scientist that he would like to have a brain transplant so that he can go farther in life. The scientist cautions the customer that buying a new brain can be expensive, though prices do vary, and he points to the different prices listed.

"Why do the prices vary?" the customer asks.

"Well," the scientist answers, "it all depends on brain capacity. For example, this first brain, selling for $10,000, once belonged to a salesman; it's a good brain, but this one here, for $20,000, belonged to an engineer. This one belonged to a doctor; it costs $30,000. And this one was a college professor's; it's $40,000."

"What about that one over there that's priced at $100,000?" the customer asks.

"Oh, that one is very expensive," the scientist answers. "That one belonged to _____" (insert here the name of someone in the group, perhaps a leader).

"Well, why is that one so expensive?"

"Because," the scientist answers, "it's never been used."

ECHO

This is an age-old stunt that is arranged prior to the performance or campfire. One person who is offstage or out of the campfire circle serves as the echo. The leader makes known his discovery that the surrounding acoustics result in an echo. He tests his observation by yelling, "Hello!" The person offstage echoes, "Hello!" Using names of individuals in the audience, the leader yells, "Mary Thompson is beautiful!" and the sentence is repeated by the echo. Then, "Harvey Greenberg is a budding genius!" and the echo is heard. Finally, "All the girls adore Frank Schmidt." There is a pause, and the echo yells, "Ridiculous!"

HEATED CONTROVERSY

This is another stunt arranged by two members of the group prior to the performance. The two individuals get into a preplanned argument about an issue that is relevant to members of the audience. If the argument is performed well, someone in the group is likely to join in. The argument is soon brought to a halt, the actors bow, and the unsuspecting "victim" is thanked for participating in the performance.

SHAKE THE DIME

The leader asks for a volunteer, who is handed a dime for verification that it is free of tape or glue. The leader then presses the dime to the volunteer's forehead for a minute while explaining that the volunteer is to see how long it takes to shake the dime from his forehead. When the leader removes his hand, the volunteer shakes his head persistently, attempting to shake off the dime, while the audience bursts out in laughter. The funny thing is, when the leader removes his hand, he also removes the dime, but it feels to the volunteer that the dime is still there.

THE BLACK EYE

Many such stunts are possible which use unsuspecting volunteers who are the last to realize what the joke is. In this stunt, the leader asks for two volunteers to engage in a contest: who can come closest to hitting the bull's-eye with one eye closed. The leader and his assistant cover one eye of each volunteer while each throws bean bags at a target. This can be fun enough to watch, but it's even more fun when the volunteers each look at the other when the contest is finished to discover their black eye — the leader and his assistant had black charcoal on their hands!

ORDER OF THE BLANKET

A few kids and a staff member or two are called forward and asked to be seated. A blanket is laid on each person's head and covers the body. The leader then tells them that they have been selected because they each have something the leader wants. They are to remove items from their person and hand them out from under the blanket until the desired object is finally turned over. So that the audience is in on the stunt, the leader points to the blanket to indicate that the blanket itself is, in fact, the desired object. Laughter is bound to erupt as unsuspecting participants hand out articles of clothing. It is even more hilarious when a male staff member (who is a "plant") hands out articles of women's underwear.

WATERMELON-EATING CONTEST

Several contestants are called forward and kneel behind a table which holds an upright slice of watermelon for each of them. With their hands behind their backs, contestants race to be the first to finish eating their slice of watermelon down to the green rind. If the slice falls over, the leader or assistant should return it to an upright position.

FORTUNE TELLER

One person is called forward to have his fortune told. A crystal ball (perhaps a softball covered with aluminum foil) is placed at the center of the table. The individual sits opposite the fortune teller, who reaches across the table and holds the hands or wrists of the unsuspecting contestant to more capably read his future. The fortune teller peers into the crystal ball and makes some minor predictions, and then forecasts a cold spot in the person's future. At this time, a jug of cold water is poured down the victim's back.

PENNY IN THE FUNNEL

A funnel is placed in the next contestant's pants, and then he is instructed to balance a penny on his nose and attempt to drop it into the funnel. After two or three successful attempts, the contestant is then asked to try it blindfolded. Once blindfolded and told to begin, water is poured into the funnel.

MARSHMALLOW RACE

Two marshmallows are placed in an aluminum pie plate filled with water. Two contestants are told that the object of this contest is to see who can be the first to blow their marshmallow to the opponent's side of the pie plate. The contestants poise themselves, ready to begin, while the leader raises his hand to announce, "One, two, three, GO," at which time his hand descends into the water and splashes both contestants.

WATER CUP RACE

Two teams line up, all members with a plastic cup attached to the top of their heads (glued to a cap or attached by the rubber bands that come with party hats). The fun comes in watching the members of the teams transfer water from cup to cup, each team trying to be the first to fill a small jug on a table at the end of the line.

DRESS-UP RACE

This is another fun race to watch. Two or more contestants race to dress up in a pile of clothes heaped on the floor in front of them. The catch is that the contestants are blindfolded as they figure out what each item is and try to put it on.

WATER BALLOON TOSS

A few teams of two members each are called forward. One member holds a basket, trash container, or plastic jug (with its top cut off) against his chest. The container has already been prepared with several pins sticking up from its top. The other member is given three water balloons to toss into the container. The object is to see who can toss the most water balloons into the container without the balloons bursting on the pins. Of course, another object is to see people get splashed with water. When a camp counselor is the one holding the container and a camper is the one throwing the balloon, the aim may change from getting the balloon into the basket to soaking the counselor.

BLOW YOUR NOSE

Each one of several contestants has a small sticker attached to the end of his or her nose. The contestants may not use their hands to remove the sticker; instead, they must blow it off. The laughs come when watching the funny faces screwed up trying to blow off the stickers.

CHEEKIE-CHEEKIE

The leader explains to a contestant that this next stunt is a "Simple Simon" game. He then says, "Cheekie-cheekie on the cheek," as he pinches the contestant on the cheek. The contestant does the same to the leader.

This is done several times. The laughs come when the contestant leaves the stage and the audience sees lipstick or charcoal all over the contestant's cheeks — lipstick or charcoal which the leader had earlier smeared on his fingers.

PUDDING FEED

One youngster and one staff member are called forward to form each team. Each youngster is blindfolded and given a spoon and container of pudding to feed to the staff member, who is then blindfolded as well. Before the leader gives the signal to begin, the youngsters' blindfolds are removed without the staff members' knowledge. They can then have lots of fun "feeding" ("smearing") the staff member until the leader gives the signal to stop.

THE HAND IS FASTER THAN THE EYE

Tell the audience that they must watch very carefully and do what you do. When you clap your hands together, they must clap theirs. No one should make a clapping sound if you don't. Then, you start slow and get progressively faster moving your hands together, sometimes clapping, sometimes almost clapping, sometimes crossing one hand over the other. Kids will laugh when they find themselves clapping their hands together when you don't. End by clapping your hands continually so that the audience seems to be applauding you; bow, thank your audience, and exit the stage.

BUCKET LINE

Acting like a game show host, the leader asks for two or three volunteers ("contestants") from the audience, who are then removed offstage. The stage is set up for the stunt: two or three tables are set up on stage and covered with sheets, making them appear as one long table. Buckets are placed upside down on the tables, each covering a different type of ball (tennis, golf, ping-pong, softball, volleyball, etc.). Someone is situated kneeling between two of the tables, with his head sticking up between them and hidden under a bucket. Then the first contestant is brought on-stage.

The contestant is told the objective: to go down the line, lift up each bucket, and name the type of ball hidden under it. The contestant who completes this task the quickest will be the winner. When the contestant lifts up the bucket with the head under it, the hidden person should scream. This will produce startling results.

The next contestant is then brought out.

Psychic

Ten Styrofoam cups are numbered and placed upside down on a table. Two individuals run this stunt, one of whom leaves the area while the other asks the audience to select a cup, under which she then hides a piece of candy. "My partner has such psychic powers," she says, "that he can identify the cup with the hidden candy without even touching the cups." After the partner is called back in, she points to cup 7 (for example) and asks her partner, "Is it cup 7?" "No," the psychic says emphatically. She points to cup 10 and asks, "Is it cup 10?" "No, the psychic replies. She points to cup 3 and asks, "Is it cup 3?" "Yes," the psychic exclaims, and that's where it is. No matter how many times the stunt is performed, the psychic gets it right, because he knows that if the cup selected is number 3, his partner points to it the third time, or if the cup selected is number 6, his partner points to it the sixth time.

The Lawnmower

One person is on hands and knees, posing as a lawnmower. The actor pulls on an imaginary cord to start the lawnmower, but it only shakes, sputters, and coughs. The actor gripes, "They can't make anything that works nowadays! Darn mower!" And so on. He tries again, with the same results. "Maybe someone else can get it to go." So he gets someone from the audience who tries, getting the same results. Another person is pulled from the audience and attempts to start the mower, again with the same results. Finally, someone else is asked to try. "Give it a really big tug. Maybe we've primed it for you," the actor says. The audience participant pulls the cord, and the mower sputters and finally starts. The actor says, "Thanks. That's terrific. All it needed was a really big jerk!"

CANDY STORE

Two members of the audience are called forward and asked to hold a prop necessary for the performance of the next skit. They are given a pole (broomhandle, yardstick, etc.) to hold up at waist level. An actor explains that he is going to play the part of the store clerk, and that the pole represents the counter at a candy store. A customer enters and asks the clerk if he has any licorice. The clerk says no. The customer then asks for jelly beans. The clerk says the store is out of them. The customer asks this time for a chocolate bar. The clerk says they have no chocolate in stock at present. Finally, the customer asks, "Well, what *do* you have?" The clerk responds, indicating the assistants holding up the pole, "All I've got is two suckers on a stick."

INDIAN BURIAL

A member of the audience is called up to lie on the floor, posing as a dead Indian. Three or four Indians are gathered nearby, one of them a woman. One Indian says, "I can't bury Chief Shortcake. My right arm is broken from when I fell off my horse." Another Indian says, "Well, I can't bury Chief Shortcake. I've grown weak with age." A third Indian says, "I can't bury Chief Shortcake, either. I have arthritis." Then, the woman gets up from kneeling by the fire and says, angrily, "All right! Squaw bury Shortcake!" and she squirts whipped cream on his face.

SPRINGTIME

The leader calls several members from the audience to the platform and gives each a role. Several are trees, some are squirrels, others are birds. Then, the leader announces that the next person will represent the most important character in this springtime scene and asks the volunteer to run through the forest. "This is a scene of springtime in the forest," the leader says. "This is one of the most amazing times of the year, when everything comes back to life. And how do we know it is spring? When we see the sap running through the trees."

ENLIGHTENMENT

A turbaned guru enters, announces he is a wise man from India, and promises that he can bring enlightenment to any who come to him. He selects a few people from the audience to come up and sit in a circle with him. He explains that he knows mystical words that will bring them to enlightenment and asks that they pronounce the words with him. Once you reach enlightenment, he says, you may leave the circle and return to the audience. Slowly, he intones, "Oh-wha-ta-goo-siam." Everyone in the circle joins in. Eventually, individuals will stand up and leave the circle when they realize they have been saying, "Oh, what a goose I am."

THERE'S A BEAR

Two leaders ask for several volunteers from the audience and line them up shoulder-to-shoulder, explaining that each one, in turn, is to imitate exactly what the leaders say and do.

At the head of the line, the first leader says, "Thar's a bar." The second leader, shoulder-to-shoulder with her, says, "Whar?" The leader answers, "Over thar," and points in the distance with her right arm. The second leader says, "Thar's a bar." The next person in line says, "Whar?" The second leader answers, "Over thar," and she also points. This continues down the line, until everyone is standing frozen with arm extended.

This litany continues again, this time everyone pointing their left arm, so that both arms are pointed. The third time down the line, everyone points with their right knee, so that they are standing on the left leg, with right knee and two arms extended. While frozen in this position, one of the leaders pushes the volunteer standing next to him, so that they all fall down in a domino effect.

THE UGLIEST CREATURE IN THE WORLD

An announcer proclaims that behind the sheet is the ugliest creature in the world. It is so ugly that women faint, children cry, and even grown men scream. It's uglier than a slug. It has to be seen to be believed. It's uglier than you could possibly imagine. Several performers are invited to look behind the sheet, and each one shrieks when he does. Finally, the announcer asks someone in the audience to come up and take a look. When he does, the person behind the sheet screams.

THE OBSTACLE COURSE

This is yet another stunt using an unsuspecting volunteer and ending as a friendly joke. A volunteer (or two for a race) walks through a short obstacle course consisting of varying-sized objects placed on the ground. Then the player is blindfolded to see if he can go through the course a second time without stepping on anything, this time being aided by the spectators' directions. He may wonder what is so funny until he discovers he has been stepping over obstacles which have been removed.

SPOOFS

Try spoofs, take-offs, or modernizations of nursery rhymes, fairy tales, and children's stories. Stories that are a part of everyone's experience make great material for farce: Little Red Riding Hood, Humpty Dumpty, Little Jack Horner, The Old Woman Who Lived in a Shoe, Jack and the Beanstalk,

Cinderella, Snow White and the Seven Dwarves, Hansel and Gretel, Rip Van Winkle, etc.

Campers could write their own scripts making light of camp life:

Camp Stick-in-the-Mud

[Two counselors are lazily lying on their beds]

COUNSELOR 1: You know, this place is really beginning to get to me. I mean, it used to be you could get the campers to serve you breakfast in bed; now you have to drag *them* out of bed.

COUNSELOR 2: Yeah, I know what you mean. They're careless, too. Just last night one of them dropped a spoonful of pudding on my foot and nearly fractured some bones. I had to limp around all night. Fortunately, that beautiful camp nurse was on duty.

C1: Don't you ever think of anything besides women?

C2: Sure, I think of *myself* being beside women.

C1: Well, anyway, there must be someone we can blame for these changes in camp.

[Enter Head Counselor, a military type who thinks he's in full command]

HC: All right, men, hit the floor. *[The two counselors rap on the floor with their knuckles]* Don't you guys have any respect?

C2: Respect? I lost that years ago when I became a camper.

HC: Look at you two lying around when there's work to be done.

C1: Uh-oh. He just said a naughty word! I'm telling the director on you.

HC: You're too much. All right, I'm here to tell you that you are shirking your responsibilities around here. Not only were you wrong yesterday in tying an anchor around a camper's neck and throwing him off the raft, but you also had no right taking your kids on a hike through the poison ivy patch this morning. I've a mind to report you to the director. The way you two act, one would think this place was for fun and games.

C1: You could have fooled me.

C2: Look, it was educational. I was teaching the kids to recognize the appearance and effects of poison ivy. It was a first-hand learning experience.

HC: Oh, yeah? Then why did you tell them it was a lettuce patch and that the cook wanted some for supper?

C2: It looked like lettuce to me; I wasn't wearing my glasses.

HC: You don't wear glasses.

C2: Yeah, that's why I couldn't see that it was poison ivy.

HC: Believe me, you two haven't heard the last of this.

[Exit HC; enter the camp Nurse]

C1: Look, it's a bird.

C2: No, it's a plane.

C1: No, it's _____, super nurse.

NU: I need some information from you two.

C2: You can have whatever you want from me.

NU: This is serious. Joey's mother called. It appears she received a letter from him telling her he's terribly homesick. How's he doing?

C1: Oh, Joey's having a great time. We always tell the kids to say they're homesick — it makes parents feel better when their kids miss them. Joey just overdid it.

NU: Oh, I see. That's very thoughtful. By the way, I thought I'd warn you: the director's on his way over here.

[Exit Nurse; enter Director]

C2: Hello, boss. What can we do for you?

DI: Look, guys, I need to have a serious talk with you.

C2: Oh, finally! I've been waiting a long time to hear about the birds and the bees.

DI: You'll have to wait till you're a bit more mature for that lecture. Look, I understand the tremendous stress that you guys must have, working with these campers as you do. But that's no excuse for encouraging Marcia to eat the raisins out where the rabbits live or putting meatloaf in Freddy's pajamas. You will remember that before the campers ever arrived here, we had many discussions on how to deal with counselor stress.

C2: Yes, I remember, but you never told us what to do when we get clobbered over the head with a baseball bat, tied to a tree for a campfire offering, or used as a target for archery practice.

C1: Not to mention how to deal with a potentially homicidal kid.

DI: Well, I guess you're right. But I did show you how to unclog a toilet.

C2: Yes, that has come in handy a number of times.

DI: Guys, being a counselor isn't really so bad. For one thing, you get meals thrown in.

C1: Yeah, whatever you don't throw out or throw up.

DI: And you get a place to sleep with a roof over your head.

C2: Yeah, a bed that's harder than concrete under a roof with more holes than Swiss cheese.

DI: Now, guys, you're forgetting one of the great joys of being a counselor: searching for stray campers.

Cl: You know, he's right! There's nothing quite like the great hunt.

C2: Yeah! It's like going on safari in Africa.

DI: Now you're talking. Hit it, guys!

[The two counselors jump off their beds. The head counselor and nurse enter from the wings, and all sing and dance the following song to the tune of "Jingle Bells":]

Crashing through the brush
With our flashlights in our hands,
We're the first-rate summer camp's
Vig-i-lan-te band.
Prowlers in the night,
The word to you's "Beware!"
If you are not caught out-right,
You'll get a healthy scare.

Chorus:

Up the hill — down the road —
Over to the beach.
There is not a single spot
Our dragnet cannot reach — hey!
Have no fear — we are here,
Our flashlights in our hands.
We're the first-rate summer camp's
Vig-i-lan-te band!

The End

Chapter 7

Storytelling

*There have been great societies that did not use the wheel, but
there have been no societies that did not tell stories.*

— Ursula LeGuin

Everybody loves a good story. This was true thousands of years ago,
when prehistoric people told tales around a campfire; it was equally true two
hundred years ago, when the campfire was again the setting for countless tales
created by courageous Americans traveling westward. A campfire seems the
ideal setting for telling stories, but it is by no means the only one. Any setting and any situation can be ripe for a story, especially bedtimes and meal-
times. Storytelling requires no special equipment, simply a voice and an
imagination. In a world where we get most of our stories canned from TV
and movie theaters, storytelling draws people together in a particularly human
way.

READING STORIES

Nothing so enthralls a group of youngsters (or adults, for that matter)
as a well-written story read with expression. Reading a story well, however,
requires preparation and practice. The novice storyteller invariably fails when
ignoring this advice. Read every story to yourself before reading it to the

group in order to determine its suitability for your audience. Read it again, preferably aloud, for practice. Go for drama; be a ham! Vary the volume and pitch of your voice; determine ahead of time what words and sentences require emphasis. Storytelling is as much about sound — what you do with your voice — as about the story itself. This includes not only your inflection but also imitations of the sea or the wind, which help pique the imagination of your listeners. Facial expressions and body gestures further contribute to the effectiveness of storytelling. This chapter includes selected stories ideal for reading aloud. Better yet, learn your story well enough so that you can tell it instead of reading it. Whether you read or tell a story which has already been written, feel free to edit — cut out sentences or paragraphs that won't likely work with your audience. Add lines which make it more personal to your listeners. Storytelling is as much an art as story writing.

TELLING STORIES

Telling one's own story can be even more absorbing than reading or telling one which has been written and published. Your own story may involve recounting an incident that actually happened (like your accidental encounter with a bee hive) or it may involve inventing a story from scratch. There is nothing like telling an original story that you made up! Spinning a yarn is as American as Mom and apple pie. But, when devising your own story, keep in mind these suggestions from the expert storytellers:

1. Think up the plot ahead of time — even if you are good at ad-libbing.
2. Don't make the plot too complicated.
3. Use your kids' own experiences in the story.
4. Don't let it drag — keep it short.
5. Get your audience to participate.

You can get your audience involved in many ways. Have them name the characters, contribute plot ideas, or create sound effects (slapping their legs to imitate thunder, for example). Even better, give them a chance to tell stories of their own. Try devising a group story, whereby each person contributes a piece of the story. One participant begins the story and tells it up to a key point. The next person continues from that point and passes the plot along until everyone has contributed.

This may be done with a small ball of string or yarn. Each person unravels the ball while telling part of the story; once unraveled, he passes it to the next person, who winds it back up while contributing to the story. The story continues until the last person in the circle brings the story to a conclusion.

A variation of this "yarn-spinning" requires a big ball of yarn and a circle of kids. The first storyteller begins the story (without unraveling the yarn) and then throws the ball to someone across the circle while holding on to the end of the yarn. Each person throws the yarn to someone else upon completing part of the story. Everyone must contribute. What results is an intricate web which follows the path of the storytelling. Then, another story can be told as you unweave the web, allowing the ball of yarn to determine the order of storytelling.

Another method that encourages group participation begins by assigning each person a word and accompanying sound effect to produce, whenever you mention that word in the telling of your story. For example, when the word "cow" is mentioned, that person says, "Moo"; when the word "car" comes up, that person says, "Honk-honk." Then, weave a story that incorporates all of the participants.

In addition to sound effects, each person can act out the word you assign. When the word "train" is spoken, the person assigned that word moves her arms like a chugging train, or perhaps even gets up and moves around the circle while imitating a locomotive.

How to Tell a Story

Mark Twain was not only a master at writing stories, he was also a master at telling stories to a live audience. One thing he understood was the effective use of a pause. In telling the following story, he said, the pause before the snapper at the end "was the most important thing in the whole story. If I got it the right length precisely, I could spring the finishing ejaculation with effect enough to make some impressible girl deliver a startled little yelp and jump out of her seat—and that was what I was after. This story was called 'The Golden Arm,' and was told in this fashion. You can practice with it yourself—and mind you look out for the pause and get it right."

The Golden Arm
by Mark Twain

Once upon a time there was a monstrous mean man, and he lived way out in the prairie all alone by himself, except that he had a wife. And by-and-by she died, and he took and toted her way out there in the prairie and buried her. Well, she had a golden arm — all solid gold, from the shoulder down. He was powerful mean — powerful; and that night he couldn't sleep, because he wanted that golden arm so bad.

When it came midnight, he couldn't stand it any more; so he got up, he did, and took his lantern and shovel and dug her up and got the golden arm; and he bent his head down against the wind, and plowed and plowed and plowed through the snow. Then all of a sudden he stopped (make a considerable pause here, and look startled, and take a listening attitude) and said: "My LAND, what's that!"

And he listened and listened and the wind said (set your teeth together and imitate the wailing and wheezing singsong of the wind), "Bzzz-z-zzz" — and then, way back yonder where the grave is, he heard a voice! he heard a voice all mixed up in the wind so that he could hardly tell 'em apart — "Bzzz-zzz — W-h-o's g-o-t m-y g-o-l-d-e-n arm? — zzz — zzz — W-h-o's g-o-t m-y g-o-l-d-e-n arm!" (You must begin to shiver violently now.)

And he began to shiver and shake, and say, "Oh, my! OH, my land!" and the wind blew the lantern out, and the snow and sleet blew in his face and almost choked him, and he started plowing knee-deep towards home almost dead, he was so scared, and pretty soon he heard the voice again, and (pause) and it was coming after him! "Bzzz — zzz — zzz — W-h-o's g-o-t m-y g-o-l-d-e-n arm?"

When he got to the pasture, he heard it again, closer now, and coming! — coming back there in the dark in the storm (repeat the wind and the voice). When he got to the house, he rushed upstairs and jumped in the bed and covered up, he and his ears, and lay there shivering and shaking — and then way out there he heard it again! — and a-coming! — and a-coming! And by-and-by, he heard (pause — awed, listening attitude) — pat — pat — pat — it's coming upstairs! Then he heard the latch, and he knew it was in the room!

Then pretty soon, he knew it was standing by the bed! (Pause.) Then — he knew it was bending down over him — and he could scarcely get his breath! Then — then — he seemed to feel something c-o-l-d, right down almost against his head! (Pause.)

Then the voice said, right at his ear — "W-h-o's g-o-t m-y g-o-l-d-e-n arm?" (You must wail it out very plaintively and accusingly; then you stare steadily and impressively into the face of the farthest-gone auditor — a girl, preferably — and let that awe-inspiring pause begin to build itself in the deep hush. When it has reached exactly the right length, jump suddenly at that girl and yell,) "You've got it!"

If you've got the pause right, she'll fetch a dear little yelp and spring right out of her shoes. But you must get the pause right; and you will find it the most troublesome and aggravating and uncertain thing you ever undertook.

STORIES I'VE BEEN TOLD

The Cabin in the Woods

We were on a dark and lonely stretch of road late one summer night and, having been cooped up in the station wagon all day, we were restless and rambunctious in the two back seats. Mom had done the whole song thing already, leading us five kids in a group-sing, so now it was Dad's turn to occupy our minds. All it took was for him to begin telling a story, and we were immediately rapt with attention:

Three of my buddies and I went out camping one night, way out in the woods, far from where we thought anyone lived. We pitched our tents and cooked dinner over a crackling fire and then decided to go for a short hike before it got too dark.

We hadn't been hiking long when we spotted a small log cabin in a clearing in the forest. A lantern in one small window shed its light into the near darkness and smoke billowed from the chimney. This might sound to you like a pleasant country cottage, but no — there was something definitely eerie — almost sinister — about this place. And I wasn't the only one who was spooked by it, for I could smell the fear on the other guys. I can't tell you what worried us; I can only say that the place was just plain weird.

But we were young, and of course none of us was going to say that we ought to leave and head back to camp. Instead, we dared Jeff — because he was the least adventurous of the four of us — to sneak up from behind the trees where we were hidden and take a peek into the window. Naturally, he couldn't refuse, because he wouldn't dare show any sign of weakness.

I regret now being a part of this whole escapade, but I have to tell you the truth, and the truth is, I encouraged him as much as the others.

Well, Jeff left us and crept quietly through the dark clearing and knelt below the window. Slowly, very slowly, he lifted himself up to peek in, and within a split second, he let out the most blood-curdling scream I had ever heard. "AAAARRGGGHHHH!" he cried out. And then he started running around in circles like a crazy man. We couldn't figure out what was going on. He ran around, waving his arms madly, all the while emitting a horrendous scream, until eventually he ran off into the forest.

Of course, there was only one thing we could do. Danny and I dared Frank to look into the window. After what we had just seen, Frank was clearly scared. We knew he was scared. He knew we knew he was scared. But there was no way he would refuse the dare and thereby appear chicken.

So Frank crept up to the house and crouched below the window. Slowly, very slowly, he raised his head to see inside. All of a sudden, he started screaming. "AAAARRGGGHHHH!" He jumped up, ran around, gesticulated wildly, almost seemed to froth at the mouth, and dashed off into the woods.

Well, that left Danny and me. At once, each of us dared the other to be the next to go. So we decided to shoot for it; you know: one person calls "odds" or "evens" and then you each make a fist and throw out some fingers. Well, I won, which means that Danny would have to be the one to go to the cabin. Normally, Danny was a bit cocky about things — being 6'5" and athletic and all — but there was a look of terror in his face. If you had seen the reaction of the other two guys after they looked in the window, you'd understand.

I watched intently as Danny moved up to the cabin and situated himself beneath the window. Slowly, he raised his head up and looked in. "AAAARRGGGHHHH!" he screamed, madly running in circles and flapping his arms. He must have run around a dozen times before he ran away into the forest.

I have to tell you now that those three guys were never the same again. After I waited back at camp for what seemed like an eternity, they finally showed up — it must have been 3:00 in the morning by the time Danny arrived. They wouldn't say anything. I tried to calm them down and cheer them up, but all they could do was shake hysterically. When Danny finally did arrive, we hightailed out of there and headed back home without even packing up camp.

But, as I said, those three were never the same again. They seemed to have lost their spirit. Just the other day I saw one of them, and it was a pitiful sight. He stared blankly ahead and looked as pale as a ghost. When I spoke to him, all he could do was grunt. It never did any good when anyone asked them what they saw, for — to this very day — if you even mention the cabin in the woods, they start shaking and seem to go into a trance. They won't say a thing.

Now, I know what you're thinking. You're wondering if I looked into that window. Didn't my curiosity get the better of me? Didn't I go up to that cabin that night to see what could be so horrible? Well, I'll tell you. The fact is, I *did* look into that window. I can't explain why the sight didn't have the same effect on me as it did on my three buddies. I can't explain it at all. Why am I now as normal as all of you? What did I see? you want to know. So far, I've never told anybody about what I saw that night, but I'm gonna tell you. I remember the sight as clearly as if it were in front of my eyes now. Are you ready for this? I crept up to the cabin, huddled beneath the window, and gradually raised myself up to look inside, and there I saw —"AAAARRGGGHHHH!"

At this point, Dad jerked the steering wheel, threw his hands up into the air, and let out a blood-curdling scream. Around a campfire, the storyteller would scream, jump up, run madly around the fire, and disappear into the woods.

And what was seen through that window? It doesn't matter. The object of telling the story is to build suspense and wonderment in your audience so that, by the time the ending is reached, they are startled and finally amused by your antics. It's a story that's as fun to tell as it is to hear.

You're It

This tale, based on one I heard several years ago, contains all the elements of the scary story: a dark and lonely setting, a repulsive pursuer, and a terrified narrator who has survived the ordeal to tell it. Before you tell it, read it to yourself two or three times, and then add your own personal touches. It is the nature of storytelling for each teller to bring something of himself to his tale. The secret to telling this story is to build suspense in your audience before hitting them with the final line.

I was only eight years old at the time, but I remember the night as vividly as if it had happened yesterday. I was never more terrified in my entire life. One look at this man's face, and you knew that you were looking at the ugliest, meanest, loneliest creature ever set on this earth.

His left eye peered out from a drooping lash while his right eye bulged from its socket. A scar ran from his forehead and passed along his cheek and down his neck to disappear beneath his dirty collar. What could have caused such a gash, I cannot say. His hair was long and matted, stuck together in clumps like that of a dead raccoon on the side of the road. What made him look even more ominous was his ragged black hat and long black cape; in his hand he held a knotty walking stick, for he was humpbacked and dragged his left leg.

It was dusk. The sun had recently fallen beneath the tree line and in the distance a light came on. A full moon was luminous in the darkening sky, and the wind was beginning to howl. I was half a mile from home, and it was then that I saw him. He stared right at me! His face had the most piteous and agonizing look. He looked painfully lonely. I can't begin to describe the eerie isolation of that gruesome man. He must not have had a friend in the world — was probably scorned even by his own mother. I was so repulsed that I had to look away. I tried to appear unshaken, but to be honest, I was beginning to tremble, and my heart was racing 100 miles an hour. Remember that I was only eight years old. I picked up my pace, eager to reach the warm security of my home. I glanced back, trying not to look at that face, only to discover that he was following me! I looked back again; there was no doubt about it: he was heading right for me!

I started to walk a little faster; so did he. What could he want with me? Would he kidnap me and take me to some lair, some cabin in the woods, and eat me? Did he steal little children to use as his slaves? Was this man — no, not man — was this creature so lonely that he took helpless kids to fill up his empty life?

I knew a dozen shortcuts home. I decided to leave the path and cut through the pines. That might throw him off, I thought. I darted into the brush, hoping to shake him, but when I glanced around, he was still in steady pursuit. All I could see was his dark, massive shape headed for me, and so I started to run, only to find myself flat on my face upon the forest floor! I must have tripped, I suppose, over some roots or vines. I quickly scrambled to my feet, just escaping his outreached hand. Now, I was running as fast as my little feet would carry me, but home was still a quarter of a mile away and I was getting breathless.

He slouched along at a pace slower than mine, but his legs were long and he was determined. I was getting ahead of him, but I knew I couldn't run the whole way home without collapsing for want of air. I needed to rest, so I hid myself beneath some bushes and tried to cover myself up with leaves and twigs. I was clever enough to leave a gap where I could peer out and make a speedy escape, if necessary. The creature reached the area where all the bushes were and slowed down, grunting, "Where are you?" He seemed to growl rather than speak. He began searching the bushes, hitting them with his stick and poking underneath. I hoped that he would give up before coming to the bushes where I was hiding, but he must have heard my trembling or my racing heart, because I saw him stop and listen before he headed straight in my direction. When he was only a few feet away, I rose up out of my bed of leaves and twigs and made a run for it, not without looking into those spooky eyes of his. That lonely beast seemed to be getting pleasure in hunting me down!

It was getting darker, and I was getting tired of running. Remember, I was only eight years old, and this monster — though slower than I — had long legs and was steady in his pursuit. My legs were weakening and I was panting for breath. I was so scared and tired that I started to weep. Yes, I have to admit it. I was racked with terror! Suddenly, out of nowhere, a bat flew by, nearly hitting my head, and I fell instinctively to the ground. I hastened to turn onto my back, only to see the dark, gruesome shape getting nearer and nearer. I could not move. I lay frozen, immobile, my eyes opened wide, my mouth agape.

And then it happened.

He stood over me, reached out his big, gloved hand, and placed it on the top of my head. "Tag," he said. "You're it!"

The Grave

A group of friends was sitting around one night, when they got to talking about the graveyard that was a little ways down the street.

"That is one spooky place," one of them said. "When I'm walking home at night, I walk twice as fast when going by the graveyard."

"I practically run," Brent stated. "It's filled with ghosts. Did you know that, if you plunge a knife into a grave while standing on it, the ghost of the deceased person will reach up and grab you and pull you into the grave?"

"That's crazy talk," Maggie retorted. "The dead have no control over the living."

"But it's true," Brent replied. "It's been documented. You wouldn't see to live another day if you showed such disrespect to the dead."

Maggie stood her ground. "No way," she exclaimed. "You won't get me to believe a half-witted story like that."

"I dare you to go into the cemetery and try it yourself," Brent taunted. "In fact, I'll give you ten dollars to try."

"All right," Maggie declared boldly, "I'll take your ten dollars. I'll go out there right now and prove you wrong."

Brent went into the kitchen and found a long butcher knife and handed it to Maggie. He gave her instructions: "Now, pick a grave, stand right on top of it, and plunge the knife as far as you can into the grave." Then he added, "It was nice knowing you."

Maggie made her way to the graveyard. She chose a grave and stood on top of it. She had to admit to herself that she was a bit nervous. In the dark, surrounded by graves, with the wind howling and a sliver of the moon hanging in the sky, she started to feel fear. But she was not going to go back on a dare. She raised the knife over her head and plunged it as far as it would go into the ground. Then, she started to leave. BUT SHE COULD NOT MOVE! Her eyes widened into a steady stare, and her mouth emitted a loud scream, but no one could hear her. She tried to lift one leg, then the other, but she would not budge. Fright consumed her as she felt herself going down, hopelessly sinking and out of control.

After an hour, when she had not returned, her friends went looking for her in the graveyard. There they found her body lying on a grave, the knife piercing through her long dress. When she had plunged the knife into the ground, it passed through her dress and pinned her to the grave. The medics later confirmed that she had died from fright.

Shaggy Dog Story

Shaggy dog stories are popular fare around campfires, in dorm rooms, on hikes, and just about anywhere people congregate. The shaggy dog story rarely has anything to do with a shaggy dog, though this one does. I have heard short shaggy dog stories, but the typical one is a long, drawn-out, elaborate concoction that ends in a fizzle and elicits several groans and occasionally a "Please, no more. Don't tell us any more!" (though, truth be told, the listener is eager for another one).

There once was a knight in a far-away land who was sent on a mission in which the safety of the kingdom was at stake.

The lord of the castle impressed upon the knight the importance of his success. "You must not fail," the lord said. "Our kingdom is in your hands. You must convey this message to the king. Should you fail, the king, the kingdom, and life as we know it will be lost. It will take you five days to reach the castle of the king, if you make haste. Now, take the best horse from the stable and ride like the wind."

The knight entered the stable and chose the finest steed he could find, though even a horse this strong might not manage a journey of five days, he thought. He saddled the horse, gathered his gear, and headed out into the world.

(At this point, in the true spirit of a shaggy dog story, the storyteller details a series of hardships which the knight experiences, perhaps craggy hills, fierce storms, and vicious highwaymen. Since shaggy dog stories are always told, not read, the storyteller can be spontaneously inventive.)

Three days had passed, and the knight realized his original concern was coming true: his horse was not going to last another two days. The knight could allow the horse and himself to rest a day, but that would put the entire mission in jeopardy. He knew he would have to trade for another horse — and soon. He had traveled the entire day without encountering a farmhouse or a single person, but luck was with him, for he came upon a lone farmhouse in the mist. He knocked upon the door of this small farmhouse, and soon an old man opened the door. He was gray and bent from years of toil, but he possessed a kindly face with thoughtful eyes.

"Sir," the knight addressed him, "I am on a crucial mission to the king's castle. I have been riding for three days, and my horse can go no farther. I ask that you trade me a horse for my fine, but exhausted, steed."

"I would be glad to help you, sir knight, if I could," the old man answered, "but I am a poor man and no longer have any horses. I have done little farming in the last two years, and the few horses I did have were taken into the king's service. I'm sorry that I can be of no help. The next farmhouse is over those hills, some twenty miles away."

Disappointed, the knight responded, "My horse cannot make it that far. Have you no other creature that can take me at least to the next farmhouse? A mule, perhaps?"

"No, I have nothing like that," the farmer said, and then his eyes brightened. "I have — no, no, that would never work."

"Go ahead," the knight urged. "Tell me what you have."

"Well, I have this huge, shaggy dog. Come in, and I'll show you." The knight entered the farmhouse and, sure enough, there stood a dog almost as big as the knight's horse. This dog was the shaggiest the knight had ever seen — and also the filthiest, smelliest, and mangiest.

"This dog will do," the knight exclaimed. "May I ride it the next twenty miles?"

"Oh, no," the farmer responded. "I can't let you take him."

"Why not?" the knight questioned. "The safety of the kingdom depends on my taking this dog."

"It would not be right," the farmer insisted. "I could never let a knight go out on a dog like this."

The Guillotine

You probably have learned about the French Revolution in history class: the peasant uprisings and the subsequent Reign of Terror in which the peasants executed the aristocrats on the guillotine while crowds gathered 'round and watched. Every aristocrat and every member of his family was rounded up and brought before the tribunal; most were put to death while crowds cheered. It was a time when vengeance became the law of the land.

One day, a French count was captured, tried, and sentenced to the guillotine. However, the members of his family were all in hiding, and the officials wanted to find them so that they, too, could be tried and executed.

"Tell us the location of your family," they demanded at the bottom of the steps leading up to the guillotine.

"I will never tell," the count responded.

They walked him up the stairs to the platform which held the guillotine. Hoping a close view of this instrument of death would strike fear in his heart and cause him to tell, they again insisted that he reveal the location of his family.

"I will never tell," the count repeated.

They forced him to kneel in front of the guillotine. "Tell us," they demanded.

"I will not tell," the count declared.

They put his head on the chopping block. "Tell us," they again insisted.

"I will not tell," the count responded.

They slowly raised the blade of the guillotine until it reached the top and was ready to drop. "This is your last chance," they warned. "Tell us."

"I will not tell," the count uttered, but fear struck him as he heard the sound of the blade being released. "Wait! I'll tell, I'll —"

But it was too late. The blade had already fallen.

The moral: Don't hatchet your counts before they chicken.

The Cruel Landlord

This story has no ending — or, rather, the group devises various creative solutions that could make it end happily for the old lady and her beautiful daughter.

Hundreds of years ago, back in the Middle Ages, the cruel lord of a castle rented out parcels of his land in return for steep payment. Each month he would personally visit each little home and collect the rent, for he loved money and loved even more watching people hand it over to him begrudgingly.

One month, as he was collecting the rent, he came to the cottage of an old lady who was working in her front garden.

"I've come to collect the rent," the landlord demanded.

"Please, sir lord," the old lady pleaded, "I have had ill fortune this month. My husband has died and I have had to work twice as hard to make ends meet. Please show mercy and give me more time to make up this month's rent."

The landlord was not one to show mercy, but he glimpsed the sight of the old lady's beautiful young daughter peering out the window of the poor hovel. A gleam came into his eye.

"All right, old hag," the landlord proclaimed. "People in these parts have the wrong notion of me. I am actually a very merciful man, as you will see. I will give you an extra month to pay your rent. But, if next month you don't pay me two months' rent, then you must give me your daughter to live in my castle."

The old lady gasped, but she was certain she would be able to raise the money, and she had no other choice, so she accepted the landlord's offer.

The month passed, and the landlord returned. The old lady and her beautiful daughter stood on the pebbled walkway to their house.

"I've come to collect the rent," the landlord said.

The old lady was distraught. "Sir lord, I have worked morning, noon, and night, but I have been unable to raise both months' rent. Surely you are a merciful man. My daughter is all that I have. Please don't take her from me. Give me another month."

"No!" the landlord shouted. "I have given you —" he continued, but noticing the neighbors gathering nearby, he softened his tone. "I have given you mercy already." Looking down upon the pebbled path on which the old lady and her beautiful daughter stood, an idea came to him by which he could take advantage of the situation: to appear merciful while still getting the beautiful daughter. "I'll tell you what I'll do," he said, getting off his horse and moving onto the pebbled path. "I will show you mercy once again. I will take a black pebble and a white pebble from your pathway and put them in this cloth bag. Your daughter will pull one pebble out of the bag. If she takes the black one, she will come to live with me in the castle. However, if she takes the white one, I will free you from your debt and she can remain here with you. That is surely a merciful offer."

The landlord stooped down to pick up two pebbles, but the beautiful daughter noticed that, instead of picking up a black and a white one, he actually gathered two black pebbles and put them in the bag.

What should the beautiful daughter do?

The Unlucky Man

A good story can be entertaining while also possessing a relevant moral.

Once upon a time, there was a man who continually moaned and groaned about how unlucky he always was. "Woe is me," he would proclaim. "Nothing ever seems to go right for me. I am a very unlucky man."

In time, he decided to go to the end of the world to find God and ask him why God made him so unlucky. So, he took to the road, and days became weeks, and weeks became months, and he traveled for well over a year.

As he walked, he passed through dangerous wolf territory and happened upon a small wolf that was too timid to attack him.

"Where are you going?" the wolf asked.

"I am going to seek God so that he can explain to me why he made me such an unlucky man."

"I wish you success on your journey," the wolf responded, "and if you find God, will you also ask him why he made me so weak and scrawny, compared to the other wolves?"

"I will do that," the man replied, and he continued on his way.

In time, he entered a large forest filled with beautiful trees and plants. He stopped to rest against a small tree that was isolated in a clearing in the woods. The small tree asked the man what he was doing, and again the man replied that he was seeking God to learn why he was so unlucky.

"If you meet him," the tree said, "would you also ask him why I am so small and leafless, compared to all of the other trees in the forest?"

"I will do that," the man replied, and he continued on his way.

As he walked on, he came upon a brightly painted cottage surrounded by a beautiful garden. Inside the cottage was the most beautiful woman the man had ever seen. She invited him for supper and fed him the most sumptuous meal he had ever eaten. She offered him a bed for the night, and he woke up the next morning fully refreshed and ready to continue on his way.

Before he departed, the beautiful woman said, "I wish you good fortune, and I ask one thing: if you do meet God, please ask him why I am so lonely."

"I will do that," the man replied, and he continued on his way.

He walked on and finally reached the end of the world, and there he found God.

"God," he said, "can you tell me why you made me such an unlucky man?"

God replied, "You're not an unlucky man at all. You simply don't see how fortunate you are. If you pay more attention to what's around you, you'll find your luck."

"Thank you," the man replied, "but I need to ask you —"

God stopped him and said, "I know everything, so I know what you're going to ask. You want the answers to the questions asked you by the wolf, the tree, and the beautiful woman. I'll tell you," and God proceeded to answer the questions.

On the way back, the man came upon the cottage in the woods, where he was greeted with great joy by the beautiful woman.

"Did you get the answer to my question?" she asked.

"Yes," the man replied. "God said that your loneliness will end when you get married."

"That is good news," the beautiful woman exclaimed. "Will you marry me?"

"I can't," the man responded, "for I must go on to find my luck. But if I meet a good man, I will send him this way."

When he reached the clearing in the forest, he explained to the tree the reason that it was so small and leafless. "Beneath you is buried a pot of gold. Your roots have not had a chance to develop fully. Once the pot of gold is removed, you will grow tall and leafy."

"Will you dig the pot out for me?" the tree asked.

"I can't," the man replied, "because I need to go find my luck. However, I will send the first good man I find to dig it up for you," and he continued on.

When the man reached the wolf, he explained to the wolf what God had told him: "The reason you are so small is simply because you don't eat enough. You should eat the first foolish creature you see."

And so the wolf did.

The Farmer

Once upon a time, there was a poor farmer who owned only one horse, which he used to help him plow the fields. One day, the horse escaped when the farmer was cleaning the stable and ran into the hills.

All of his neighbors sympathized with him. "How unfortunate you are," they said. "What bad luck!"

"Bad luck, good luck? I don't know," the farmer said, and he continued on with his work.

The next day, the horse returned from the hills, followed by a half dozen wild horses.

"What good luck!" the neighbors exclaimed.

"Good luck, bad luck? I don't know," the farmer said, and he continued on with his work.

The next day, the farmer's son was trying to break one of the wild horses, and he fell off and broke his leg.

"What bad luck!" the neighbors exclaimed.

"Bad luck, good luck? I don't know," the farmer said, and he continued on with his work.

The next day, the military came to the village to draft one able-bodied man from each home, but because the farmer was too old and the son had broken his leg, the military passed by the farmer's house.

"What good luck!" the neighbors exclaimed.

"Good luck, bad luck? I don't know," the farmer said, and he continued on with his work.

This is a good place for the story to end, though it could continue indefinitely. By now, however, the moral is clear. The acceptance of the flow and flux of life is central to Chinese Daoist philosophy, from where this story may have derived.

The Rabbi's Prayers

Long ago, a rabbi and his followers were wandering the countryside. As evening approached, they stopped at an old farmhouse and knocked at the door. An old and weary-looking couple appeared and welcomed them.

"We are traveling and are very thirsty," the rabbi said. "Would you be kind enough to provide us with something to quench our thirst?"

The old man smiled and answered, "We have but one old cow which barely gives enough milk for the two of us, but you are welcome to what I milked from her today." And he gave the rabbi and his followers the day's milk.

The rabbi then explained, "We are also very hungry after our long day's journey. Can you offer us any food for our dinner?"

The old woman responded, "We are poor, but please come in and share with us the little we have." The rabbi and his followers entered and ate supper with the old couple.

After dinner, the rabbi asked if the old couple would lodge his followers and himself for the night. The old man told him that they were welcome to stay in the barn, and he provided them with blankets and tried to make them comfortable.

The next morning, the rabbi put his hands on the cow and prayed fervently, whereupon the cow suddenly died.

After the next day of traveling, the rabbi knocked upon the door of another house and asked for food and drink. The couple who owned the house were willing to give the travelers only a jug of water and a few slices of bread.

"Would you be kind enough to put us up for the night?" the rabbi asked.

The master of the house told them they could sleep on the dirt floor of the barn, but he did not offer them blankets or comfort.

The next morning, the rabbi put his hands on the farm's crumbling stone wall and prayed fervently, whereupon the stone wall was restored to its original condition. The rabbi's followers looked at each other with astonishment.

One of them exclaimed, "We don't understand, rabbi. The first couple we met gave us everything they had, and then their only cow was killed. This couple barely offered us any concern, and yet their stone wall was restored as good as new."

"Never question the workings of God," the rabbi responded firmly. "You cannot understand God's ways. The fact is that, beneath the wall, an immense treasure was buried a number of years ago which this couple would have discovered were they to repair their wall. Yesterday, when the first couple's cow died, the angel of death was going to swoop down and take the old woman, but he took the cow instead."

Paradise

Telling jokes is also fun around a campfire or wherever people get together. Adapt this joke by adjusting gender, if necessary, and by substituting the names provided with names of people in the group. Select kids who have a good sense of humor and who can enjoy a joke in which they are the object of the punch line.

Evan, Mark, and Dan all entered heaven to find it remarkably different from what they had expected. Everywhere they looked they saw beautiful girls, and every guy they saw walked by with a gorgeous woman on each arm.

"This is awesome!" exclaimed Evan.

"Heaven is better than we could have ever imagined," Mark agreed.

"Let's split up and see what we can do for ourselves," Dan suggested.

An hour later, Mark and Dan came upon Evan enjoying the company of a big, ugly girl. Mark and Dan were astounded.

"What's going on here, Evan?" Mark asked. "I don't understand. There are thousands of beautiful girls all around."

"I don't know what happened, either," responded Evan. "All I know is that I backed up while talking to a girl and accidentally stepped on a duck, and this is who I've become attracted to."

Mark and Dan decided to mill around and meet more girls. Later, Dan encountered Mark sidling up to a big, ugly, hairy girl.

"You, too, Mark?" Dan asked, astonished. "There are millions of beautiful girls here. What happened?"

"I can't explain it," Mark replied. "I was milling around and accidentally stepped on a duck, and now I can't help myself from wanting nothing else but to be with this girl."

It was only an hour or so later when Mark and Evan encountered Dan walking along with a knockout, gorgeous bombshell on his arm.

"Wow!" said Evan. "I can't believe it! How did this happen?"

"I can't explain it either," the beautiful girl responded. "I accidentally stepped on a duck, and now I can't help but be attracted to Dan."

The Starry Sky

Two friends went camping, and after putting up their tent and telling campfire stories, they fell fast asleep.

A few hours later, Matt woke his friend up and said, "Tom, wake up. Look up into the sky and tell me what you see."

"I see a sky filled with millions of stars," Tom replied.

"What does that tell you?" asked Matt.

"Well, it tells me many things. It tells me that we live in a vast galaxy in which each of us is as small as a speck of light in the night sky. It tells me that God has created a universe in which there is order and beauty, and that everything is all right. By making some calculations, I can tell it is about three o'clock in the morning. And it looks as though we should have a beautiful day tomorrow."

"Is that all?" asked Matt.

"Yeah. Why? What does it tell you?"

"Tom, you fool, it tells me that our tent was stolen while we were sleeping!"

The Fishing Expedition

Matt and Tom had decided to spend their time fishing while they were on their camping trip. They had spent over five hundred dollars on fishing supplies: the finest rods and reels, and even a canoe. The first day, they caught nothing. The second day, nothing still. This continued until the last day, when one of them finally caught a fish.

They drove home, glum and disappointed. Finally, Matt said to Tom, "Can you believe it? This one fish ended up costing us over five hundred dollars!"

Tom replied, "Well, then, it's a good thing we didn't catch more than one!"

The Adopted Twins

A struggling young couple was forced to give up their new-born twins for adoption. Years later, however, the mother longed to discover what had become of the twins. Her husband agreed to help her find them, and they learned that the twins had been separated, that one had been adopted by an Hispanic family and had been named Juan, and that the other had been adopted by an Arab family and had been named Amal.

After considerable effort, the husband and wife tracked down the location of Juan and received permission from the parents to meet with him. They were extremely proud of the young man that he had become.

After they left him, the husband asked his wife, "Like you, I am so happy that we saw Juan. Shall we start tracking down the location of Amal?"

The wife replied, "No need to bother. Once you've seen Juan, you've seen Amal."

Teddy Takes Charge

True stories — whether about heroes or ordinary people — can possess as much power to captivate and inspire as fiction.

The silence of the Dakota range was broken by an insistent pounding on the cabin door, followed by a loud command: "Paddock, come out of there!"

Instantly, Paddock knew from the voice that the man outside his door was the city slicker from the east, the one with the round glasses that everyone called "Four Eyes." To his face, though, this newcomer from New York was usually called "Teddy," and Paddock had bragged throughout town that he was going to shoot him.

Paddock opened the door.

"I've heard tell that you don't much like me and want to kill me," Teddy announced. "Well, let's get it over with."

Paddock hadn't expected this. He thought his threats would be enough to frighten the young man and send him running back east. But here he was, at the front door, armed and ready for a gunfight.

"Er, I think you've got it wrong, Teddy," Paddock stammered. "That's not what I said at all. There's been some sort of misunderstanding."

Then Paddock shut the door.

Teddy had taken charge of the situation, and as word spread of his courageous encounter, the respect of the townspeople grew. They had kept their distance from this young fellow who was so different from them — born to a wealthy family and educated at Harvard — who had recently become a neighbor after purchasing a ranch in the Great Plains. Though he was not experienced at working on a ranch, Teddy worked as hard as any man, riding alongside the cowboys for hours at a time, driving herds, and branding cattle. They had to respect him for his determination and audacity.

It had been Teddy's lifelong dream to live a life of strenuous activity and adventure. His mother had told him stories of frontiersmen like Daniel Boone and Davy Crockett, and his father had always encouraged him to strive to be his best. He devoured every adventure story and nature book he could find. He loved the outdoors, and spent hours at a time hiking and exploring the woods and hills, observing the wildlife and gathering specimens. But again and again, he would be driven back to his sickbed, awake all night, gasping for breath, not certain whether his lungs would take in more oxygen.

Teddy had been born with a weak and sickly body; when he was three, he had his first major asthma attack. For days and sometimes weeks, Teddy lay in bed, nearly suffocating, often wondering if he would be able take another breath. And when the attacks had subsided, he lay fatigued, relieved to have survived, but dreading the onset of the next attack at some undetermined hour. The attacks were so severe that his parents feared for his life.

One day, his father said to him, "You have the mind, Teddy, but you have not the body, and without the help of the body, the mind cannot go as far as it should. You must make your body. It will be hard, but I know you will do it." His father had set down a challenge, and Teddy resolved that very day to make his body work. He knew that if he wanted to live life on his own terms, he would have to take charge of his health. Day after day, he went to the gym and pushed his muscles to their limit. It was grueling and demanding exercise. There were times he wanted to give up, but he didn't. His determination to live a life of adventure drove him daily to persevere. In time, he even began to enjoy the feel of pushing his muscles, and he began to notice his body growing stronger, more forceful, more resilient. He learned the value of pushing himself, of testing his limits, of living a strenuous life.

Teddy had taken charge of his health, and he had improved. When he was fourteen, he was put to the test. Traveling alone to Maine, two youths his age taunted him, making fun of his puny body and his thick eyeglasses. After he had been provoked enough, he took the action which he thought to be common among strong men: he fought his antagonists, punching with all of his force ... and he lost. He was not as strong as he had thought. He was no match for the two teens, and he came away the worst for it.

Having been bullied and beaten was a humiliating defeat, but it was also an opportunity for Teddy to realize that he must struggle even harder to over-come his physical weakness. With more resolve than ever, he went back to the gym and pushed himself harder, even receiving his father's permission to start boxing lessons. Teddy took charge, and as the years passed, he devel-oped "the doctrine of the strenuous life," the belief that it's better to be a "doer of deeds," to be "actually in the arena" amidst "the dust and sweat and blood," than to live, without effort, the life of ease. Years later, he would state, "Far better it is to dare mighty things, to win glorious triumphs, even though checkered by failure, than to rank with those poor spirits who neither enjoy much nor suffer much, because they live in that grey twilight that knows nei-ther victory nor defeat."

And that is exactly how Teddy lived his life ... how he approached his studies at Harvard ... how he won the respect of the rugged cowboys of the Dakota Badlands ... how he led a group of men in the Spanish-American War ... how he devoted himself to his family ... how he fought to conserve the natural America that he loved so much. It was with that same bold and mighty spirit that he led the country when he became president of the United States. He had come a long way from those days as a puny kid, but for Theodore Roosevelt, the only way to live was to challenge yourself, to overcome obsta-cles, and to spend yourself in a worthy cause.

"Nothing in the world is worth having or worth doing unless it means effort, pain, difficulty," Theodore Roosevelt once said. "I have never in my life envied a human being who led an easy life. I have envied a great many people who led difficult lives and led them well." Roosevelt's motto for liv-ing was, "Do what you can, with what you have, where you are."

Annie Got Her Gun

At a very young age, Annie Moses loved to tramp through the woods and fields. Her father took her with him when he went hunting and trap-ping, and he taught her how to trap squirrels and birds for dinner. But when she was only five, her father died, altering Annie's life forever. To support the family, her mother had to work odd jobs and was often away from the house. So when Annie returned home with animals she had trapped, her mother did not mind, because it brought food upon the family table. Annie was permitted to trap, her mother decided, but she was forbidden to touch her father's old rifle that hung over the fireplace. Guns were not for little girls, she said.

But Annie was fascinated with her father's old rifle. At age eight, she still remembered their hunting trips together, recalling exactly how he would raise the rifle, take aim, and shoot. Though Annie was small, she was strong and fiercely independent. When her mother wasn't looking, she climbed upon a chair and took the rifle down. Resting the barrel of the rifle on the porch railing, Annie aimed at a squirrel and fired. The squirrel fell. Annie's first shot hit its target.

By the time she was fourteen, Annie had her own sixteen-gauge shotgun and was hunting for a living. She sold the game she shot for food and for fur, making enough to pay off her family's mortgage. When she reached the age of fifteen, Annie left the countryside to live with her married sister in Cincinnati, Ohio. While walking through the streets with her brother-in-law, Joe, they passed a shooting gallery, a novelty to Annie, who had never heard of shooting for sport. Joe took her inside. If she was able to hit five targets in a row, the owner declared, there would be no charge. Little did anyone know what this girl could do. One-two-three-four-five; in rapid succession, Annie hit each target she fired at. Stunned, the owner gave her another free round. She fired six shots and hit six targets. This was clearly no ordinary girl.

Someone suggested a match between Annie and a professional sharpshooter named Frank Butler. Frank agreed. When he arrived and discovered that his adversary was a young girl, he was reluctant to compete in an uneven match, but people had already crowded around to watch, so the competition began.

"Pull!" Frank shouted, and a clay disk was hurled into the sky. Frank aimed, shot, and hit. "Dead!" the referee exclaimed, signifying that Frank had hit the moving target.

"Pull!" Annie shouted, then aimed and fired. "Dead!" was the referee's verdict.

Frank and Annie alternated again and again, each hitting the target every time. The crowd grew; the tension built. When it came time for Frank to shoot for the twenty-fifth time, he shouted,

"Pull!" The target flew through the air, and Frank shot. This time he missed. The professional had missed his mark, and Annie had won the competition.

She also won Frank Butler's heart. As a gentleman, Frank accepted his defeat with grace, recognizing Annie's superior skill. As a gentleman, he also wooed her. In less than a year, they joined together in marriage and soon after joined together in business, entering in wild west shows. Annie was everyone's favorite; in front of large and excited audiences, she would perform stunts that amazed and awed her onlookers. She would shoot the ash off the end of a cigarette hanging from Frank's mouth. She would ride fast on horseback and hit difficult targets. She would even shoot a playing card that had been thrown into the air, putting five or six holes in it before it reached the ground. The Butlers became so popular that their tour performed not only in America, but in other parts of the world as well.

Except that they weren't known as the Butlers. Annie preferred to use her stage name — Annie Oakley.

"Aim at a high mark and you'll hit it," Annie once advised. "No, not the first time, nor the second time, and maybe not the third. But keep on aiming and keep on shooting, for only practice will make you perfect. Finally, you'll hit the bull's eye of success."

CLASSIC STORIES AND STORY-POEMS FOR READING ALOUD

Fairy tales are not only for little children, and neither is love. Love conquers all, even...

The Selfish Giant *by Oscar Wilde*

Every afternoon, as they were coming from school, the children used to go and play in the Giant's garden.

It was a large lovely garden, with soft green grass. Here and there over the grass stood beautiful flowers like stars, and there were twelve peach-trees that in the spring-time broke out into delicate blossoms of pink and pearl, and in the autumn bore rich fruit. The birds sat on the trees and sang so sweetly that the children used to stop their games in order to listen to them. "How happy we are here!" they cried to each other.

One day the Giant came back. He had been to visit his friend the Cornish ogre, and had stayed with him for seven years. After the seven years were over he had said all that he had to say, for his conversation was limited, and he determined to return to his own castle. When he arrived he saw the children playing in the garden.

"What are you doing here?" he cried in a very gruff voice, and the children ran away.

"My own garden is my own garden," said the Giant; "anyone can understand that, and I will allow nobody to play in it but myself."

So he built a high wall all round it, and put up a notice-board.

TRESPASSERS
WILL BE
PROSECUTED

He was a very selfish Giant.

The poor children had now nowhere to play. They tried to play on the road, but the road was very dusty and full of hard stones, and they did not like it. They used to wander round the high walls when their lessons were over, and talk about the beautiful garden inside.

"How happy we were there!" they said to each other.

Then the Spring came, and all over the country there were little blossoms and little birds. Only in the garden of the Selfish Giant it was still winter. The birds did not care to sing in it as there were no children, and the trees forgot to blossom. Once a beautiful flower put its head out from the grass, but when it saw the notice-board it was so sorry for the children that it slipped back into the ground again, and went off to sleep. The only people who were pleased were the Snow and the Frost. "Spring has forgotten this garden," they cried, "so we will live here all the year round." The Snow covered up the grass with her great white cloak, and the Frost painted all the trees silver. Then they invited the North Wind to stay with them, and he came. He was wrapped in furs, and he roared all day about the garden, and blew the chimney-pots down. "This is a delightful spot," he said, "we must ask the Hail on a visit." So the Hail came. Every day for three hours he rattled on the roof of the castle till he broke most of the slates, and then he ran round and round the garden as fast as he could go. He was dressed in grey, and his breath was like ice.

"I cannot understand why the Spring is so late in coming," said the Selfish Giant, as he sat at the window and looked out at his cold, white garden; "I hope there will be a change in the weather."

But the Spring never came, nor the Summer. The Autumn gave golden fruit to every garden, but to the Giant's garden she gave none. "He is too selfish," she said. So it was always Winter there, and the North Wind and the Hail, and the Frost, and the Snow danced about through the trees.

One morning the Giant was lying awake in bed when he heard some lovely music. It sounded so sweet to his ears that he thought it must be the King's musicians passing by. It was really only a little linnet singing outside his window, but it was so long since he had heard a bird sing in his garden that it seemed to him to be the most beautiful music in the world. Then the

Hail stopped dancing over his head, and the North Wind ceased roaring, and a delicious perfume came to him through the open casement. believe the Spring has come at last," said the Giant; and he jumped out of bed and looked out.

What did he see?

He saw the most wonderful sight. Through a little hole in the wall the children had crept in, and they were sitting in the branches of the trees. In every tree that he could see there was a little child. And the trees were so glad to have the children back again that they had covered themselves with blossoms, and were waving their arms gently above the children's heads. The birds were flying about and twittering with delight, and the flowers were looking up through the green grass and laughing. It was a lovely scene, only in one corner it was still winter. It was the farthest corner of the garden, and in it was standing a little boy. He was so small that he could not reach up to the branches of the tree, and he was wandering all round it, crying bitterly. The poor tree was still quite covered with frost and snow, and the North Wind was blowing and roaring above it. "Climb up! little boy," said the Tree, and it bent its branches down as low as it could; but the boy was too tiny.

And the Giant's heart melted as he looked out. "How selfish I have been!" he said; "now I know why the Spring would not come here. I will put that poor little boy on the top of the tree, and then I will knock down the wall, and my garden shall be the children's playground for ever and ever." He was really very sorry for what he had done.

So he crept downstairs and opened the front door quite softly, and went out into the garden. But when the children saw him they were so frightened that they all ran away, and the garden became winter again. Only the little boy did not run, for his eyes were so full of tears that he did not see the Giant coming.

And the Giant stole up behind him and took him gently in his hand, and put him up into the tree. And the tree broke at once into blossom, and the birds came and sang on it, and the little boy stretched out his two arms and flung them round the Giant's neck, and kissed him. And the other children, when they saw that the Giant was not wicked any longer, came running back, and with them came the Spring. "It is your garden now, little children," said the Giant, and he took a great axe and knocked down the wall. And when the people were going to market at twelve o'clock they found the Giant playing with the children in the most beautiful garden they had ever seen.

All day long they played, and in the evening they came to the Giant to bid him good-bye.

"But where is your little companion?" he said: "the boy I put into the tree." The Giant loved him the best because he had kissed him.

"We don't know," answered the children: "he has gone away."

"You must tell him to be sure and come tomorrow," said the Giant. But the children said that they did not know where he lived, and had never seen him before; and the Giant felt very sad.

Every afternoon, when school was over, the children came and played with the Giant. But the little boy whom the Giant loved was never seen again. The Giant was very kind to all the children, yet he longed for his first little friend, and often spoke of him. "How I would like to see him!" he used to say.

Years went over, and the Giant grew very old and feeble. He could not play about any more, so he sat in a huge armchair, and watched the children at their games, and admired his garden. "I have many beautiful flowers," he said; "but the children are the most beautiful flowers of all."

One winter morning he looked out of his window as he was dressing. He did not hate the Winter now, for he knew that it was merely the Spring asleep, and that the flowers were resting.

Suddenly he rubbed his eyes in wonder and looked and looked. It certainly was a marvelous sight. In the farthest corner of the garden was a tree quite covered with lovely white blossoms. Its branches were all golden, and silver fruit hung down from them, and underneath it stood the little boy he had loved.

Downstairs ran the Giant in great joy, and out into the garden. He hastened across the grass, and came near to the child. And when he came quite close his face grew red with anger, and he said, "Who hath dared to wound thee?" For on the palms of the child's hands were the prints of two nails, and the prints of two nails were on the little feet.

"Who hath dared to wound thee?" cried the Giant; "tell me, that I may take my big sword and slay him."

"Nay!" answered the child: "but these are the wounds of Love."

"Who art thou?" said the Giant, and a strange awe fell on him, and he knelt before the little child.

And the child smiled on the Giant, and said to him, "You let me play once in your garden; today you shall come with me to my garden, which is Paradise."

And when the children ran in that afternoon, they found the Giant lying dead under the tree, all covered with white blossoms.

Some people think doodling is a great waste of time, but not for...

The Boy Who Drew Cats *by Lafcadio Hearn*

A long, long time ago, in a small country village in Japan, there lived a poor farmer and his wife, who were very good people. They had a number of children, and found it very hard to feed them all. The elder son was strong enough when only fourteen years old to help his father; and the little girls learned to help their mother almost as soon as they could walk.

But the youngest, a little boy, did not seem to be fit for hard work. He was very clever — cleverer than all his brothers and sisters; but he could never grow very big. So his parents thought it would be better for him to become a priest than to become a farmer. They took him with them to the village-temple one day, and asked the good old priest who lived there if he would have their little boy for his acolyte, and teach him all that a priest ought to know.

The old man spoke kindly to the lad, and asked him some hard questions. So clever were the answers that the priest agreed to take the little fellow into the temple as an acolyte, and to educate him for the priesthood.

The boy learned quickly what the old priest taught him, and was very obedient in most things. But he had one fault. He liked to draw cats during study-hours, and to draw cats even where cats ought not to have been drawn at all.

Whenever he found himself alone, he drew cats. He drew them on the margins of the priest's books, and on all the screens of the temple, and on the walls, and on the pillars. Several times the priest told him this was not right; but he did not stop drawing cats. He drew them because he could not really help it. He had what is called "the genius of an artist," and just for that reason he was not quite fit to be an acolyte;— a good acolyte should study books.

One day after he had drawn some very clever pictures of cats upon a paper screen, the old priest said to him severely: "My boy, you must go away from this temple at once. You will never make a good priest, but perhaps you will become a great artist. Now let me give you a last piece of advice, and be sure you never forget it. *Avoid large places at night;— keep to small!*"

The boy did not know what the priest meant by saying, "*Avoid large places at night;— keep to small.*" He thought and thought, while he was tying up his little bundle of clothes to go away; but he could not understand those words, and he was afraid to speak to the priest any more, except to say goodby.

He left the temple very sorrowfully, and began to wonder what he should do. If he went straight home he felt sure his father would punish him for having been disobedient to the priest; so he was afraid to go home. All at once he remembered that at the next village, twelve miles away, there was a very big temple. He had heard there were several priests at that temple; and he made up his mind to go to them and ask them to take him for their acolyte.

Now that big temple was closed up but the boy did not know this fact. The reason it had been closed up was that a goblin had frightened the priests away, and had taken possession of the place. Some brave warriors had afterward gone to the temple at night to kill the goblin; but they had never been seen alive again. Nobody had ever told these things to the boy; — so he walked all the way to the village hoping to be kindly treated by the priests.

When he got to the village, it was already dark, and all the people were in bed; but he saw the big temple on a hill at the other end of the principal street, and he saw there was a light in the temple. People who tell the story say the goblin used to make that light, in order to tempt lonely travelers to ask for shelter. The boy went at once to the temple, and knocked. There was no sound inside. He knocked and knocked again; but still nobody came. At last he pushed gently at the door, and was quite glad to find that it had not been fastened. So he went in, and saw a lamp burning — but no priest.

He thought some priest would be sure to come very soon, and he sat down and waited. Then he noticed that everything in the temple was gray with dust, and thickly spun over with cobwebs. So he thought to himself that the priests would certainly like to have an acolyte, to keep the place clean. He wondered why they had allowed everything to get so dusty. What most pleased him, however, were some big white screens, good to paint cats upon. Though he was tired, he looked at once for a writing pad, and found one and ground some ink, and began to paint cats.

He painted a great many cats upon the screen; and then he began to feel very, very sleepy. He was just on the point of lying down to sleep beside one of the screens, when he suddenly remembered the words, "*Avoid large places;— keep to small!*"

The temple was very large; he was all alone; and as he thought of these words — though he could not quite understand them — he began to feel for the first time a little afraid; and he resolved to look for a *small place* in which to sleep. He found a little cabinet, with a sliding door, and went into it, and shut himself up. Then he lay down and fell fast asleep.

Very late in the night he was awakened by a most terrible noise — a noise of fighting and screaming. It was so dreadful that he was afraid even to look through a chink in the little cabinet; he lay very still, holding his breath for fright.

The light that had been in the temple went out; but the awful sounds continued, and became more awful, and all the temple shook. After a long time silence came; but the boy was still afraid to move. He did not move until the light of the morning sun shone into the cabinet through the chinks of the little door.

Then he got out of his hiding place very cautiously, and looked about. The first thing he saw was that all the floor of the temple was covered with blood. And then he saw, lying dead in the middle of it, an enormous, monstrous rat — a goblin-rat — bigger than a cow!

But who or what could have killed it? There was no man or other creature to be seen. Suddenly the boy observed that the mouths of all the cats he had drawn the night before, were red and wet with blood. Then he knew that the goblin had been killed by the cats which he had drawn. And then also, for the first time, he understood why the wise old priest had said to him, "*Avoid large places at night;— keep to small.*"

Afterward that boy became a very famous artist. Some of the cats which he drew are still shown to travelers in Japan.

At first, it seems like a hopelessly wasted summer morning, but then comes...

Tom Sawyer's Great, Magnificent Inspiration
by Mark Twain

Saturday morning was come, and all the summer world was bright and fresh, and brimming with life. There was a song in every heart; and if the heart was young the music issued at the lips. There was cheer in every face and a spring in every step. The locust trees were in bloom and the fragrance of the blossoms filled the air. Cardiff Hill, beyond the village and above it, was green with vegetation, and it lay just far enough away to seem a Delectable Land, dreamy, reposeful, and inviting.

Tom appeared on the sidewalk with a bucket of whitewash and a long-handled brush. He surveyed the fence, and all gladness left him and a deep melancholy settled down upon his spirit. Thirty yards of board fence nine feet high. Life to him seemed hollow, and existence but a burden. Sighing he dipped his brush and passed it along the topmost plank; repeated the operation; did it again; compared the insignificant whitewashed streak with the far-reaching continent of unwhitewashed fence, and sat down on a tree-box discouraged....

He began to think of the fun he had planned for this day, and his sorrows multiplied. Soon the free boys would come tripping along on all sorts of delicious expeditions, and they would make a world of fun of him for having to work — the very thought of it burnt him like fire. He got out his worldly wealth and examined it — bits of toys, marbles, and trash; enough to buy an exchange of *work*, maybe, but not half enough to buy so much as half an hour of pure freedom. So he returned his straitened means to his pocket, and gave up the idea of trying to buy the boys. At this dark and hopeless moment an inspiration burst upon him! Nothing less than a great, magnificent inspiration.

He took up his brush and went tranquilly to work. Ben Rogers hove in sight presently — the very boy, of all boys, whose ridicule he had been dreading. Ben's gait was the hop-skip-and-jump — proof enough that his heart was light and his anticipations high. He was eating an apple, and giving a long, melodious whoop, at intervals, followed by a deep-toned ding-dong-dong, ding-dong-dong, for he was personating a steamboat. As he drew near, he slackened speed, took the middle of the street, leaned far over to starboard and rounded to ponderously and with laborious pomp and circumstance — for he was personating the *Big Missouri*, and considered himself to be drawing nine feet of water. He was boat and captain and engine bells combined, so he had to imagine himself standing on his own hurricane deck giving the orders and executing them:

"Stop her, sir! Ting-a-ling-ling!" The headway ran almost out and he drew up slowly toward the sidewalk.

"Ship up to back! Ting-a-ling-ling!" His arms straightened and stiffened down his sides.

"Set her back on the stabboard! Ting-a-ling-ling! Chow! ch-chow-wow! Chow!" His right hand, meantime, describing stately circles, for it was representing a forty-foot wheel.

"Let her go back on the labboard! Ting-a-ling-ling! Chow-ch-chow-chow!" The left hand began to describe circles.

"Stop the stabboard! Ting-a-ling-ling! Stop the labboard! Come ahead on the stabboard! Stop her! Let your outside turn over slow! Ting-a-ling-ling! Chow-ow-ow! Get out that head-line! *Lively* now! Come — out with your spring-line — what're you about there! Take a turn round that stump with the bight of it! Stand by that stage, now — let her go! Done with the engines, sir! Ting-a-ling-ling! *Sh't! s'h't! sh't!*" (trying the gauge cocks).

Tom went on whitewashing — paid no attention to the steamboat. Ben stared a moment and then said:

"Hi-*yi! You're* up a stump, ain't you!"

No answer. Tom surveyed his last touch with the eye of an artist, then he gave his brush another gentle sweep and surveyed the result, as before. Ben ranged up alongside of him. Tom's mouth watered for the apple, but he stuck to his work. Ben said:

"Hello, old chap, you got to work, hey?"

Tom wheeled suddenly and said:

"Why, it's you, Ben! I warn't noticing."

"Say — *I'm* going in a-swimming, *I* am. Don't you wish you could? But of course you'd druther *work* — wouldn't you? Course you would!"

Tom contemplated the boy a bit, and said:

"What do you call work?"

"Why, ain't *that* work?"

Tom resumed his whitewashing, and answered carelessly:

"Well, maybe it is, and maybe it ain't. All I know, is, it suits Tom Sawyer."

"Oh, come, now, you don't mean to let on that you *like* it?"

The brush continued to move.

"Like it? Well, I don't see why I oughtn't to like it. Does a boy get a chance to whitewash a fence every day?"

That put the thing in a new light. Ben stopped nibbling his apple. Tom swept his brush daintily back and forth — stepped back to note the effect — added a touch here and there — criticized the effect again — Ben watching every move and getting more and more interested, more and more absorbed. Presently he said:

"Say, Tom, let *me* whitewash a little."

Tom considered, was about to consent; but he altered his mind:

"No — no — I reckon it wouldn't hardly do, Ben. You see, Aunt Polly's awful particular about this fence — right here on the street, you know — but if it was the back fence I wouldn't mind and *she* wouldn't. Yes, she's awful particular about this fence; it's got to be done very careful; I reckon there ain't one boy in a thousand, maybe two thousand, that can do it the way it's got to be done."

"No — is that so? Oh come, now — lemme just try. Only just a little — I'd let *you*, if you was me, Tom."

"Ben, I'd like to, honest injun; but Aunt Polly — well, Jim wanted to do it, but she wouldn't let him; Sid wanted to do it, and she wouldn't let Sid. Now don't you see how I'm fixed? If you was to tackle this fence and anything was to happen to it —"

"Oh, shucks, I'll be just as careful. Now lemme try. Say — I'll give you the core of my apple."

"Well, here — No, Ben, now don't. I'm afeard —"

"I'll give you *all* of it!"

Tom gave up the brush with reluctance in his face, but alacrity in his heart. And while the late steamer *Big Missouri* worked and sweated in the sun, the retired artist sat on a barrel in the shade close by, dangled his legs, munched his apple, and planned the slaughter of more innocents. There was no lack of material; boys happened along every little while; they came to jeer, but remained to whitewash. By the time Ben was fagged out, Tom had traded the next chance to Billy Fisher for a kite, in good repair; and when *he* played out, Johnny Miller bought in for a dead rat and a string to swing it with — and so on, and so on, hour after hour. And when the middle of the afternoon came, from being a poor poverty-stricken boy in the morning, Tom was literally rolling in wealth. He had besides the things before mentioned, twelve marbles, part of a jew's-harp, a piece of blue bottle glass to look through, a spool cannon, a key that wouldn't unlock anything, a fragment of chalk, a glass stopper of a decanter, a tin soldier, a couple of tadpoles, six firecrackers, a kitten with only one eye, a brass doorknob, a dog collar — but no dog — the handle of a knife, four pieces of orange peel, and a dilapidated old window sash.

He had had a nice, good, idle time all the while — plenty of company — and the fence had three coats of whitewash on it! If he hadn't run out of whitewash, he would have bankrupted every boy in the village.

Tom said to himself that it was not such a hollow world, after all. He had discovered a great law of human action, without knowing it — namely, that in order to make a man or a boy covet a thing, it is only necessary to make the thing difficult to attain. If he had been a great and wise philosopher, like the writer of this book, he would now have comprehended that Work consists of whatever a body is *obliged* to do, and that Play consists of whatever a body is not obliged to do. And this would help him to understand why constructing artificial flowers or performing on a treadmill is work, while rolling tenpins or climbing Mont Blanc is only amusement. There are wealthy gentlemen in England who drive four-horse passenger coaches twenty or thirty miles on a daily line, in the summer, because the privilege costs them considerable money; but if they were offered wages for the service, that would turn it into work and then they would resign.

The boy mused a while over the substantial change which had taken place in his worldly circumstances, and then wended toward headquarters to report.

Aunt Marilla had thought she'd heard everything, until she listened to...

Anne's Confession *by Lucy Maud Montgomery*

On the Monday evening before the picnic, Marilla came down from her room with a troubled face.

"Anne," she said to that small personage, who was shelling peas by the spotless table and singing, "did you see anything of my amethyst brooch? I thought I stuck it in my pincushion when I came home from church yesterday evening, but I can't find it anywhere."

"I — I saw it this afternoon when you were away at the Aid Society," said Anne, a little slowly. "I was passing your door when I saw it on the cushion, so I went in to look at it."

"Did you touch it?" said Marilla sternly.

"Y-e-e-s," admitted Anne, "I took it up and I pinned it on my breast just to see how it would look."

"You had no business to do anything of the sort. It's very wrong in a little girl to meddle. You shouldn't have gone into my room in the first place and you shouldn't have touched a brooch that didn't belong to you in the second. Where did you put it?"

"Oh, I put it back on the bureau. I hadn't it on a minute. Truly, I didn't mean to meddle, Marilla. I didn't think about its being wrong to go in and try on the brooch; but I see now that it was and I'll never do it again. That's one good thing about me. I never do the same naughty thing twice."

"You didn't put it back," said Marilla. "That brooch isn't anywhere on the bureau. You've taken it out or something, Anne."

"I did put it back," said Anne quickly — pertly, Marilla thought. "I don't just remember whether I stuck it on the pincushion or laid it in the china tray. But I'm perfectly certain I put it back."

"I'll go and have another look," said Marilla, determining to be just. "If you put that brooch back it's there still. If it isn't I'll know you didn't, that's all!"

Marilla went to her room and made a thorough search, not only over the bureau but in every other place she thought the brooch might possibly be. It was not to be found and she returned to the kitchen.

"Anne, the brooch is gone. By your own admission you were the last person to handle it. Now, what have you done with it? Tell me the truth at once. Did you take it out and lose it?"

"No, I didn't," said Anne solemnly, meeting Marilla's angry gaze squarely. "I never took the brooch out of your room and that is the truth, if I was to be led to the block for it — although I'm not very certain what a block is. So there, Marilla."

Anne's "so there" was only intended to emphasize her assertion, but Marilla took it as a display of defiance.

"I believe you are telling me a falsehood, Anne," she said sharply. "I know you are. There now, don't say anything more unless you are prepared to tell the whole truth. Go to your room and stay there until you are ready to confess."

"Will I take the peas with me?" said Anne meekly.

"No, I'll finish shelling them myself. Do as I bid you."

When Anne had gone Marilla went about her evening tasks in a very disturbed state of mind. She was worried about her valuable brooch. What if Anne had lost it? And how wicked of the child to deny having taken it, when anybody could see she must have! With such an innocent face, too!

"I don't know what I wouldn't sooner have had happen," thought Marilla, as she nervously shelled the peas. "Of course, I don't suppose she meant to steal it or anything like that. She's just taken it to play with or help along that imagination of hers. She must have taken it, that's clear, for there hasn't been a soul in that room since she was in it, by her own story, until I went up tonight. And the brooch is gone, there's nothing surer. I suppose she has lost it and is afraid to own up for fear she'll be punished. It's a dreadful thing to think she tells falsehoods. It's a far worse thing than her fit of temper. It's a fearful responsibility to have a child in your house you can't trust. Slyness and untruthfulness — that's what she has displayed. I declare I feel worse about that than about the brooch. If she'd only have told the truth about it I wouldn't mind so much."

Marilla went to her room at intervals all through the evening and searched for the brooch, without finding it. A bedtime visit to the east gable produced no result. Anne persisted in denying that she knew anything about the brooch but Marilla was only the more firmly convinced that she did.

She told Matthew the story the next morning. Matthew was confounded and puzzled; he could not so quickly lose faith in Anne but he had to admit that circumstances were against her.

"You're sure it hasn't fell down behind the bureau?" was the only suggestion he could offer.

"I've moved the bureau and I've taken out the drawers and I've looked in every crack and cranny" was Marilla's positive answer. "The brooch is gone and that child has taken it and lied about it. That's the plain, ugly truth, Matthew Cuthbert, and we might as well look it in the face."

"Well now, what are you going to do about it?" Matthew asked forlornly, feeling secretly thankful that Marilla and not he had to deal with the situation. He felt no desire to put his oar in this time.

"She'll stay in her room until she confesses," said Marilla grimly, remembering the success of this method in the former case. "Then we'll see. Perhaps we'll be able to find the brooch if she'll only tell where she took it; but in any case she'll have to be severely punished, Matthew."

"Well now, you'll have to punish her," said Matthew, reaching for his hat. "I've nothing to do with it, remember. You warned me off yourself."

Marilla felt deserted by everyone. She could not even go to Mrs. Lynde for advice. She went up to the east gable with a very serious face and left it with a face more serious still. Anne steadfastly refused to confess. She persisted in asserting that she had not taken the brooch. The child had evidently been crying and Marilla felt a pang of pity which she sternly repressed. By night she was, as she expressed it, "beat out."

"You'll stay in this room until you confess, Anne. You can make up your mind to that," she said firmly.

"But the picnic is tomorrow, Marilla," cried Anne. "You won't keep me from going to that, will you? You'll just let me out for the afternoon, won't you? Then I'll stay here as long as you like AFTERWARDS cheerfully. But I MUST go to the picnic."

"You'll not go to picnics nor anywhere else until you've confessed, Anne."

"Oh, Marilla," gasped Anne.

But Marilla had gone out and shut the door.

Wednesday morning dawned as bright and fair as if expressly made to order for the picnic. Birds sang around Green Gables; the Madonna lilies in the garden sent out whiffs of perfume that entered in on viewless winds at every door and window, and wandered through halls and rooms like spirits of benediction. The birches in the hollow waved joyful hands as if watching for Anne's usual morning greeting from the east gable. But Anne was not at her window. When Marilla took her breakfast up to her she found the child sitting primly on her bed, pale and resolute, with tight-shut lips and gleaming eyes.

"Marilla, I'm ready to confess."

"Ah!" Marilla laid down her tray. Once again her method had succeeded; but her success was very bitter to her. "Let me hear what you have to say then, Anne."

"I took the amethyst brooch," said Anne, as if repeating a lesson she had learned. "I took it just as you said. I didn't mean to take it when I went in. But it did look so beautiful, Marilla, when I pinned it on my breast that I was overcome by an irresistible temptation. I imagined how perfectly thrilling it would be to take it to Idlewild and play I was the Lady Cordelia Fitzgerald. It would be so much easier to imagine I was the Lady Cordelia if I had a real amethyst brooch on. Diana and I make necklaces of roseberries but what are roseberries compared to amethysts? So I took the brooch. I thought I could put it back before you came home. I went all the way around by the road to lengthen out the time. When I was going over the bridge across the Lake of Shining Waters I took the brooch off to have another look at it. Oh, how it did shine in the sunlight! And then, when I was leaning over the bridge, it just slipped through my fingers — so — and went down — down — down, all purplysparkling, and sank forevermore beneath the Lake of Shining Waters. And that's the best I can do at confessing, Marilla."

Marilla felt hot anger surge up into her heart again. This child had taken and lost her treasured amethyst brooch and now sat there calmly reciting the details thereof without the least apparent compunction or repentance.

"Anne, this is terrible," she said, trying to speak calmly. "You are the very wickedest girl I ever heard of"

"Yes, I suppose I am," agreed Anne tranquilly. "And I know I'll have to be punished. It'll be your duty to punish me, Marilla. Won't you please get it over right off because I'd like to go to the picnic with nothing on my mind."

"Picnic, indeed! You'll go to no picnic today, Anne Shirley. That shall be your punishment. And it isn't half severe enough either for what you've done!"

"Not go to the picnic!" Anne sprang to her feet and clutched Marilla's hand. "But you PROMISED me I might! Oh, Marilla, I must go to the picnic. That was why I confessed. Punish me any way you like but that. Oh, Marilla, please, please, let me go to the picnic. Think of the ice cream! For anything you know I may never have a chance to taste ice cream again."

Marilla disengaged Anne's clinging hands stonily.

"You needn't plead, Anne. You are not going to the picnic and that's final. No, not a word."

Anne realized that Marilla was not to be moved. She clasped her hands together, gave a piercing shriek, and then flung herself face downward on the bed, crying and writhing in an utter abandonment of disappointment and despair.

"For the land's sake!" gasped Marilla, hastening from the room. "I believe the child is crazy. No child in her senses would behave as she does. If she isn't she's utterly bad. Oh dear, I'm afraid Rachel was right from the first. But I've put my hand to the plow and I won't look back."

That was a dismal morning. Marilla worked fiercely and scrubbed the porch floor and the dairy shelves when she could find nothing else to do. Neither the shelves nor the porch needed it — but Marilla did. Then she went out and raked the yard.

When dinner was ready she went to the stairs and called Anne. A tear-stained face appeared, looking tragically over the banisters.

"Come down to your dinner, Anne."

"I don't want any dinner, Marilla," said Anne, sobbingly. "I couldn't eat anything. My heart is broken. You'll feel remorse of conscience someday, I expect, for breaking it, Marilla, but I forgive you. Remember when the time comes that I forgive you. But please don't ask me to eat anything, especially boiled pork and greens. Boiled pork and greens are so unromantic when one is in affliction."

Exasperated, Marilla returned to the kitchen and poured out her tale of woe to Matthew, who, between his sense of justice and his unlawful sympathy with Anne, was a miserable man.

"Well now, she shouldn't have taken the brooch, Marilla, or told stories about it," he admitted, mournfully surveying his plateful of unromantic pork and greens as if he, like Anne, thought it a food unsuited to crises of feeling, "but she's such a little thing — such an interesting little thing. Don't you think it's pretty rough not to let her go to the picnic when she's so set on it?"

"Matthew Cuthbert, I'm amazed at you. I think I've let her off entirely too easy. And she doesn't appear to realize how wicked she's been at all — that's what worries me most. If she'd really felt sorry it wouldn't be so bad. And you don't seem to realize it, neither; you're making excuses for her all the time to yourself — I can see that."

"Well now, she's such a little thing," feebly reiterated Matthew. "And there should be allowances made, Marilla. You know she's never had any bringing up."

"Well, she's having it now," retorted Marilla.

The retort silenced Matthew if it did not convince him. That dinner was a very dismal meal. The only cheerful thing about it was Jerry Buote, the hired boy, and Marilla resented his cheerfulness as a personal insult.

When her dishes were washed and her bread sponge set and her hens fed Marilla remembered that she had noticed a small rent in her best black lace shawl when she had taken it off on Monday afternoon on returning from the Ladies' Aid.

She would go and mend it. The shawl was in a box in her trunk. As Marilla lifted it out, the sunlight, falling through the vines that clustered thickly about the window, struck upon something caught in the shawl — something that glittered and sparkled in facets of violet light. Marilla snatched at it with a gasp. It was the amethyst brooch, hanging to a thread of the lace by its catch!

"Dear life and heart," said Marilla blankly, "what does this mean? Here's my brooch safe and sound that I thought was at the bottom of Barry's pond. Whatever did that girl mean by saying she took it and lost it? I declare I believe Green Gables is bewitched. I remember now that when I took off my shawl Monday afternoon I laid it on the bureau for a minute. I suppose the brooch got caught in it somehow. Well!"

Marilla betook herself to the east gable, brooch in hand. Anne had cried herself out and was sitting dejectedly by the window.

"Anne Shirley," said Marilla solemnly, "I've just found my brooch hanging to my black lace shawl. Now I want to know what that rigmarole you told me this morning meant."

"Why, you said you'd keep me here until I confessed," returned Anne wearily, "and so I decided to confess because I was bound to get to the picnic. I thought out a confession last night after I went to bed and made it as interesting as I could. And I said it over and over so that I wouldn't forget it. But you wouldn't let me go to the picnic after all, so all my trouble was wasted."

Marilla had to laugh in spite of herself. But her conscience pricked her.

"Anne, you do beat all! But I was wrong — I see that now. I shouldn't have doubted your word when I'd never known you to tell a story. Of course, it wasn't right for you to confess to a thing you hadn't done — it was very wrong to do so. But I drove you to it. So if you'll forgive me, Anne, I'll forgive you and we'll start square again. And now get yourself ready for the picnic."

Anne flew up like a rocket.

"Oh, Marilla, isn't it too late?"

"No, it's only two o'clock. They won't be more than well gathered yet and it'll be an hour before they have tea. Wash your face and comb your hair and put on your gingham. I'll fill a basket for you. There's plenty of stuff baked in the house. And I'll get Jerry to hitch up the sorrel and drive you down to the picnic ground."

"Oh, Marilla," exclaimed Anne, flying to the washstand. "Five minutes ago I was so miserable I was wishing I'd never been born and now I wouldn't change places with an angel!"

That night a thoroughly happy, completely tired-out Anne returned to Green Gables in a state of beatification impossible to describe.

"Oh, Marilla, I've had a perfectly scrumptious time. Scrumptious is a new word I learned today. I heard Mary Alice Bell use it. Isn't it very expressive? Everything was lovely. We had a splendid tea and then Mr. Harmon Andrews took us all for a row on the Lake of Shining Waters — six of us at a time. And Jane Andrews nearly fell overboard. She was leaning out to pick water lilies and if Mr. Andrews hadn't caught her by her sash just in the nick of time she'd fallen in and prob'ly been drowned. I wish it had been me. It would have been such a romantic experience to have been nearly drowned. It would be such a thrilling tale to tell. And we had the ice cream. Words fail me to describe that ice cream. Marilla, I assure you it was sublime."

That evening Marilla told the whole story to Matthew over her stocking basket.

"I'm willing to own up that I made a mistake," she concluded candidly, "but I've learned a lesson. I have to laugh when I think of Anne's 'confession,' although I suppose I shouldn't for it really was a falsehood. But it doesn't seem as bad as the other would have been, somehow, and anyhow I'm responsible for it. That child is hard to understand in some respects. But I believe she'll turn out all right yet. And there's one thing certain, no house will ever be dull that she's in."

What had I to fear? Nobody would ever discover the murder, unless from the sound of...

The Telltale Heart *by Edgar Allan Poe*

True! Nervous — very nervous, dreadfully nervous I had been and am. But why will you say that I am mad? The disease had sharpened my senses — not destroyed, not dulled them. Above all was the sense of hearing acute. I heard all things in the heaven and in the earth. I heard many things in hell. How then am I mad? Hearken, and observe how healthily, how calmly I can tell you the whole story.

It is impossible to say how the idea first entered my brain. But once conceived, it haunted me day and night. Object there was none. Passion there was none. I loved the old man. He had never wronged me. He had never given me insult. For his gold I had no desire. I think it was his eye! Yes, it was this! He had the eye of a vulture, a pale blue eye, with a film over it. Whenever it fell upon me my blood ran cold; and so by degrees, very gradually, I made up my mind to take the life of the old man, and thus rid myself of the eye forever.

Now this is the point. You fancy me mad. Madmen know nothing. But you should have seen *me*. You should have seen how wisely I proceeded. With what caution, with what foresight, with what dissimulation I went to work! I was never kinder to the old man than during the whole week before I killed him.

And every night, about midnight, I turned the latch of his door and opened it — oh, so gently! And then, when I had made an opening sufficient for my head, I put in a dark lantern, all closed, closed so that no light shone out, and then I thrust in my head. Oh, you would have laughed to see how cunningly I thrust it in! I moved it slowly — very, very slowly, so that I might not disturb the old man's sleep. It took me an hour to place my whole head within the opening so far that I could see him as he lay upon his bed. Ha! Would a madman have been so wise as this? And then, when my head was well in the room, I undid the lantern cautiously — oh, so cautiously — cautiously (for the hinges creaked) — I undid it just so much that a single thin ray fell upon the vulture eye. And this I did for seven long nights, every night just at midnight, but I found the eye always closed; and so it was impossible to do the work. For it was not the old man who vexed me, but his Evil Eye.

And every morning when the day broke, I went boldly into the chamber and spoke courageously to him, calling him by name in a hearty tone, and inquiring how he had passed the night. So you see he would have been a very profound old man indeed to suspect that every night, just at twelve, I looked in upon him while he slept.

Upon the eighth night I was more than usually cautious in opening the door. A watch's minute hand moves more quickly than did mine. Never before that night had I *felt* the extent of my own powers — of my sagacity. I could scarcely contain my feelings of triumph. To think that there I was, opening the door, little by little, and he not even dreaming of my secret deeds or thoughts! I fairly chuckled at the idea. And perhaps he heard me, for he moved on the bed suddenly, as if startled. Now you may think that I drew back —

but no. His room was as black as pitch with the thick darkness (for the shutters were close fastened, through fear of robbers), and so I knew that he could not see the opening of the door, and I kept pushing it on steadily, steadily.

I had my head in, and was about to open the lantern, when my thumb slipped upon the tin fastening, and the old man sprang up in bed, crying out, "Who's there?"

I kept quite still and said nothing. For a whole hour I did not move a muscle, and in the meantime I did not hear him lie down. He was still sitting up in the bed listening — just as I have done, night after night, hearkening to the death watches in the wall.

Presently I heard a slight groan, and I knew it was the groan of mortal terror. It was not a groan of pain or of grief. Oh, no! It was the low stifled sound that arises from the bottom of the soul when overcharged with awe. I knew the sound well. Many a night, just at midnight, when all the world slept, it has welled up from my own bosom, deepening, with its dreadful echo, the terrors that distracted me. I say I knew it well. I knew what the old man felt, and pitied him, although I chuckled at heart. I knew that he had been lying awake ever since the first slight noise, when he had turned in the bed. His fears had been growing upon him ever since. He had been trying to fancy them causeless, but could not. He had been saying to himself, "It is nothing but the wind in the chimney. It is only a mouse crossing the floor." Or, "It is merely a cricket which has made a single chirp." Yes, he had been trying to comfort himself with these suppositions, but he had found them all in vain. *All in vain*, because death, in approaching him had stalked with his black shadow before him, and enveloped the victim. And it was the mournful influence of the unperceived shadow that caused him to feel, although he neither saw nor heard — to *feel* the presence of my head within the room.

When I had waited a long time, very patiently, without hearing him lie down, I resolved to open a little, a very, very little crevice in the lantern. So I opened it — you cannot imagine how stealthily, stealthily — until at length a single dim ray, like the thread of the spider, shot from out the crevice and fell full upon the vulture eye.

It was open, wide, wide open, and I grew furious as I gazed upon it. I saw it with perfect distinctness — all a dull blue, with a hideous veil over it that chilled the very marrow in my bones. But I could see nothing else of the old man's face or person, for I had directed the ray, as if by instinct, precisely upon the damned spot.

And have I not told you that what you mistake for madness is but overacuteness of the senses? Now, I say, there came to my ears a low, dull, quick sound, such as a watch makes when enveloped in cotton. I knew *that* sound well, too. It was the beating of the old man's heart. It increased my fury, as the beating of a drum stimulates the soldier into courage.

But even yet I refrained and kept still. I scarcely breathed. I held the lantern motionless. I tried to see how steadily I could maintain the ray upon the eye. Meantime the hellish tattoo of the heart increased. It grew quicker and quicker, and louder and louder every instant. The old man's terror *must* have been extreme! Do you mark me well? I have told you that I am nervous; so I am. And now at the dead hour of the night, amid the dreadful silence of that old house, so strange a noise as this excited me to uncontrollable terror. Yet for some minutes longer I refrained and stood still. But the beating grew louder, louder! I thought the heart must burst. And now a new anxiety seized me. The sound would be heard by a neighbor! The old man's hour had come! With a loud yell, I threw open the lantern and leaped into the room. He shrieked once — once only. In an instant I dragged him to the floor, and pulled the heavy bed over him. I then smiled gaily, to find the deed so far done. But, for many minutes, the heart beat on with a muffled sound. This, however, did not vex me; it would not be heard through the wall. At length it ceased. The old man was dead. I removed the bed and examined the corpse. Yes, he was stone, stone dead. I placed my hand upon the heart and held it there many minutes. There was no pulsation. He was stone dead. His eye would trouble me no more.

If you still think me mad, you will think so no longer when I describe the wise precautions I took for the concealment of the body. The night waned, and I worked hastily but in silence. First of all I dismembered the corpse. I cut off the head and the arms and the legs.

I then took up three planks from the flooring of the chamber, and deposited all between the scantlings. I then replaced the boards so cleverly, so cunningly, that no human eye — not even *his*— could have detected anything wrong. There was nothing to wash out, no stain of any kind, no bloodspot whatever. I had been too wary for that. A tub had caught all — ha! ha!

When I had made an end of these labors, it was four o'clock — still dark as midnight. As the bell sounded the hour, there came a knocking at the street door. I went down to open it with a light heart, for what had I *now* to fear? There entered three men, who introduced themselves, with perfect suavity, as officers of the police. A shriek had been heard by a neighbor during the night, suspicion of foul play had been aroused, information had been lodged at the police office, and they (the officers) had been deputed to search the premises.

I smiled, for *what* had I to fear? I bade the gentlemen welcome. The shriek, I said, was my own in a dream. The old man, I mentioned, was absent in the country. I took my visitors all over the house. I bade them search —

search *well.* I led them at length to *his* chamber. I showed them his treasures, secure, undisturbed. In the enthusiasm of my confidence I brought chairs into the room, and desired them *here* to rest from their fatigues, while I myself, in the wild audacity of my perfect triumph, placed my own seat upon the very spot beneath which reposed the corpse of the victim.

The officers were satisfied. My manner had convinced them. I was singularly at ease. They sat, and while I answered cheerily, they chatted of familiar things. But ere long I felt myself getting pale and wished them gone. My head ached and I fancied a ringing in my ears. But still they sat and still chatted. The ringing became more distinct. It continued and became more distinct. I talked more freely to get rid of the feeling, but it continued and gained definiteness, until at length I found that the noise was *not* within my ears.

No doubt I now grew *very* pale, but now I talked more fluently and with heightened voice. Yet the sound increased. And what could I do? It was a low, dull, quick sound, much such a sound as a watch makes when enveloped in cotton. I gasped for breath — and yet the officers heard it not. I talked more quickly, more vehemently — but the noise steadily increased. I arose and argued about trifles, in a high key and with violent gesticulations — but the noise steadily increased. Why *would* they not be gone? I paced the floor to and fro with heavy strides, as if excited to fury by the observations of the men — but the noise steadily increased.

Oh God! what *could* I do? I foamed — I raved — I swore! I swung the chair upon which I had been sitting, and grated it upon the boards, but the noise arose over all and continually increased. It grew louder — louder — *louder!* And still the men chatted pleasantly and smiled. Was it possible they heard not? Almighty God? No, no! They heard! They suspected! They *knew!* They were making a mockery of my horror! This I thought and this I think. But anything was better than this agony! Anything was more tolerable than this derision! I could bear those hypocritical smiles no longer! I felt that I must scream or die! And now, again — hark! Louder! Louder! Louder! *Louder!*

"Villains!" I shrieked. "Dissemble no more! I admit the deed! Tear up the planks! Here, here! It is the beating of his hideous heart!"

"But you have a home," he said. "Yes — in the grave!" she answered....

The Adventures of the German Student
by Washington Irving

On a stormy night, in the tempestuous times of the French Revolution, a young German was returning to his lodgings, at a late hour, across the old part of Paris. The lightning gleamed, and the loud claps of thunder rattled through the lofty, narrow streets — but I should first tell you something about this young German.

Gottfried Wolfgang was a young man of good family. He had studied for some time at Gottingen, but being of a visionary and enthusiastic character, he had wandered into those wild and speculative doctrines which have so often bewildered German students. His secluded life, his intense application, and the singular nature of his studies, had an effect on both mind and body. His health was impaired; his imagination diseased. He had been indulging in fanciful speculation on spiritual essences until, like Swedenborg, he had an ideal world of his own around him. He took up a notion, I do not know from what cause, that there was an evil influence hanging over him; an evil genius or spirit seeking to ensnare him and ensure his perdition. Such an idea working on his melancholy temperament produced the most gloomy effects. He became haggard and desponding. His friends discovered the mental malady that was preying upon him, and determined that the best cure was a change of scene; he was sent, therefore, to finish his studies amidst the splendors and gaieties of Paris.

Wolfgang arrived in Paris at the breaking out of the Revolution. The popular delirium at first caught his enthusiastic mind, and he was captivated by the political and philosophical theories of the day: but the scenes of blood which followed shocked his sensitive nature; disgusted him with society and the world, and made him more than ever a recluse. He shut himself up in a solitary apartment in the *Pays Latin*, the quarter of students. There in a gloomy street not far from the monastic walls of the Sorbonne, he pursued his favorite speculations. Sometimes he spent hours together in the great libraries of Paris, those catacombs of departed authors, rummaging among their hoards of dusty and obsolete works in quest of food for his unhealthy appetite. He was, in a manner, a literary ghoul, feeding in the charnel-house of decayed literature.

Wolfgang, though solitary and recluse, was of an ardent temperament, but for a time it operated merely upon his imagination. He was too shy and ignorant of the world to make any advances to the fair, but he was a passionate admirer of female beauty, and in his lonely chamber would often lose himself in reveries on forms and faces which he had seen, and his fancy would deck out images of loveliness far surpassing the reality.

While his mind was in this excited and sublimated state, he had a dream which produced an extraordinary effect upon him. It was of a female face of transcendent beauty. So strong was the impression it made, that he dreamt of it again and again. It haunted his thoughts by day, his slumbers by night; in fine, he became passionately enamored of this shadow of a dream. This lasted so long, that it became one of those fixed ideas which haunt the minds of melancholy men, and are at times mistaken for madness.

Such was Gottfried Wolfgang, and such his situation at the time I mentioned. He was returning home late one stormy night, through some of the old and gloomy streets of the *Marais*, the ancient part of Paris. The loud claps of thunder rattled among the high houses of the narrow streets. He came to the Place de Greve, the square where public executions are performed. The lightning quivered about the pinnacles of the ancient Hotel de Ville, and shed flickering gleams over the open space in front. As Wolfgang was crossing the square, he shrunk back with horror at finding himself close by the guillotine. It was the height of the reign of terror, when this dreadful instrument of death stood ever ready, and its scaffold was continually running with blood of the virtuous and the brave. It had that very day been actively employed in the work of carnage, and there it stood in grim array amidst a silent and sleeping city, waiting for fresh victims.

Wolfgang's heart sickened within him, and he was turning shuddering from the horrible engine, when he beheld a shadowy form cowering as it were at the foot of the steps which led up to the scaffold. A succession of vivid flashes of lightning revealed it more distinctly. It was a female figure, dressed in black. She was seated on one of the lower steps of the scaffold, leaning forward, her face hid in her lap, and her long disheveled tresses hanging to the ground, streaming with the rain which fell in torrents. Wolfgang paused. There was something awful in this solitary monument of woe. The female had the appearance of being above the common order. He knew the times to be full of vicissitude, and that many a fair head, which had once been pillowed on down, now wandered houseless. Perhaps this was some poor mourner whom the dreadful axe had rendered desolated, and who sat here heartbroken on the strand of existence, from which all that was dear to her had been launched into eternity.

He approached, and addressed her in the accents of sympathy. She raised her head and gazed wildly at him. What was his astonishment at beholding, by the bright glare of the lightning, the very face which had haunted him in his dreams. It was pale and disconsolate, but ravishingly beautiful.

Trembling with violent and conflicting emotions, Wolfgang again accosted her. He spoke something of her being exposed at such an hour of the night, and to the fury of such a storm, and offered to conduct her to her friends. She pointed to the guillotine with a gesture of dreadful signification.

"I have no friends on earth!" said she.

"But you have a home," said Wolfgang.

"Yes — in the grave!"

The heart of the student melted at the words.

"If a stranger dare make an offer," said he, "without danger of being misunderstood, I would offer my humble dwelling as a shelter; myself as a devoted friend. I am friendless myself in Paris, and a stranger in the land; but if my life could be of service, it is at your disposal, and should be sacrificed before harm or indignity should come to you."

There was an honest earnestness in the young man's manner that had its effect. His foreign accent, too, was in his favor; it showed him not to be a hackneyed inhabitant of Paris. Indeed there is an eloquence in true enthusiasm that is not to be doubted. The homeless stranger confided herself implicitly to the protection of the student.

He supported her faltering steps across the Pont Neuf, and by the place where the statue of Henry the Fourth had been overthrown by the populace. The storm had abated, and the thunder rumbled at a distance. All Paris was quiet; that great volcano of human passion slumbered for a while, to gather fresh strength for the next day's eruption. The student conducted his charge through the ancient streets of the *Pays Latin*, and by the dusky walls of the Sorbonne to the great, dingy hotel which he inhabited. The old portress who admitted them stared with surprise at the unusual sight of the melancholy Wolfgang with a female companion.

On entering his apartment, the student, for the first time, blushed at the scantiness and indifference of his dwelling. He had but one chamber — an old-fashioned saloon — heavily carved and fantastically furnished with the remains of former magnificence, for it was one of those hotels in the quarter of Luxembourg Palace which had once belonged to nobility. It was lumbered with books and papers, and all the usual apparatus of a student, and his bed stood in a recess at one end.

When lights were brought, and Wolfgang had a better opportunity of contemplating the stranger, he was more than ever intoxicated by her beauty. Her face was pale, but of a dazzling fairness, set off by a profusion of raven hair that hung clustered about it. Her eyes were large and brilliant, with a singular expression that approached almost to wildness. As far as her black dress permitted her shape to be seen, it was of perfect symmetry. Her whole appearance was highly striking, though she was dressed in the simplest style. The only thing approaching to an ornament which she wore was a broad, black band round her neck, clasped by diamonds.

The perplexity now commenced with the student how to dispose of the helpless being thus thrown upon his protection. He thought of abandoning his chamber to her, and seeking shelter for himself elsewhere. Still he was so fascinated by her charms, there seemed to be such a spell upon his thoughts and senses, that he could not tear himself from her presence. Her manner, too, was singular and unaccountable. She spoke no more of the guillotine. Her grief had abated. The attentions of the student had first won her confidence, and then, apparently, her heart. She was evidently an enthusiast like himself, and enthusiasts soon understand each other.

In the infatuation of the moment Wolfgang avowed his passion for her. He told her the story of his mysterious dream, and how she had possessed his heart before he had ever seen her. She was strangely affected by his recital, and acknowledged to have felt an impulse towards him equally unaccountable. It was the time for wild theory and wild actions. Old prejudices and superstitions were done away; everything was under the sway of the "Goddess of reason." Among other rubbish of the old times, the forms and ceremonies of marriage began to be considered superfluous binds for honorable minds. Social compacts were the vogue. Wolfgang was too much of a theorist not to be tainted by the liberal doctrines of the day.

"Why should we separate?" said he: "our hearts are united; in the eye of reason and honor we are as one. What need is there of sordid forms to bind high souls together?"

The stranger listened with emotion: she had evidently received illumination of the same school.

"You have no home nor family," continued he: "let me be everything to you, or rather let us be everything to one another. If form is necessary, form shall be observed — there is my hand. I pledge myself to you forever."

"For ever?" said the stranger, solemnly.

"For ever!" repeated Wolfgang.

The stranger clasped the hand extended to her: "Then I am yours," murmured she, and sunk upon his bosom.

The next morning the student left his bride sleeping, and sallied forth at an early hour to seek more spacious apartments, suitable to the change in his situation. When he returned, he found the stranger lying with her head hanging over the bed, and one arm thrown over it. He spoke to her, but received no reply. He advanced to awaken her from her uneasy posture. On taking her hand, it was cold — there was no pulsation — her face was pallid and ghastly. In a word — she was a corpse.

Horrified and frantic, he alarmed the house. A scene of confusion ensued. The police were summoned. As the officer of police entered the room, he started back on beholding the corpse.

"Great heaven!" cried he, "How did this woman come here?"

"Do you know anything about her?" said Wolfgang eagerly.

"Do I?" exclaimed the police officer. "She was guillotined yesterday!"

He stepped forward; undid the black collar round the neck of the corpse, and the head rolled on the floor!

The student burst into a frenzy. "The fiend! The fiend has gained possession of me!" shrieked he: "I am lost for ever!"

They tried to soothe him, but in vain. He was possessed with the frightful belief that an evil spirit had reanimated the dead body to ensnare him. He went distracted, and died in a madhouse.

Here the old gentleman with the haunted head finished the narrative.

"And is this really a fact?" said the inquisitive gentleman.

"A fact not to be doubted," replied the other. "I had it from the best authority. The student told it to me himself. I saw him in a madhouse at Paris."

It was past endurance. I could stand it no longer. I hated John Claverhouse. I resolved to kill the man with the...

Moon-Face *by Jack London*

John Claverhouse was a moon-faced man. You know the kind, cheekbones wide apart, chin and forehead melting into the cheeks to complete the perfect round, and the nose, broad and pudgy, equidistant from the circumference, flattened against the very center of the face like a dough ball upon the ceiling. Perhaps that is why I hated him, for truly he had become an offense to my eyes, and I believed the earth to be cumbered with his presence. Perhaps my mother may have been superstitious of the moon and looked upon it over the wrong shoulder at the wrong time.

Be that as it may, I hated John Claverhouse. Not that he had done me what society would consider a wrong or an ill turn. Far from it. The evil was of deeper, subtler sort, so elusive, so intangible, as to defy clear, definite analysis in words. We all experience such things at some period in our lives. For the first time we see a certain individual, one who the very instant before we did not dream existed; and yet, at the first moment of meeting, we say, "I do not like that man." Why do we not like him? Ah, we do not know why; we know only that we do not. We have taken a dislike, that is all. And so I with John Claverhouse.

What right had such a man to be happy? Yet he was an optimist. He was always gleeful and laughing. All things were always all right, curse him! Other men could laugh, and it did not bother me. I even used to laugh myself, before I met John Claverhouse.

But his laugh! It irritated me, maddened me, as nothing else under the sun could irritate or madden me. It haunted me, gripped hold of me, and would not let me go. It was a huge, Gargantuan laugh. Waking or sleeping, it was always with me, whirring and jarring across my heartstrings like an enormous rasp. At break of day it came whooping across the fields to spoil my pleasant morning reverie. Under the aching noonday glare, when the green things drooped and the birds withdrew to the depths of the forest, and all nature drowsed, his great "Ha! Ha!" and "Ho! Ho!" rose up to the sky and challenged the sun. And at black midnight, from the lonely crossroads where he turned from town into his own place, came his plaguey cachinnations to rouse me from my sleep and make me writhe and clench my nails into my palms.

I went forth privily in the nighttime and turned his cattle into his fields, and in the morning heard his whooping laugh as he drove them out again. "It is nothing," he said; "the poor dumb beasties are not to be blamed for straying into fatter pastures."

He had a dog he called Mars, a big, splendid brute, part deerhound and part bloodhound, and resembling both. Mars was a great delight to him, and they were always together. But I bided my time and one day when opportunity was ripe lured the animal away and settled for him with strychnine and beefsteak. It made positively no impression on John Claverhouse. His laugh was as hearty and frequent as ever, and his face as much like the full moon as it always had been.

Then I set fire to his haystacks and his barn. But the next morning, being Sunday, he went forth blithe and cheerful.

"Where are you going?" I asked him as he went by the crossroads.

"Trout," he said, and his face beamed like a full moon. "I just dote on trout."

Was there ever such an impossible man! His whole harvest had gone up in his haystacks and barn. It was uninsured, I knew. And yet, in the face of famine and the rigorous winter, he went out gaily in quest of a mess of trout, forsooth, because he "doted" on them! Had gloom but rested, no matter how lightly, on his brow, or had his bovine countenance grown long and serious and less like the moon, or had he removed that smile but once from off his face, I am sure I could have forgiven him for existing. But no, he grew only more cheerful under misfortune.

I insulted him. He looked at me in slow and smiling surprise.

"I fight you? Why?" he asked slowly. And then he laughed. "You are so funny! Ho! Ho! You'll be the death of me! He! He! He! Oh! Ho! Ho! Ho!"

What would you? It was past endurance. By the blood of Judas, how I hated him. Then there was that name — Claverhouse! What a name! Wasn't it absurd? Claverhouse! Merciful heaven, *why* Claverhouse? Again and again I asked myself that question. I should not have minded Smith, or Brown, or Jones — but *Claverhouse!* I leave it to you. Repeat it to yourself — Claverhouse. Just listen to the ridiculous sound of it — Claverhouse! Should a man live with such a name? I ask you. "No," you say. And "no" said I.

But I bethought me of this mortgage. What of his crops and barn destroyed, I knew he would be unable to meet it. So I got a shrewd, close-mouthed, tightfisted money lender to get the mortgage transferred to him. I did not appear, but through this agent I forced the foreclosure, and but few days (no more, believe me, than the law allowed) were given John Claverhouse to remove his goods and chattels from the premises. Then I strolled down to see how he took it, for he had lived there upward of twenty years. But he met me with his saucer-eyes twinkling and the light glowing and spreading in his face till it was a full-risen moon.

"Ha! Ha! Ha!" he laughed. "The funniest tyke, that youngster of mine! Did you ever hear the like? Let me tell you. He was down playing by the edge of the river when a piece of the bank caved in and splashed him. 'Oh, papa!' he cried, 'a great big puddle flewed up and hit me.'"

He stopped and waited for me to join him in his infernal glee.

"I don't see any laugh in it," I said shortly, and I know my face went sour.

He regarded me with wonderment, and then came the damnable light, glowing and spreading, as I have described it, till his face shone soft and warm like the summer moon, and then the laugh—"Ha! Ha! That's funny! You don't see it, eh? He! He! Ho! Ho! Ho! He doesn't see it! Why, look here. You know a puddle—"

But I turned on my heel and left him. That was the last. I could stand it no longer. The thing must end right there, I thought, curse him. The earth should be quit of him. And as I went over the hill, I could hear his monstrous laugh reverberating against the sky.

Now, I pride myself on doing things neatly, and when I resolved to kill John Claverhouse I had it in my mind to do so in such a fashion that I should not look back upon it and feel ashamed. I hate bungling, and I hate brutality. To me there is something repugnant in merely striking a man with one's naked fist—faugh! It is sickening! So, to shoot, or stab, or club John Claverhouse (oh, that name!) did not appeal to me. And not only was I impelled to do it neatly and artistically, but also in such manner that not the slightest possible suspicion could be directed against me.

To this end I bent my intellect, and after a week of profound incubation, I hatched the scheme. Then I set to work. I bought a water-spaniel bitch, five months old, and devoted my whole attention to her training. Had anyone spied upon me, they would have remarked that this training consisted entirely of one thing—retrieving. I taught the dog, which I called Bellona, to fetch sticks I threw into the water, and not only to fetch, but to fetch at once, without mouthing or playing with them. The point was that she was to stop for nothing, but to deliver the stick in all haste. I made a practice of running away and leaving her to chase me, with the stick in her mouth, till she caught me. She was a bright animal and took to the game with such eagerness that I was soon content.

After that, at the first casual opportunity, I presented Bellona to John Claverhouse. I knew what I was about, for I was aware of a little weakness of his and of a little private sinning of which he was regularly and inveterately guilty.

"No," he said when I placed the end of the rope in his hand. "No, you don't mean it." And his mouth opened wide and he grinned all over his damnable moon-face.

"I — I kind of thought, somehow, you didn't like me," he explained. "Wasn't it funny for me to make such a mistake?" And at the thought he held his sides with laughter.

"What is her name?" he managed to ask between paroxysms.

"Bellona," I said.

"He! He!" he tittered. "What a funny name!"

I gritted my teeth, for his mirth put them on edge, and snapped out between them, "She was the wife of Mars, you know."

Then the light of the full moon began to suffuse his face, until he exploded with, "That was my other dog. Well, I guess she's a widow now. Oh! Ho! Ho! E! He! He! Ho!" he whooped after me, and I turned and fled swiftly over the hill.

The week passed by, and on Saturday evening I said to him, "You go away Monday, don't you?"

He nodded his head and grinned.

"Then you won't have another chance to get a mess of those trout you just dote on."

But he did not notice the sneer. "Oh, I don't know," he chuckled. "I'm going up tomorrow to try pretty hard."

Thus was assurance made doubly sure, and I went back to my house hugging myself with rapture.

Early next morning I saw him go by with a dipnet and gunnysack, and Bellona trotting at his heels. I knew where he was bound and cut out by the back pasture and climbed through the underbrush to the top of the mountain. Keeping carefully out of sight, I followed the crest along for a couple of miles to a natural amphitheater in the hills, where the little river raced down out of a gorge and stopped for breath in a large and placid rockbound pool. That was the spot! I sat down on the croup of the mountain, where I could see all that occurred, and lighted my pipe.

Ere many minutes had passed John Claverhouse came plodding up the bed of the stream. Bellona was ambling about him, and they were in high feather, her short snappy barks mingling with his deeper chest notes. Arrived at this pool, he threw down the dipnet and sack and drew from his hip pocket what looked like a large fat candle. But I knew it to be a stick of "giant," for such was his method of catching trout. He dynamited them. He attached the fuse by wrapping the "giant" tightly in a piece of cotton. Then he ignited the fuse and tossed the explosive into the pool.

Like a flash, Bellona was into the pool after it. I could have shrieked aloud for joy. Claverhouse yelled at her, but without avail. He pelted her with clods of rocks, but she swam steadily on till she got the stick of "giant" in her mouth, when she whirled about and headed for shore. Then, for the first time, he realized his danger and started to run. As foreseen and planned by me, she made the bank and took out after him. Oh, I tell you, it was great! As I have said, the pool lay in a sort of amphitheater. Above and below, the stream could be crossed on steppingstones. And around and around, up and down and across the stones, raced Claverhouse and Bellona. I could never have believed that such an ungainly man could run so fast. But run he did, Bellona hotfooted after him, and gaining. And then, just as she caught up, he in full stride and she leaping with nose at his knee, there was a sudden flash, a burst of smoke, a terrific detonation, and where man and dog had been the instant before there was naught to be seen but a big hole in the ground.

"Death from accident while engaged in illegal fishing." That was the verdict of the coroner's jury, and that is why I pride myself on the neat and artistic way in which I finished off John Claverhouse. There was no bungling, no brutality, nothing of which to be ashamed in the whole transaction, as I am sure you will agree. No more does his infernal laugh go echoing among the hills, and no more does his fat moon-face rise up to vex me. My days are peaceful now, and my night's sleep deep.

It seemed a foolproof plan...

The Ransom of Red Chief *by O. Henry (abridged)*

It looked like a good thing: but wait till I tell you. We were down South, in Alabama — Bill Driscoll and myself— when this kidnapping idea struck us. It was, as Bill afterward expressed it, "during a moment of temporary mental insanity"; but we didn't find that out till later.

There was a town down there, as flat as a pancake, and called Summit, of course. It contained inhabitants as harmless and content as you could imagine.

Bill and me had about six hundred dollars, and we needed just two thousand dollars more to pull off a money-raising scheme in Illinois with. We talked it over on the front steps of the hotel. The love of family, says we, is strong in rural communities; therefore and for other reasons, a kidnapping project ought to do better here than in areas where newspapers send reporters out in to stir up talk about such things. We knew that Summit couldn't get after us with anything stronger than constables and maybe some lackadaisical bloodhounds. So, it looked good.

We selected for our victim the only child of a prominent citizen named Ebenezer Dorset. The father was respectable, and the kid was a boy of ten, with freckles and red hair. Bill and me figured that Ebenezer would melt down for a ransom of two thousand dollars to a cent. But wait till I tell you.

About two miles from Summit was a little mountain, covered with dense cedar trees. On the rear elevation of this mountain was a cave. There we stored provisions. One evening after sundown, we drove in a buggy past old Dorset's house. The kid was in the street, throwing rocks at a kitten on the opposite fence.

"Hey, little boy!" says Bill, "would you like to have a bag of candy and a nice ride?"

The boy catches Bill neatly in the eye with a piece of brick.

"That will cost the old man an extra five hundred dollars," says Bill, climbing over the wheel.

That boy put up a fight like a bear; but, at last, we got him down in the bottom of the buggy and drove away. We took him up to the cave and I hitched the horse in the woods. After dark I drove the buggy to the little village, three miles away, where we had hired it, and walked back to the mountain.

Bill was repairing the scratches and bruises on his face. At the entrance of the cave, the boy was standing with two buzzard tailfeathers stuck in his red hair. He points a stick at me when I come up, and says:

"Ha! cursed paleface, do you dare to enter the camp of Red Chief, the terror of the plains?"

"He's all right now," says Bill, rolling up his trousers and examining some bruises on his shins. "We're playing Indian. I'm Old Hank, the Trapper, Red Chief's captive, and I'm to be scalped at daybreak. By Geronimo! that kid can kick hard."

Yes, sir, that boy seemed to be having the time of his life. The fun of camping out in a cave had made him forget that he was a captive, himself. He immediately named me Snake-eye, the Spy, and announced that, when his braves returned from the warpath, I was to be broiled at the stake at the rising of the sun.

Then we had supper; and he filled his mouth full of bacon and bread and gravy, and began to talk. He made a during-dinner speech something like this:

"I like this fine. I never camped out before; but I had a pet 'possum once, and I was nine last birthday. I hate to go to school. Rats ate up sixteen of Jimmy Talbot's aunt's speckled hen's eggs. Are there any real Indians in these woods? I want some more gravy. Does the trees moving make the wind blow? We had five puppies. What makes your nose so red, Hank? My father has lots of money. Are the stars hot? I whipped Ed Walker twice, Saturday. I don't like girls. You can't catch toads unless with a string. Do oxen make any noise? Why are oranges round? Have you got beds to sleep on in this cave? Amos Murray has got six toes. A parrot can talk, but a monkey or a fish can't. How many does it take to make twelve?"

Every few minutes he would remember that he was a pesky redskin, and pick up his stick rifle and tiptoe to the mouth of the cave to spot the scouts of the hated paleface. Now and then he would let out a war-whoop that made Old Hank the Trapper shiver. That boy had Bill terrorized from the start.

"Red Chief," says I to the kid, "would you like to go home?"

"Aw, what for?" says he. "I don't have any fun at home. I hate to go to school. I like to camp out. You won't take me back home again, Snake-eye, will you?"

"Not right away," says I. "We'll stay here in the cave a while."

"All right!" says he. "That'll be fine. I never had such fun in all my life."

We went to bed about eleven o'clock. We spread down some wide blankets and quilts and put Red Chief between us. We weren't afraid he'd run away. He kept us awake for three hours, jumping up and reaching for his rifle and screeching: "Hist! pard," in mine and Bill's ears, as the fancied crackle of a twig or the rustle of a leaf revealed to his young imagination the stealthy approach of the outlaw band. At last, I fell into a troubled sleep, and dreamed that I had been kidnapped and chained to a tree by a ferocious pirate with red hair.

Just at daybreak, I was awakened by a series of awful screams from Bill. They weren't yells, or howls, or shouts, or whoops, or yalps, such as you'd expect from a manly set of vocal organs — they were simply indecent, terrifying, humiliating screams, such as women emit when they see ghosts or caterpillars. It's an awful thing to hear a strong, desperate, fat man scream out of control in a cave at daybreak.

I jumped up to see what the matter was. Red Chief was sitting on Bill's chest, with one hand looped in Bill's hair. In the other he had the sharp case-knife we used for slicing bacon; and he was industriously and realistically trying to take Bill's scalp, according to the sentence that had been pronounced upon him the evening before.

I got the knife away from the kid and made him lie down again. But, from that moment, Bill's spirit was broken. He laid down on his side of the bed, but he never closed an eye again in sleep as long as that boy was with us. I dozed off for a while, but along toward sun-up I remembered that Red Chief had said I was to be burned at the stake at the rising of the sun. I wasn't nervous or afraid; but I sat up and lit my pipe and leaned against a rock.

"What you getting up so soon for, Sam?" asked Bill.

"Me?" says I. "Oh, I got a kind of a pain in my shoulder. I thought sitting up would rest it."

"You're a liar!" says Bill. "You're afraid. You was to be burned at sunrise, and you was afraid he'd do it. And he would, too, if he could find a match. Ain't it awful, Sam? Do you think anybody will pay out money to get a little imp like that back home?"

"Sure," said I. "A rowdy kid like that is just the kind that parents dote on. Now, you and the Chief get up and cook breakfast, while I go up on the top of this mountain and investigate."

I went up on the peak of the little mountain and ran my eye over the vicinity. Over toward Summit I expected to see the sturdy citizens of the village armed with scythes and pitchforks beating the countryside for the dastardly kidnappers. But what I saw was a peaceful landscape dotted with one man plowing with a mule. Nobody was dragging the creek; nobody dashed hither and yon, bringing tidings of no news to the distracted parents. There was a peaceful attitude of sleepiness pervading the village.

"Perhaps," says I to myself, "it has not yet been discovered that the wolves have taken away the tender lamb from the fold. Heaven help the wolves!" says I, and I went down the mountain to breakfast.

When I got to the cave I found Bill backed up against the side of it, breathing hard, and the boy threatening to smash him with a rock half as big as a cocoanut.

"He put a red-hot boiled potato down my back," explained Bill, "and then mashed it with his foot; and I boxed his ears. Have you got a gun about you, Sam?

I took the rock away from the boy and kind of patched up the argument. "I'll fix you," says the kid to Bill. "No man ever yet struck the Red Chief but what he got paid for it. You better beware!"

After breakfast the kid takes a piece of leather with strings wrapped around it out of his pocket and goes outside the cave unwinding it.

"What's he up to now?" says Bill, anxiously. "You don't think he'll run away, do you, Sam?"

"No fear of it," says I. "He don't seem to be much of a home body. But we've got to fix up some plan about the ransom. There don't seem to be much excitement around Summit on account of his disappearance; but maybe they haven't realized yet that he's gone. His folks may think he's spending the night with Aunt Jane or one of the neighbors. Anyhow, he'll be missed to-day. Tonight we must get a message to his father demanding the two thousand dollars for his return."

Just then we heard a kind of war-whoop, such as David might have emitted when he knocked out the champion Goliath. It was a sling that Red Chief had pulled out of his pocket, and he was whirling it around his head.

I dodged, and heard a heavy thud and a kind of a sigh from Bill, like a horse gives out when you take his saddle off. A rock the size of an egg had caught Bill just behind his left ear. He loosened himself all over and fell in the fire across the frying pan of hot water for washing the dishes. I dragged him out and poured cold water on his head for half an hour.

By and by, Bill sits up and feels behind his ear and says: "You won't go away and leave me here alone, will you, Sam?"

I went out and caught that boy and shook him until his freckles rattled.

"If you don't behave," says I, "I'll take you straight home. Now, are you going to be good, or not?"

"I was only funning," says he sullenly. "I didn't mean to hurt Old Hank. But what did he hit me for? I'll behave, Snake-eye, if you won't send me home, and if you'll let me play the Black Scout to-day."

"I don't know the game," says I. "That's for you and Mr. Bill to decide. He's your playmate for the day. I'm going away for a while, on business. Now, you come in and make friends with him and say you are sorry for hurting him, or home you go, at once."

I made him and Bill shake hands, and then I took Bill aside and told him I was going to Poplar Cove, a little village three miles from the cave, and find out what I could about how the kidnapping had been regarded in Summit. Also, I thought it best to send a no-nonsense letter to old man Dorset that day, demanding the ransom and dictating how it should be paid.

"You know, Sam," says Bill, "I've stood by you without batting an eye in earthquakes, fire and flood — in poker games, police raids, train robberies and cyclones. I never lost my nerve yet till we kidnapped that two-legged sky-rocket of a kid. He's got me going. You won't leave me long with him, will you, Sam?"

"I'll be back some time this afternoon," says I. "You must keep the boy amused and quiet till I return. And now we'll write the letter to old Dorset."

Bill and I got paper and pencil and worked on the letter while Red Chief, with a blanket wrapped around him, strutted up and down, guarding the mouth of the cave. Bill begged me tearfully to make the ransom fifteen hundred dollars instead of two thousand.

"I ain't attempting," says he, "to belittle parental affection, but we're dealing with humans, and it ain't human for anybody to give up two thousand dollars for that forty-pound chunk of freckled wildcat. I'm willing to take a chance at fifteen hundred dollars. You can charge the difference up to me."

So, to relieve Bill, I agreed, and we collaborated a letter that ran this way:

Ebenezer Dorset, Esq.:

We have your boy concealed in a place far from Summit. It is useless for you or the most skillful detectives to attempt to find him. Absolutely, the only terms on which you can have him restored to you are these: We demand fifteen hundred dollars in large bills for his return; the money to be left at midnight tonight at the same spot and in the same box as your reply — as hereinafter described. If you agree to these terms, send your answer in writing by a solitary messenger tonight at half-past eight o'clock. After crossing Owl Creek, on the road to Poplar Cove, there are three large trees about a hundred yards apart, close to the fence of the wheat field on the right-hand side. At the bottom of the fence-post, opposite the third tree, will be found a small box. The messenger will place the answer in this box and return immediately to Summit.

If you attempt any treachery or fail to comply with our demand as stated, you will never see your boy again.

If you pay the money as demanded, he will be returned to you safe and well within three hours. These terms are final, and if you do not agree to them, no further communication will be attempted.

TWO DESPERATE MEN.

I addressed this letter to Dorset, and put it in my pocket. As I was about to start, the kid comes up to me and says:

"Aw, Snake-eye, you said I could play the Black Scout while you was gone."

"Play it, of course," says I. "Mr. Bill will play with you. What kind of a game is it?"

"I'm the Black Scout," says Red Chief, "and I have to ride to the stockade to warn the settlers that the Indians are coming. I'm tired of playing Indian myself. I want to be the Black Scout."

"All right," says I. "It sounds harmless to me. I guess Mr. Bill will help you foil the pesky savages."

"What am I to do?" asks Bill, looking at the kid suspiciously.

"You are the hoss," says Black Scout. "Get down on your hands and knees. How can I ride to the stockade without a hoss?"

"You'd better keep him interested," said I, "till we get the scheme going. Loosen up."

Bill gets down on his all fours, and a look comes in his eye like a rabbit's when you catch it in a trap.

"How far is it to the stockade, kid?" he asks, in a husky manner of voice.

"Ninety miles," says the Black Scout. "And you have to hump yourself to get there on time. Whoa, now!"

The Black Scout jumps on Bill's back and digs his heels in his side.

"For Heaven's sake," says Bill, "hurry back, Sam, as soon as you can. I wish we hadn't made the ransom more than a thousand. Say, you quit kicking me or I'll get up and warm you good."

I walked over to Poplar Cove and sat around the post-office and store, talking with the men that came in to trade. One guy says that he hears Summit is all upset on account of Elder Ebenezer Dorset's boy having been lost or stolen. That was all I wanted to know. I bought some smoking tobacco, referred casually to the price of black-eyed peas, posted my letter and came away. The postmaster said the mail-carrier would come by in an hour to take the mail on to Summit.

When I got back to the cave Bill and the boy were not to be found. I explored the vicinity of the cave, and risked a yodel or two, but there was no response. So I lighted my pipe and sat down on a mossy bank to await developments.

In about half an hour I heard the bushes rustle, and Bill wabbled out into the little glade in front of the cave. Behind him was the kid, stepping softly like a scout, with a broad grin on his face. Bill stopped, took off his hat and wiped his face with a red handkerchief. The kid stopped about eight feet behind him.

"Sam," says Bill, "I suppose you'll think I'm a renegade, but I couldn't help it. The boy is gone. I have sent him home. All is off. There was martyrs in old times," goes on Bill, "that suffered death rather than give up the particular graft they enjoyed. None of 'em ever was subjugated to such supernatural tortures as I have been. I tried to be faithful to our articles of depredation; but there came a limit."

"What's the trouble, Bill?" I asks him.

"I was rode," says Bill, "the ninety miles to the stockade, not barring an inch. Then, when the settlers was rescued, I was given oats. Sand don't taste too good. And then, for an hour I had to try to explain to him why there was nothin' in holes, how a road can run both ways and what makes the grass green. I tell you, Sam, a human can only stand so much. I takes him by the neck of his clothes and drags him down the mountain. On the way he kicks my legs black-and-blue from the knees down; and I've got two or three bites on my thumb and hand.

"But he's gone," continues Bill, "gone home. I showed him the road to

Summit and kicked him about eight feet nearer there at one kick. I'm sorry we lose the ransom; but it was either that or Bill Driscoll to the madhouse."

Bill is puffing and blowing, but there is a look of ineffable peace and growing content on his rose-pink features.

"Bill," says I, "there isn't any heart disease in your family, is there?"

"No," says Bill, "nothing chronic except malaria and accidents. Why?"

"Then you might turn around," says I, "and have a look behind you."

Bill turns and sees the boy, and loses his complexion and sits down plump on the ground and begins to pluck aimlessly at grass and little sticks. For an hour I was afraid for his mind. And then I told him that my scheme was to put the whole job through immediately and that we would get the ransom and be off with it by midnight if old Dorset fell in with our proposition. So Bill braced up enough to give the kid a weak sort of a smile and a promise to play the Russian in a Japanese war with him as soon as he felt a little better.

I had a scheme for collecting that ransom without danger of being caught by counterplots. The tree under which the answer was to be left — and the money later on — was close to the road fence with big, bare fields on all sides. If a gang of constables should be watching for any one to come for the note they could see him a long way off crossing the fields or in the road. But no, sirree! At half-past eight I was up in that tree as well hidden as a tree toad, waiting for the messenger to arrive.

Exactly on time, a half-grown boy rides up the road on a bicycle, locates the box at the foot of the fence-post, slips a folded piece of paper into it and pedals away again back toward Summit.

I waited an hour and then concluded the thing was square. I slid down the tree, got the note, slipped along the fence till I struck the woods, and was back at the cave in another half an hour. I opened the note, got near the lantern and read it to Bill. It was written with a pen, and the sum and substance of it was this:

Two Desperate Men.

Gentlemen: I received your letter to-day by post, in regard to the ransom you ask for the return of my son. I think you are a little high in your demands, and I hereby make you a counter-proposition, which I am inclined to believe you will accept. You bring Johnny home and pay me two hundred and fifty dollars in cash, and I agree to take him off your hands. You had better come at night, for the neighbors believe he is lost, and I couldn't be responsible for what they would do to anybody they saw bringing him back.

Very respectfully,
EBENEZER DORSET.

"Great pirates of Penzance!" says I; "of all the impudent —"

But I glanced at Bill, and hesitated. He had the most appealing look in his eyes I ever saw on the face of a dumb or a talking brute.

"Sam," says he, "what's two hundred and fifty dollars, after all? We've got the money. One more night of this kid will send me to a bed in an asylum. Besides being a thorough gentleman, I think Mr. Dorset is a spendthrift for making us such a liberal offer. You ain't going to let the chance go, are you?"

"Tell you the truth, Bill," says I, "this little kid has somewhat got on my nerves too. We'll take him home, pay the ransom and make our getaway."

We took him home that night. We got him to go by telling him that his father had bought a silver-mounted rifle and a pair of moccasins for him, and we were going to hunt bears the next day.

It was just twelve o'clock when we knocked at Ebenezer's front door. Just at the moment when I should have been removing the fifteen hundred dollars from the box under the tree, according to the original proposition, Bill was counting out two hundred and fifty dollars into Dorset's hand.

When the kid found out we were going to leave him at home he started up a howl and fastened himself as tight as a leech to Bill's leg. His father peeled him away gradually, like a porous plaster.

"How long can you hold him?" asks Bill.

"I'm not as strong as I used to be," says old Dorset, "but I think I can promise you ten minutes."

"Enough," says Bill. "In ten minutes I shall cross the Central, Southern and Middle Western States, and be legging it for the Canadian border."

And, as dark as it was, and as fat as Bill was, and as good a runner as I am, he was a good mile and a half out of Summit before I could catch up with him.

In a kingdom by the sea, I loved a girl by the name of...

Annabel Lee *by Edgar Allan Poe*

> It was many and many a year ago,
>   In a kingdom by the sea,
> That a maiden there lived whom you may know
>   By the name of Annabel Lee;
> And this maiden she lived with no other thought
>   Than to love and be loved by me.

She was a child and *I* was a child,
   In this kingdom by the sea,
But we loved with a love that was more than love —
   I and my Annabel Lee —
With a love that the winged seraphs of heaven
   Coveted her and me.

And this was the reason that, long ago,
   In this kingdom by the sea,
A wind blew out of a cloud by night
   Chilling my Annabel Lee;
So that her highborn kinsmen came
   And bore her away from me,
To shut her up in a sepulcher
   In this kingdom by the sea.

The angels, not half so happy in heaven,
   Went envying her and me:
Yes! that was the reason (as all men know,
   In this kingdom by the sea)
That the wind came out of the cloud, chilling
   And killing my Annabel Lee.

But our love it was stronger by far than the love
   Of those who were older than we —
   Of many far wiser than we —
And neither the angels in heaven above
   Nor the demons down under the sea,
Can ever dissever my soul from the soul
   Of the beautiful Annabel Lee:

For the moon never beams without bringing me dreams
   Of the beautiful Annabel Lee;
And the stars never rise but I see the bright eyes
   Of the beautiful Annabel Lee;
And so, all the nighttide, I lie down by the side
Of my darling, my darling, my life and my bride,
   In her sepulcher there by the sea —
   In her tomb by the side of the sea.

Will the skipper's fair daughter survive...

The Wreck of the Hesperus
by Henry Wadsworth Longfellow

It was the schooner Hesperus,
    That sailed the wintry sea;
And the skipper had taken his little daughtèr,
    To bear him company.

Blue were her eyes as the fairy-flax,
    Her cheeks like the dawn of day,
And her bosom white as the hawthorn buds,
    That ope in the month of May.

The skipper he stood beside the helm,
    His pipe was in his mouth,
And he watched how the veering flaw did blow
    The smoke now West, now South.

Then up and spake an old Sailòr,
    Had sailed to the Spanish Main,
"I pray thee, put into yonder port,
    For I fear a hurricane."

"Last night, the moon had a golden ring,
    And to-night no moon we see!"
The skipper, he blew a whiff from his pipe,
    And a scornful laugh laughed he.

Colder and louder blew the wind,
    A gale from the Northeast,
The snow fell hissing in the brine,
    And the billows frothed like yeast.

Down came the storm, and smote amain
    The vessel in its strength;
She shuddered and paused, like a frighted steed,
    Then leaped her cable's length.

"Come hither! come hither! my little daughtèr,
  And do not tremble so;
For I can weather the roughest gale
  That ever wind did blow."

He wrapped her warm in his seaman's coat
  Against the stinging blast;
He cut a rope from a broken spar,
  And bound her to the mast.

"O father! I hear the church-bells ring,
  Oh say, what may it be?"
"'Tis a fog-bell on a rock-bound coast!"—
  And he steered for the open sea.

"O father! I hear the sound of guns,
  Oh say, what may it be?"
"Some ship in distress, that cannot live
  In such an angry sea!"

"O father! I see a gleaming light,
  Oh say, what may it be?"
But the father answered never a word,
  A frozen corpse was he.

Lashed to the helm, all stiff and stark,
  With his face turned to the skies,
The lantern gleamed through the gleaming snow
  On his fixed and glassy eyes.

Then the maiden clasped her hands and prayed
  That savèd she might be;
And she thought of Christ, who stilled the wave,
  On the Lake of Galilee.

And fast through the midnight dark and drear,
  Through the whistling sleet and snow,
Like a sheeted ghost, the vessel swept
  Tow'rds the reef of Norman's Woe.

And ever the fitful gusts between
   A sound came from the land;
It was the sound of the trampling surf
   On the rocks and the hard sea-sand.

The breakers were right beneath her bows,
   She drifted a dreary wreck,
And a whooping billow swept the crew
   Like icicles from her deck.

She struck where the white and fleecy waves
   Looked soft as carded wool,
But the cruel rocks, they gored her side
   Like the horns of an angry bull.

Her rattling shrouds, all sheathed in ice,
   With the masts went by the board;
Like a vessel of glass, she stove and sank,
   Ho! ho! the breakers roared!

At daybreak, on the bleak sea-beach,
   A fisherman stood aghast,
To see the form of a maiden fair,
   Lashed close to a drifting mast.

The salt sea was frozen on her breast,
   The salt tears in her eyes;
And he saw her hair, like the brown seaweed,
   On the billows fall and rise.

Such was the wreck of the Hesperus,
   In the midnight and the snow!
Christ save us all from a death like this,
   On the reef of Norman's Woe!

All seems nearly lost, until it's...

Casey at the Bat *by Ernest Lawrence Thayer*

It looked extremely rocky for the Mudville nine that day;
The score stood two to four, with but one inning left to play.

So, when Cooney died at second, and Burrows did the same,
A pallor wreathed the features of the patrons of the game.

A straggling few got up to go, leaving there the rest,
With that hope which springs eternal within the human breast.
For they thought: "If only Casey could get a whack at that,"
They'd put even money now, with Casey at the bat.

But Flynn preceded Casey, and likewise so did Blake,
And the former was a pudd'n, and the latter was a fake.
So on that stricken multitude a deathlike silence sat;
For there seemed but little chance of Casey's getting to the bat.

But Flynn let drive a single, to the wonderment of all.
And the much-despised Blakey "tore the cover off the ball."
And when the dust had lifted, and they saw what had occurred,
There was Blakey safe at second, and Flynn a-huggin' third.

Then from the gladdened multitude went up a joyous yell —
It rumbled in the mountaintops, it rattled in the dell;
It struck upon the hillside and rebounded on the flat;
For Casey, mighty Casey, was advancing to the bat.

There was ease in Casey's manner as he stepped into his place,
There was pride in Casey's bearing and a smile on Casey's face;
And when responding to the cheers he lightly doffed his hat,
No stranger in the crowd could doubt 'twas Casey at the bat.

Ten thousand eyes were on him as he rubbed his hands with dirt,
Five thousand tongues applauded when he wiped them on his shirt;
Then when the writhing pitcher ground the ball into his hip,
Defiance glanced in Casey's eye, a sneer curled Casey's lip.

And now the leather-covered sphere came hurtling through the air,
And Casey stood a-watching it in haughty grandeur there.
Close by the sturdy batsman the ball unheeded sped;
"That ain't my style," said Casey. "Strike one," the umpire said.

From the benches, black with people, there went up a muffled roar,
Like the beating of the storm waves on the stern and distant shore.
"Kill him! Kill the umpire!" shouted someone in the stand;
And it's likely they'd have killed him had not Casey raised his hand.

With a smile of Christian charity great Casey's visage shone;
He stilled the rising tumult, he made the game go on;
He signaled to the pitcher, and once more the spheroid flew;
But Casey still ignored it, and the umpire said, "Strike two."

"Fraud!" cried the maddened thousands, and the echo answered "Fraud!"
But one scornful look from Casey and the audience was awed;
They saw his face grow stern and cold, they saw his muscles strain,
And they knew that Casey wouldn't let the ball go by again.

The sneer is gone from Casey's lips, his teeth are clenched in hate,
He pounds with cruel vengeance his bat upon the plate;
And now the pitcher holds the ball, and now he lets it go,
And now the air is shattered by the force of Casey's blow.

Oh, somewhere in this favored land the sun is shining bright,
The band is playing somewhere, and somewhere hearts are light;
And somewhere men are laughing, and somewhere children shout,
But there is no joy in Mudville — mighty Casey has struck out.

There's a moral here: consider all the facts or you'll be like...

The Blind Men and the Elephant
by John Godfrey Saxe

It was six men of Indostan
　　To learning much inclined,
Who went to see the Elephant
　　(Though all of them were blind),
That each by observations
　　Might satisfy his mind.

The *First* approached the Elephant,
　　And happening to fall
Against his broad and sturdy side,
　　At once began to bawl:
"God bless me! but the Elephant
　　Is very like a wall!"

The *Second*, feeling of the tusk,
   Cried, "Ho! what have we here
So very round and smooth and sharp?
   To me 'tis mighty clear
This wonder of an Elephant
   Is very like a spear!"

The *Third* approached the animal,
   And happening to take
The squirming trunk within his hands,
   Thus boldly up and spake:
"I see," quoth he, "the Elephant
   Is very like a snake!"

The *Fourth* reached out an eager hand,
   And felt about the knee.
"What most this wondrous beast is like
   Is mighty plain," quoth he;
"'Tis clear enough the Elephant
   Is very like a tree!"

The *Fifth* who chanced to touch the ear,
   Said: "E'en the blindest man
Can tell what this resembles most;
   Deny the fact who can,
This marvel of an Elephant
   Is very like a fan!"

The *Sixth* no sooner had begun
   About the beast to grope,
Than, seizing on the swinging tail
   That fell within his scope,
"I see," quoth he, "the Elephant
   Is very like a rope!"

And so these men of Indostan
   Disputed loud and long,
Each in his own opinion
   Exceeding stiff and strong,
Though each was partly in the right,
   And all were in the wrong!

Moral

So oft in theologic wars,
    The disputants, I ween,
Rail on in utter ignorance
    Of what each other mean,
And prate about an Elephant
    Not one of them has seen!

Listen carefully to the tale of...

Little Orphant Annie *by James Whitcomb Riley*

Little Orphant Annie's come to our house to stay,
An' wash the cups an' saucers up, an' brush the crumbs away,
An' shoo the chickens off the porch, an' dust the hearth, an' sweep,
An' make the fire, an' bake the bread, an' earn her board-an'-keep;
An' all us other childern, when the supper things is done,
We set around the kitchen fire an' has the mostest fun
A-list'nin' to the witch-tales 'at Annie tells about,
An' the Gobble-uns 'at gits you
            Ef you
                Don't
                    Watch
                        Out!

Onc't they was a little boy wouldn't say his prayers, —
So when he went to bed at night, away up stairs,
His Mammy heerd him holler, an' his Daddy heerd him bawl,
An' when they turn't the kivvers down, he wasn't there at all!
An' they seeked him in the rafter-room, an' cubby-hole, an' press,
An' seeked him up the chimbly-flue, an' ever'wheres, I guess;
But all they ever found was thist his pants an' roundabout —
An' the Gobble-uns'll git you
            Ef you
                Don't
                    Watch
                        Out!

An' one time a little girl 'ud allus laugh an' grin,
An' make fun of ever'one, an' all her blood an' kin;

An' onc't, when they was "company," an' ole folks was there,
She mocked 'em an' shocked 'em, an' said she didn't care!
An' thist as she kicked her heels, an' turn't to run an' hide,
They was two great big Black Things a-standin' by her side,
An' they snatched her through the ceilin' 'fore she knowed what she's about!
An' the Gobble-uns'll git you
        Ef you
          Don't
            Watch
              Out!

An' little Orphant Annie says when the blaze is blue,
An' the lamp-wick sputters, an' the wind goes *woo-oo!*
An' you hear the crickets quit, an' the moon is gray,
An' the lightnin'-bugs in dew is all squenched away,—
You better mind yer parents, an' yer teachers fond an' dear,
An' churish them 'at loves you, an' dry the orphant's tear,
An' he'p the pore an' needy ones 'at clusters all about,
Er the Gobble-uns'll git you
        Ef you
          Don't
            Watch
              Out!

There are strange things done in the midnight sun...

The Cremation of Sam McGee *by Robert W. Service*

There are strange things done in the midnight sun
  By the men who moil for gold;
The Arctic trails have their secret tales
  That would make your blood run cold;
The Northern Lights have seen queer sights,
  But the queerest they ever did see
Was that night on the marge of Lake Lebarge
  I cremated Sam McGee.

Now Sam McGee was from Tennessee, where the cotton blooms and blows.
Why he left his home in the South to roam 'round the Pole, God only knows.
He was always cold, but the land of gold seemed to hold him like a spell;
Though he'd often say in his homely way that "he'd sooner live in hell."

On a Christmas Day we were mushing our way over the Dawson trail.
Talk of your cold! through the parka's fold it stabbed like a driven nail.
If our eyes we'd close, then the lashes froze till sometimes we couldn't see;
It wasn't much fun, but the only one to whimper was Sam McGee.

And that very night, as we lay packed tight in our robes beneath the snow,
And the dogs were fed, and the stars o'erhead were dancing heel and toe,
He turned to me, and "Cap," says he, "I'll cash in this trip, I guess;
And if I do, I'm asking that you won't refuse my last request."

Well, he seemed so low that I couldn't say no; then he says with a sort of
    moan:
"It's the cursed cold, and it's got right hold till I'm chilled clean through to
    the bone.
Yet 'taint being dead — it's my awful dread of the icy grave that pains;
So I want you to swear that, foul or fair, you'll cremate my last remains."

A pal's last need is a thing to heed, so I swore I would not fail;
And we started on at the streak of dawn; but God! he looked ghastly pale.
He crouched on the sleigh, and he raved all day of his home in Tennessee;
And before nightfall a corpse was all that was left of Sam McGee.

There wasn't a breath in that land of death, and I hurried, horror-driven,
With a corpse half hid that I couldn't get rid, because of a promise given;
It was lashed to the sleigh, and it seemed to say: "You may tax your brawn
    and brains,
But you promised true, and it's up to you to cremate those last remains."

Now a promise made is a debt unpaid, and the trail has its own stern code.
In the days to come, though my lips were dumb, in my heart how I cursed
    that load.
In the long, long night, by the lone firelight, while the huskies, round in a
    ring,
Howled out their woes to the homeless snows — O God! how I loathed the
    thing.

And every day that quiet clay seemed to heavy and heavier grow;
And on I went, though the dogs were spent and the grub was getting low;
The trail was bad, and I felt half mad, but I swore I would not give in;
And I'd often sing to the hateful thing, and it hearkened with a grin.

Till I came to the marge of Lake Lebarge, and a derelict there lay;
It was jammed in the ice, but I saw in a trice it was called the "Alice May."
And I looked at it, and I thought a bit, and I looked at my frozen chum;
Then "Here," said I, with a sudden cry, "is my cre-ma-tor-eum."

Some planks I tore from the cabin floor, and I lit the boiler fire;
Some coal I found that was lying around, and I heaped the fuel higher;
The flames just soared, and the furnace roared — such a blaze you seldom see;
And I burrowed a hole in the glowing coal, and I stuffed in Sam McGee.

Then I made a hike, for I didn't like to hear him sizzle so;
And the heavens scowled, and the huskies howled, and the wind began to
   blow.
It was icy cold, but the hot sweat rolled down my cheeks, and I don't know
   why;
And the greasy smoke in an inky cloak went streaking down the sky.

I do not know how long in the snow I wrestled with grisly fear;
But the stars came out and they danced about ere again I ventured near;
I was sick with dread, but I bravely said: "I'll just take a peep inside.
I guess he's cooked, and it's time I looked;" ... then the door I opened wide.

And there sat Sam, looking cool and calm, in the heart of the furnace roar;
And he wore a smile you could see a mile, and he said: "Please close that door.
It's fine in here, but I greatly fear you'll let in the cold and storm —
Since I left Plumtree, down in Tennessee, it's the first time I've been warm."

There are strange things done in the midnight sun
   By the men who moil for gold;
The Arctic trails have their secret tales
   That would make your blood run cold;
The Northern Lights have seen queer sights,
   But the queerest they ever did see
Was that night on the marge of Lake Lebarge
   I cremated Sam McGee.

MORE SUGGESTED READINGS FOR CAMPFIRES, RAINY DAYS, BEDTIME, AND OTHER OCCASIONS

Short Stories

Collier, John. "Thus I Refute Beelzy"
Harris, Joel Chandler. "The Wonderful Tar-Baby Story"
Jacobs, W. W. "The Monkey's Paw"
Maupassant, Guy de. "The Necklace" and "The Piece of String"
McManus, Patrick. "The Mountain Man" and "Rancid Crabtree"
O. Henry. "The Gift of the Magi"
Stockton, Frank R. "The Lady or the Tiger"
Twain, Mark. "The Celebrated Jumping Frog of Calaveras County"
Wilde, Oscar. "The Devoted Friend"
Williams, Margery. *The Velveteen Rabbit*

Short Story Collections

Most books on this list are available in paperback editions.

Andersen, Hans Christian. *Fairy Tales.*

Asher, Sandy. *But That's Another Story.* New York: Walker Books for Young Readers, 1999.

Bennett, William J. *The Book of Virtues.* New York: Simon & Schuster, 1993.

Bradbury, Ray. *The Illustrated Man.* New York: Bantam, 1951.

_____. *The Machineries of Joy.* New York: Bantam, 1964.

_____. *The Martian Chronicles.* New York: Bantam, 1950.

Canfield, Jack, et al., ed. *Chicken Soup for the Preteen Soul: 101 Stories of Changes, Choices, and Growing Up for Kids Ages 9–13.* Deerfield Beach, FL: HCI Teens, 2000.

_____, et al., ed. *Chicken Soup for the Teenage Soul on Love and Friendship.* Deerfield Beach, FL: HCI Teens, 2002.

_____, et al., ed. *Chicken Soup for the Teenage Soul: 101 Stories of Life, Love, and Learning.* Deerfield Beach, FL: Health Communications, Inc., 1997.

_____, et al., ed. *Chicken Soup for the Teenage Soul III: More Stories of Life, Love, and Learning.* Deerfield Beach, FL: HCI Teens, 2004.

_____, et al., ed. *Chicken Soup for the Teenage Soul IV: More Stories of Life, Love, and Learning.* Deerfield Beach, FL: HCI Teens, 2004

Christensen, Jo-Anne. *Campfire Ghost Stories.* Auburn, WA: Lone Pine Publishing, 2002.

Crutcher, Chris. *Athletic Shorts: Six Short Stories.* New York: Greenwillow Books, 1989.

Dahl, Roald, ed. *Roald Dahl's Book of Ghost Stories.* New York: Noonday Press, 1983.

Forgey, William W. *Campfire Stories: More Things That Go Bump in the Night.* Old Saybrook, CT: The Globe Pequot Press, 1998.

_____. *Campfire Stories: Things That Go Bump in the Night.* Old Saybrook, CT: The Globe Pequot Press, 1985.

Gallo, Donald R., ed. *Join In: Multiethnic Short Stories by Outstanding Writers for Young Adults.* New York: Bantam Doubleday Dell, 1993.

_____. *Sixteen: Short Stories by Outstanding Writers for Young Adults.* New York: Bantam Doubleday Dell, 1984.

_____. *Visions: Nineteen Short Stories by Outstanding Writers for Young Adults.* New York: Bantam Doubleday Dell, 1987.

_____, ed. *Ultimate Sports: Short Stories by Outstanding Writers for Young Adults.* New York: Bantam Doubleday Dell, 1995.

Herriot, James. *All Creatures Great and Small.* New York: Bantam Books, 1972.

Kipling, Rudyard. *Just So Stories.* New York: Signet Classic, 2002.

Leeming, David, and Jake Page. *Myths, Legends, and Folktales of America: An Anthology.* New York: Oxford University Press, 1999.

MacDonald, Margaret Read. *Twenty Tellable Tales: Audience Participation Folktales for the Beginning Storyteller.* Chicago: American Library Association, 2005.

McManus, Patrick F. *A Fine and Pleasant Misery.* New York: Holt, Rinehart & Winston, 1978.

Schwartz, Alvin. *More Scary Stories to Tell in the Dark.* New York: Harper Trophy, 1984.

_____. *Scary Stories to Tell in the Dark.* New York: Harper Trophy, 1981.

_____. *Scary Stories III.* New York: Harper Trophy, 1991.

Stone, Tom B. *Scream Around the Campfire.* New York: Bantam Doubleday Dell, 1998.

The Usborne Book of Puzzle Adventures. Tulsa, OK: EDC Publishing, 1988.

Wang, Ping. *American Visa: Short Stories.* Minneapolis: Coffee House Press, 1994.

Wilde, Oscar. *Complete Fairy Tales of Oscar Wilde.* New York: Penguin Books, 1990.

Young, Richard, and Judy Dockney Young. *The Scary Story Reader.* Little Rock, AR: August House, 1993.

Story-Poems

Due to their compelling rhythm and intriguing narrative, story-poems are especially fitting for reading aloud.

Bennett, Rowena. "The Witch of Willowby Wood"
Carroll, Lewis. "The Walrus and the Carpenter"
Field, Eugene. "The Duel"

Fields, James T. "The Tempest"
Foss, Sam Walter. "The House by the Side of the Road"
Johnson, James Weldon. "The Creation"
Longfellow, Henry Wadsworth. "Paul Revere's Ride"
Service, Robert W. "The Spell of the Yukon"

Lyrical Poems

Many young people find beauty and meaning in the eloquence of lyrical poetry. Shel Silverstein's *Where the Sidewalk Ends* appeals to all ages, though it is usually considered a children's book. Kahlil Gibran's *The Prophet* expresses universal truths, and selections like "Of Friendship" and "Of Love" can be especially effective with groups that have grown together. Poems on love, such as those by Amy Lowell, Edna St. Vincent Millay, and Pablo Neruda, have special appeal to many girls at this age. Like music, poetry can express what seems inexpressible and, because of rhythm, length, and power, can be ideal for reading aloud.

BOOKS ON STORYTELLING

de Vos, Gail. *Storytelling for Young Adults: A Guide to Tales for Teens.* 2d ed. Westport, CT: Libraries Unlimited, 2003.

_____, et al. *Telling Tales: Storytelling in the Family.* Edmonton: The University of Alberta Press, 2003.

MacDonald, Margaret Read. *The Parents Guide to Storytelling: How to Make Up New Stories and Retell Old Favorites.* New York: HarperCollins Children's Books, 1995.

Chapter 8

Songs

Nothing draws people together like music; nothing is quite so pleasing to the human spirit than voices lifted together in song. Whether around a campfire or on a hike, at work or at conference, at mealtime or at vespers, music can unite and uplift. The power of music to transform people cannot be overestimated.

Get people singing together and you have harmony of spirit, if not also of sound. Guitar, piano, flute, recorder, and other instrumental accompaniment often help to enrich the sound, but they are by no means necessary. The only instruments required are those which singers take with them wherever they go: their voices and their hearts.

When songs are part of a program, such as a campfire or service, consider the following suggestions:

1. Begin with songs which everyone knows or which are easy to learn.
2. Vary your program. Include lively and upbeat songs along with quiet and peaceful ones. End evening programs with the latter type.
3. Have fun with the music: harmonize; act; invent lyrics.
4. Your kids will come with their personal favorites. Encourage them to lead songs. Each generation cherishes its own music.
5. Know when to stop.

Many of the following songs are traditional folk songs that have lasted for decades and will retain their power for generations to come.

MUSIC AND LYRICS

If You're Happy

If you're   hap-py and you know it, clap your

hands. (clap, clap) If you're hap-py and you know it, clap your

hands. (clap, clap) If you're hap-py and you know it, Then your

life will sure-ly show it. If you're hap-py and you know it, clap your

hands.   (clap,   clap)

Hokey-Pokey

Singers stand in a circle and act out the words, putting their right foot in towards the center of the circle, putting it outside the circle, and so forth, as the lyrics indicate.

You put your right foot in, You take your

right foot out, You put your right foot in and you

shake it all a-bout. Then you do the-ho-key po-key, And you

turn your-self a-bout. And that's what it's all a - bout.

2. Left foot
3. Right hand
4. Left hand
5. Right shoulder
6. Left shoulder
7. Right hip
8. Left hip
9. Whole self

My Bonnie

Scottish Song

back, bring back, Bring back my

Bon-nie to me, to me. Bring

back, bring back, Oh bring back my

Bon - nie to me.____

2. Last night as I lay on my pillow,
Last night as I lay on my bed,
Last night as I lay on my pillow,
I dreamt that my Bonnie was dead.

3. The heather is blooming around me,
The blossoms of Spring now appear,
The meadows with green-ry surround me,
Oh Bonnie I wish you were here.

4. O blow, ye winds, over the ocean,
O blow, ye winds, over the sea,
O blow, ye winds, over the ocean,
And bring back my Bonnie to me.

First variation: when you reach a word that begins with the letter B, you stand up;
for the next B, you sit down, etc., throughout the entire song. Try it as fast as you can.

Second variation: as an action song, try these movements when singing each of the
following words:
bonnie - hug yourself
lies - tilt head to rest on hands, palms together, which rest on shoulder
over - draw an arc in the air
ocean/sea - draw waves in the air
bring back - motion to "come back"
O - make O with hands
to - raise two fingers

John Brown's Baby

Civil War Song

John   Brown's   ba -   by   had   a

cold   u - pon   its chest.   John Brown's ba - by had   a

cold   u - pon   its chest.   John Brown's ba - by had   a

cold u - pon its chest. So they   rubbed it with cam - phor - a - ted

Refrain

oil.   Glo -   ry,   glo - ry, hal - le - lu   -   jah,

Glo - ry, glo - ry, hal - le - lu - jah,

Glo - ry, glo - ry, hal - le - lu - jah, They

rubbed it with cam - phor - a - ted oil.

This action song is something like BINGO; each time the stanza is sung, an action or sound is substituted for a word until the final time through, most of the song is acted out. The first time, the stanza is sung through as written; the second time, replace "baby" with a cradling motion as though you're rocking a baby; the third time, replace "cold" with a cough; the fourth time, replace "chest" with a tap upon the chest; the fifth time, replace "rubbed" with a rubbing motion upon the chest; and the sixth time, replace "camphorated oil" with a sniffling sound.

Row, Row, Row Your Boat

Round

Row,   row,   row   your   boat

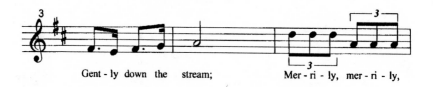

Gent - ly down the   stream;   Mer - ri - ly, mer - ri - ly,

mer-ri-ly, mer-ri-ly, Life   is but   a   dream.

For an action song, make the following motions for each line:

"Row, row, row your boat"	make motions as though rowing a boat
"Gently down the stream"	move fingers and hands to make motion resembling a rippling stream
"Merrily, merrily..."	hold both hands up and bounce back and forth to the rhythm of the music
"Life is but a dream"	hold palms together, hands next to one cheek, with eyes closed, as though asleep

Each time the song is sung, a line can be substituted with a motion, so that the final rendition of the song is performed with no sound, only actions.

Frère Jacques

French round

Frè - re　Jac - ques,　Frè - re　Jac - ques,
Are　you　sleep - ing,　Are　you　sleep - ing,

Dor - mez　vous,　　　Dor - mez　vous?
Broth - er　John,　　　Broth - er　John?

Son - nez les ma - tin - es,　Son - nez les ma - tin - es,
Morn-ing bells are ring - ing,　Morn-ing bells are ring - ing,

Din,　din,　don,　　Din,　din,　don.
Ding,　ding,　dong,　Ding,　ding,　dong.

Music Alone Shall Live

German Canon

All things shall per - ish from

un - der the sky;

Mu - sic a - lone shall live,

mu - sic a - lone shall live,

Mu - sic a - lone shall live,

nev - er to die.

Make New Friends

Make new friends but keep the old;

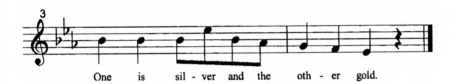

One is sil - ver and the oth - er gold.

He's Got the Whole World

Spiritual

He's got the   whole___   world___

in His   hands,   He's got the whole   wide   world___

in His   hands,   He's got the whole   world___

in His   hands,   He's got the whole   world   in   His

hands.

2. He's got the wind and rain in His hands,
He's got the sun and moon in His hands...
3. He's got the itty bitty baby...
4. He's got you and me, brother...
5. He's got everybody...
6. He's got the whole world...

Michael, Row the Boat Ashore

Spiritual

2. Sister, help to trim the sail...
3. Jordan river is chilly and cold...
4. Jordan river is deep and wide...
5. Jordan's stream is wide and deep...
6. Michael, row the boat ashore...

Who Did?

Who did, who did, who did, who did,

who did swal - low Jo, Jo, Jo, Jo?

Who did, who did, who did, who did,

who did swal - low Jo, Jo, Jo, Jo?

Who did swal - low Jo - nah,__

Who   did   swal - low   Jo   -   nah,__

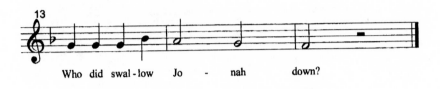

Who did swal - low   Jo   -   nah   down?

2. Whale did, whale did, whale did, whale did,
Whale did swallow Jo, Jo, Jo, Jo...
Whale did swallow Jonah down.

3. Gabriel, Gabriel, Gabriel, Gabriel.
Gabriel blow your trum, trum, trum, trum....
Gabriel blow your trumpet loud.

4. Daniel, Daniel, Daniel, Daniel,
Daniel in the li, li, li, li....
Daniel in the lions' den.

Rocka My Soul

So low, you can't get un - der it;

So wide, you can't get a - round___ it; You

must go in at the door.

Jacob's Ladder

We are   climb - ing   Ja - cob's

lad - der;   We   are   climb - ing

Ja - cob's   lad - der;   We   are

climb - ing   Ja - cob's   lad - der,

Sol - diers   of   the   cross.___

2. Every rung goes higher, higher...
3. Sinner, do you love my Jesus?...
4. If you love him, why not serve him?...
5. We are climbing higher, higher...

On Top of Old Smoky

American Song

2. Well, courtin's a pleasure and parting is grief,
But a false-hearted lover is worse than a thief.

3. A thief will but rob you and take all you save,
But a false-hearted lover will send you to your grave.

4. The grave will decay you, will turn you to dust,
Not one boy in a hundred a poor girl can trust.

5. He'll hug you and kiss you and tell you more lies
Than cross ties on the railroad or stars in the skies.

6. They'll tell you they love you to give your heart ease,
As soon as your back's turned, they'll court as they please.

Study War No More

2. Goin' to lay down my sword and shield...
3. Goin' to try on my long white robe...
4. Goin' to try on my starry crown...

Billy Boy

English Song

"Oh,___ where have you been, Bil - ly

Boy, Bil - ly Boy? Oh,___ where have you

been, charm - ing Bil - ly?"   "I have

been to seek a wife, she's the joy___ of my

life, She's a young thing and can - not leave her

moth - er!"___

2.   "Did she bid you come in, Billy Boy, Billy Boy?
Did she bid you come in, charming Billy?"
"Yes, she bid me to come in,
There's a dimple in her chin,
She's a young thing and cannot leave her mother!"

3.   "Did she set'for you a chair, Billy Boy, Billy Boy?
Did she set for you a chair, charming Billy?"
"Yes, she set for me a chair,
She has ringlets in her hair,
She's a young thing and cannot leave her mother!"

4.   "Can she bake a cherry pie, Billy Boy, Billy Boy?
Can she bake a cherry pie, charming Billy?"
"She can bake a cherry pie,
Quick as'a cat can wink her eye,
She's a young thing and cannot leave her mother!"

5.   "How old is she, Billy Boy, Billy Boy?
How old is she, charming Billy?"
"Three times six and four times sev'n,
Twenty eight and elev'n,
She's a young thing and cannot leave her mother!"

The Ash Grove

Welsh Song

1. Down yon - der green val - ley where stream - lets me - an - der, When twi - light is fa - ding I pen - sive - ly roam, 'Twas there while the black - birds were

Or at the bright noon - tide in sol - i - tude wan - der A - mid the dark shades of the lone - ly Ash Grove.

joy   of   my   heart!   A -

round   us   for   glad - ness   the

blue - bells   were   ring - ing;   Ah,

then   lit - tle   thought   I   how

soon   we   would   part.

There Is a Tavern in the Town

There
Oh

is a tav - ern in the
dig my grave both wide and

town, in the town, And there my dear love sits him
deep, wide and deep, Put tomb - stones at my head and

down, sits him down,___ And___ drinks his wine 'mid the
feet, head and feet,___ And___ on my breast carve a

laugh - ter___ free, And nev - er, nev - er thinks of
tur - tle___ dove, To sig - ni - fy I died of

Refrain

me.___
love.___

Fare thee

11
well, for I must leave thee, do not let the part - ing grieve thee, And re -

13
mem - ber that the best of friends must   part,   must   part.   A -

15
dieu,   a - dieu,   kind   friends,   a - dieu,   a - dieu,   a - dieu.   I

17
can   no   long - er   stay   with   you,   stay   with   you.___   I'll___

19
hang   my   harp   on   a   weep - ing   wil - low   tree,   And

21
may   the   world   go   well   with   thee.

Home on the Range

Cowboy Song

Oh,   give   me   a   home   where the

buf - fa - lo   roam,   Where the   deer   and the

an - te - lope play;___   Where

sel - dom   is   heard   a   dis - cour - ag - ing

word   And the skies   are not   cloud - y   all

day.___   Home,

home on   the   range,___   where the

deer   and the   an -   te - lope   play;___

Where   sel - dom   is   heard   a dis -

cour - ag - ing   word   And the   skies   are   not

cloud - y   all   day.___

Buffalo Gals

American Minstrel Song

As   I   was   lum - b'ring
I   asked her   would she
I   asked her   would she

down   the   street,   Down   the   street,
have   some talk,   Have   some talk,
have   a   dance,   Have   a   dance,

down   the   street,   A   hand - some gal   I
have   some talk;   Her feet   cover'd up   the
have   a   dance;   I   thought that   I   might

chanced to   meet,   Oh,   she was   fair   to
whole   side - walk, As   she stood close to
get   a   chance   To   shake a   foot   with

Refrain

view.   Buf - fa - lo   gals,   won't you
me.
her.

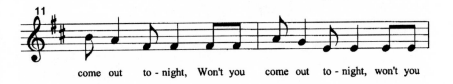

come out   to - night, Won't you   come out   to - night, won't you

come out   to - night?   Buf - fa - lo   gals,   won't you

come out to - night, And   dance by the light of the   moon?

Erie Canal

American Song

I've got a___ mule, her
We bet - ter get a - long on our

name is Sal, Fif - teen miles on the
way, old pal, Fif - teen miles on the

Er - ie Can - al.___ She's a good old work - er and a
Er - ie Can - al.___ Cause you bet your life I'd nev - er

good old pal, Fif - teen miles on the
part with Sal, Fif - teen miles on the

Er - ie Can - al.___ We've haul'd some barg - es
Er - ie Can - al.___ Git up there, mule, here comes

11

in   our   day,   Fill'd   with   lum - ber,
a   lock,   We'll   make   Rome   'bout

13

coal   and   hay,   And   we   know   ev - 'ry
six   o' - clock,___   One   more   trip   and

15

inch   of   the   way   From   Al - ba - ny___   to___
back   we'll   go   Right   back   home___   to

Refrain

17

Buf - fa - lo.___   Low   bridge!
Buf - fa - lo.___

19

ev - 'ry - bod - y   down!   Low   bridge,   for   we're

go - ing through   a   town,   And   you'll

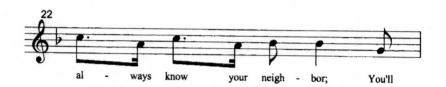

al - ways know   your   neigh - bor;   You'll

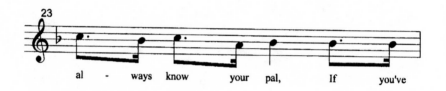

al - ways know   your   pal,   If   you've

ev - er nav - i - gat - ed   on   the

Er - ie   Can - al.

I Was Born About Ten Thousand Years Ago

(To the tune of "She'll Be Comin' Round the Mountain")

1. I was born about ten thousand years ago,
There's a lot of famous folks I used to know.
I was in the ark with Noah, I was in the whale with Jonah,
And there's no one who can prove it isn't so!

2. You can stop me if you heard this one before,
'Bout the apple too delicious to ignore,
Adam said to Eve, "We're cheating
If that apple we start eating,"
I came by and I'm the guy what et the core.

3. Old King Solomon was very wise, they claim,
With a thousand wives, he knew them all by name,
That's because I used to list 'em
With my alphabetic system,
In my little book, each time he took a dame!

4. Isabella sent Columbus with a crew,
On a little trip across the ocean blue,
But to me she said, "Hey, fella,
You stay here with Isabella,"
I'm the stowaway of fourteen ninety two.

5. I was on the shore with Washington, I swear,
When he tossed a coin across the Delaware,
But nobody has believed it
When I tell 'em I retrieved it
And I bought me boots, they cost a buck a pair.

TAG If you've any doubt, remove it,
'Cause there's no one to disprove it,
I was born about ten thousand years ago!

She'll Be Comin'
Round the Mountain

American Song

She'll be com-in' round the moun-tain when she comes, She'll be com-in' round the moun-tain when she comes, She'll be com-in' round the moun-tain, she'll be com-in' round the moun-tain, she'll be com-in' round the moun-tain when she comes.___

2. She'll be drivin' six white horses when she comes....

3. Oh, we'll all go out to meet her when she comes....

4. Oh, we'll kill the old red rooster when she comes....

A slightly more ribald version than the original:

1. She'll be coming 'round the mountain when she comes....

2. Singing, "I will if you will so will I...."

3. Oh, she has a lovely naval uniform....

4. Oh, she has a lovely bottom set of teeth....

5. Oh, she has a lovely titillating smile....

Oh! Susanna

Stephen Foster

I___   come   from   Al - a -
It___   rained   all   night   the

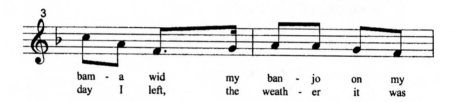

bam - a   wid   my   ban - jo   on   my
day   I   left,   the   weath - er   it   was

knee,   I'm   gwan   to   Lou - si -
dry,   The   sun   so   hot   I

an - na,   My___   true   love   for   to
froze   to   death,   Su - san - na   don't   you

Refrain

see.   Oh!   Su - san - na,   Oh!
cry.

don't you cry for   me,   I've___   come from Al - a -

bam - a wid   my ban - jo   on my   knee.

2. I had a dream the other night
When everything was still,
I thought I saw Susanna
A-coming down the hill.
The buckwheat cake was in her mouth,
The tear was in her eye,
Says I, I'm coming from the South,
Susanna, don't you cry.

Blue Tail Fly

Jimmy Crack Corn

When   I   was   young,   I   used   to   wait   on

mas-ter and hand   him   his   plate.   I   brought his bot-tle when

he   got dry and   brushed a - way   the   blue - tail   fly.

Jim - my crack   corn   and   I   don't   care,

Jim - my crack   corn   and   I   don't   care,

Jim - my crack corn and I don't care, My

mas - ter's gone a - way.___

2. He used to ride each afternoon,
I'd follow with a hick'ry broom.
The pony kicked his legs up high,
When bitten by the blue-tail fly.

3. The pony jump, he run, he pitch,
He threw my master in the ditch.
He died and the jury wondered why,
The verdict was the blue-tail fly.

4. Old master's dead and gone to rest,
They say things happen for the best.
I won't forget until I die
Old master and the blue-tail fly.

Goober Peas

Civil War Song

Sit - ting by the road - side on a sum - mer day, Chat - ting with my mess - mates, pass - ing time a - way, Ly - ing in the shad - ow un - der - neath the trees, Good - ness how de - li - cious,

eat-ing goo - ber peas!

Refrain

Peas! Peas!

Peas! Peas! Eat - ing goo - ber peas!

Good - ness how de - li-cious, eat-ing goo - ber peas!

2. When a horseman passes the soldiers have a rule,
To cry out at their loudest, "Mister here's your mule."
But another pleasure enchantinger than these,
Is wearing out your grinders, eating goober peas! REFRAIN

3. Just before the battle, the general hears a row.
He says, "The Yanks are coming, I hear their rifles now.
He turns 'round in wonder, and what d'you think he sees?
The Georgia Militia eating goober peas! REFRAIN

4. I think my song has lasted almost long enough;
The subject's interesting, but rhymes are mighty rough.
I wish this war was over, when, free from rags and fleas,
We'd kiss our wives and sweethearts and gobble goober peas. REFRAIN

Yankee Doodle

dan - dy, Mind the mu - sic

and the step, And with the girls be hand - y.

2. And there was Captain Washington
Upon a slapping stallion,
And giving orders to his men,
I guess there was a million. REFRAIN

3. And there I see a little keg,
Its heads were made of leather,
They knocked upo't with little sticks,
To call the folks together. REFRAIN

4. And there they'd fife away like fun,
And play on cornstalk fiddles,
And some had ribbons red as blood,
All bound around their middles. REFRAIN

5. The troopers too would gallop up
And fire right in our faces;
It scared me almost half to death
To see them run such races. REFRAIN

I've Been Working on the Railroad

American Song

I've been work - ing on the rail - road,

All the live - long day.

I've been work - ing on the rail - road, to

pass the time a - way.

Don't you hear the whis - tle blow - ing

Rise up ear - ly in the morn;

Some-one's in the kitch-en I know - o - o - o.

Some-one's in the kitch-en with Di - nah!

Strum-min' on the old ban - jo.

Fee Fi fidd - lee - i - o

Fee - fi - fidd - lee - i - o - o - o - o.

Fee Fi fidd - lee - i - o

Strum-min' on the old ban - jo.

Red River Valley

American Song

From this val - ley they say you are
Come and sit by my side if you

go - ing.___ We will miss your bright
love me,___ Do not hast - en to

eyes and sweet smile;___ For they
bid me a - dieu;___ But re -

say you are tak - ing the sun - shine___
mem - ber the Red Riv - er Val - ley___

That___ bright - ens our path - ways a -
And the one who has loved you so

while.___
true.___

The Midnight Special

American Song

Wake up ev - 'ry morn - ing,___

Same old at - mos - phere.

Yearn - ing for new plac - es,___

Seems I like it an - y - where but here.

Refrain

Let the Mid - night Spe - cial

shine her light on me.

Let the Mid - night Spe - cial

shine her ev - er - lov - in' light on

me.

2. Don't know where it's going,
I don't even care.
Any place it's going,
Let her take me, let her take me there.
REFRAIN

3. Don't we all get tired
Of the same routine?
Longing for some somewhere,
For a place that we have never seen.
REFRAIN

Clementine

Percy Montrose, 1883

In a cav - ern in a can - yon, Ex - ca - vat - ing for a mine, Dwelt a min - er for - ty - nin - er, And his daugh - ter, Clem - en - tine.

Refrain

Oh my dar - ling, oh my dar - ling, Oh my dar - ling Clem - en - tine! You are lost and gone for - ev - er, Dread - ful sor - ry, Clem - en - tine.

2.   Light she was and like a fairy,
And her shoes were number nine,
Herring boxes without topses,
Sandals were for Clementine.

3.   Drove she ducklings to the water,
Ev'ry morning just at nine,
Hit her foot against a splinter,
Fell into the foaming brine.

4.   Ruby lips above the water,
Blowing bubbles soft and fine,
But, alas, I was no swimmer,
So I lost my Clementine.

5.   Then the miner, forty-niner,
Soon began to peak and pine,
Thought he oughter join his daughter,
Now he's with his Clementine.

6.   In my dreams she still does haunt me,
Robed in garments soaked in brine,
Though in life I used to hug her,
Now she's dead, I draw the line.

The Cat Came Back

Harry S. Miller, 1893

There was old Farm - er John - son, he had

troub - les of his own,___ He had an old yel - low cat

that would-n't leave home; He tried ev - 'ry-thing he knew to

keep the cat a-way, E - ven gave it to a preach - er who was

Refrain

go - ing far a-way. But the

cat came back could - n't stay no long - er, Yes, the

cat came back, the ver - y next day, The

cat came back, thought he was a gon - er, But the

cat came back for it would - n't stay a - way.

2. The cat it had some company one night out in the yard,
Somebody threw a boot, and they threw it mighty hard;
Caught the cat behind the ear, he thought it rather slight,
When along there came a brickbat and knocked the cat out of sight.

3. The man around the corner swore he'd kill the cat on sight,
He loaded up his shotgun with nails and dynamite;
He waited and he waited for the cat to come around,
Ninety seven pieces of the man is all they found.

4. He gave it to a little boy with a dollar note,
Told him for to take it up the river in a boat;
They tied a rope around its neck, it must have weighed a pound,
Now they drag the river for a little boy that's drowned.

Shenandoah

American Song

Oh Shen - an - doah, I long to hear you, A - way you rol - ling ri - ver,___ Oh Shen - an - doah, I long to hear you, A - way, we're bound a - way 'Cross the wide Mis - sou - ri.

2. Oh Shenandoah, I love your daughter...
3. Oh Shenandoah, I'm bound to leave you...

HIKING SONGS

Marching to Pretoria *(from the Boer War, c. 1900)*

I'm with you and you're with me and
So we are all together,
So we are all together,
So we are all together.
Sing with me, I'll sing with you and
So we will sing together
As we march along.

Chorus: We are marching to Pretoria,
Pretoria, Pretoria.
We are marching to Pretoria,
Pretoria, Hurrah.

Verse 2: We have food, the food is good, and
So let us eat together,
So let us eat together,
So let us eat together.
When we eat, it is a treat,
So we will sing together,
As we march along.

The Caissons Go Rolling Along *(1917 version)*

Over hill, over dale,
We have hit the dusty trail,
And those caissons go rolling along.
In and out, hear them shout,
Counter march and right about,
And the Caissons go rolling along.

Refrain: For it's hi! hi! hee!
In the field artillery,
Shout your numbers loud and strong,
And where e'er you go,
You will always know
That the Caissons go rolling along.

Verse 2: In the storm, in the night,
Action left or action right
See those Caissons go rolling along.

Limber front, limber rear,
Prepare to mount your cannoneer
And those Caissons go rolling along.

Verse 3:　Was it high, was it low,
Where the heck did that one go?
As those Caissons go rolling along.
Was it left, was it right,
Now we won't get home tonight
And those Caissons go rolling along.

Waltzing Matilda (1903; Australian)

Once a jolly swagman camped by a billabong,
Under the shade of a coolibah tree,
And he sang as he watched and waited 'til his billy boiled,
"Who'll come a-Waltzing Matilda with me?"
Waltzing Matilda, Waltzing Matilda,
"You'll come a-Waltzing Matilda with me."
And he sang as he watched and waited 'til his billy boiled,
"You'll come a-Waltzing Matilda with me."

Down came a jumbuck to drink at the billabong,
Up got the swagman and grabbed him with glee,
And he sang as he stowed that jumbuck in his tucker bag,
"You'll come a-Waltzing Matilda with me."
Waltzing Matilda, Waltzing Matilda,
"You'll come a-Waltzing Matilda with me."
And he sang as he stowed that jumbuck in his tucker bag,
"You'll come a-Waltzing Matilda with me."

Down came the squatter, mounted on his thoroughbred,
Up came the troopers, one, two, three,
"Where's the jolly jumbuck you've got in your tucker bag?"
"You'll come a-Waltzing Matilda with me."
Waltzing Matilda, Waltzing Matilda,
"You'll come a-Waltzing Matilda with me."
"Who's that jolly jumbuck you've got in your tucker bag?"
"You'll come a-Waltzing Matilda with me."

Up got the swagman and jumped into the billabong.
"You'll never catch me alive," said he,
And his ghost may be heard as you pass by that billabong,
"You'll come a-Waltzing Matilda with me."

Waltzing Matilda, Waltzing Matilda
"Who'll come a-Waltzing Matilda with me?"
And his ghost may be heard as you pass by that billabong,
"Who'll come a-Waltzing Matilda with me?"

When the Saints Go Marching In *(1895)*

This song can be sung in a call-and-response manner, in which the leader sings out "Oh, when the saints," and the audience responds with "Oh, when the saints."

Verse 1: We are trav'ling in the footsteps
Of those who've gone before
And we'll all be reunited,
On a new and sunlit shore.

Verse 2: Oh, when the saints go marching in,
Oh, when the saints go marching in,
Lord, how I want to be in that number
When the saints go marching in.

Verse 3: And when the sun begins to shine
And when the sun begins to shine
Lord, how I want to be in that number
When the sun begins to shine.

Verse 4: Oh, when the trumpet sounds its call

Verse 5: Oh, when the saints go marching in

When Johnny Comes Marching Home *(Civil War song)*

When Johnny comes marching home again, hurrah! Hurrah!
We'll give him a hearty welcome then, hurrah! Hurrah!
The men will cheer and the boys will shout
The ladies they will all turn out
And we'll all feel gay when Johnny comes marching home.

The old church bell will peal with joy, hurrah! Hurrah!
To welcome home our darling boy, hurrah! Hurrah!
The village lads and lassies say
With roses they will strew the way
And we'll all feel gay when Johnny comes marching home.

Get ready for the Jubilee, hurrah! Hurrah!
We'll give the hero three times three, hurrah! Hurrah!

The laurel wreath is ready now
To place upon his loyal brow
And we'll all feel gay when Johnny comes marching home.

Let love and friendship on that day, hurrah! Hurrah!
Their choicest pleasures then display, hurrah! Hurrah!
And let each one perform some part
To fill with joy the warrior's heart
And we'll all feel gay when Johnny comes marching home.

Tramp! Tramp! Tramp! (The Boys Are Marching) (Civil War song)

Verse 1: In our prison cell I sit, thinking Mother, dear, of you,
And our bright and happy home so far away,
And the tears, they fill my eyes 'spite of all that I can do,
Tho' I try to cheer my comrades and be gay.

Chorus: Tramp, tramp, tramp, the boys are marching,
Cheer up, comrades, they will come.
And beneath the starry flag we shall breathe the air again,
Of the free land in our own beloved home.

Verse 2: In the battle front we stood, when their fiercest charge they made,
And they swept us off a hundred men or more,
But before we reached their lines, they were beaten back dismayed,
And we heard the cry of vict'ry o'er and o'er.

Verse 3: So within the prison cell we are waiting for the day,
That shall come to open wide the iron door.
And the hollow eye grows bright, and the poor heart almost gay,
As we think of seeing home and friends once more.

ECHO SONGS

Sippin' Cider Through a Straw (1919)

Verse 1: The prettiest girl (echoed by group), I ever saw (echo),
Was sippin' cider (echo), through a straw (echo).
(All sing together) The prettiest girl I ever saw
Was sippin' cider through a straw.

Verse 2: I asked that girl, "How do you draw That apple cider through a straw?"

Verse 3: She smiled at me and said that I Might come up close and give a try.

Verse 4: Then cheek to cheek and jaw to jaw, We sipped that cider through a straw.

Verse 5: And all at once that straw did slip; I'd sip some cider from her lip.

Verse 6: The parson came to her backyard, A-sippin' cider from a straw.

Verse 7: And now I've got a mother-in-law, And forty-nine kids to call me Pa.

Verse 8: The moral of this little tale, Is sip your cider from a pail!

The Bear Song *(The Other Day)*

This song is sung to the tune of "Sippin' Cider Through a Straw." This makes a good hiking song, the leader hearing his or her line echoed by the hikers behind.

1. The other day (echoed by group),
   I met a bear (echo),
   In tennis shoes (echo),
   a dandy pair (echo).

   (All sing) The other day, I met a bear,
   In tennis shoes, a dandy pair.

2. He looked at me,
   I looked at him.
   He sized up me,
   And I sized up him.

3. He said to me,
   "Why don't you run?
   I see you ain't
   Got any gun."

4. And so I ran
   Away from there,
   But right behind me
   Came that bear.

5. Ahead of me,
   I saw a tree,
   I saw a tree,
   Oh gracious me!

6. The only branch
   Was ten feet up,
   So I'd have to jump
   And trust my luck.

7. And so I jumped
   Into the air,
   And missed that branch
   Away up there.

8. Now don't you fret,
   Now don't you frown,
   'Cause I caught that branch
   On the way back down.

9. The moral is
   No shocking news:
   Don't talk to bears
   In tennis shoes.

10. That's all there is,
    There ain't no more,
    Unless I meet
    That bear once more.

MOTION SONGS

Do Your Ears Hang Low?

To the tune of "Turkey in the Straw"

Do your ears hang low? (place thumbs on ears and let fingers hang down)
Do they wobble to and fro? (wobble fingers)
Can you tie 'em in a knot? (make action of tying a knot)
Can you tie 'em in a bow? (make action of tying a bow)
Can you throw 'em over your shoulder, (make action of tossing over your shoulder)
Like a continental soldier?
Do you ears hang low?

Have You Ever Gone Fishing?

To the tune of "Turkey in the Straw" (or "Do Your Ears Hang Low?")

Have you ever gone fishing (cast out your pole and reel the line in)
On a bright and sunny day (hold your hands in a circle in the sky)
With all the little fishies swimming up and down the bay? (place palms together and move hand like swimming fish)
With your hands in your pockets (slap your pockets)
And your pockets in your pants (slap your hips)
All the little fishies do the hootchy-kootchy dance. (dance)
Tra-la-la-la-la, Tra-la-la-la
With your hands in your pockets (slap your pockets)
And your pockets in your pants. (slap your hips)

Father Abraham

Father Abraham had seven sons;
Seven sons had Father Abraham.
And they didn't laugh, and they didn't cry;
All they did was go like this.

After the group sings, "go like this," the leader shouts out a new motion (for example: "right arm"). A new motion is introduced each time the song is sung, while all previous motions are continued. There are variations to the motions, and you can feel free to add your own.

1st time: right arm is raised and beats out the rhythm of the song
2nd time: left arm

3rd time: right leg kicks out
4th time: left leg
5th time: nod your head
6th time: turn around in a circle
Last time: "Sit down!"

A Hot Time in the Old Town

Late last night, when we were all in bed (a-sleeping)
Old Lady Leary hung a lantern in the shed
And when the cow kicked it over,
She winked her eye and said,
"There'll be a hot time in the old town tonight!"
Fire! Fire! Fire!

1st time: sing all of the words through
2nd time: replace the word "bed" with both hands against your cheek, as a gesture of sleeping.
3rd time: continue previous action and substitute hanging out a imaginary lantern
4th time: substitute "cow kicked it over" with kicking motion
5th time: substitute "wink" with a wink
6th time: substitute "hot time" with a fanning motion
7th time: substitute "fire" with hand thrown into the air

Little Bunny Foo-Foo

(Sung)   Little Bunny Foo-Foo, (raise two fingers)
           Hopping through the forest (bounce hands up and down)
           Scooping up the field mice, (make a scooping motion)
           And bopping them on the head. (slap palm with fist)

(Spoken) Down came the Good Fairy, and she said:
           Little Bunny Foo-Foo, (wag index finger sideways)
           I don't want to see you (wag index finger sideways)
           Scooping up the field mice, (make a scooping motion)
           And bopping them on the head. (slap palm with fist)
           I'll give you 3 chances,
           And if you don't behave,
           I will turn you into a Goon!

(Sung)   Little Bunny Foo-Foo,
           Hopping through the forest

Scooping up the field mice,
And bopping them on the head.

(Spoken) Down came the Good Fairy, and she said:
Little Bunny Foo-Foo,
I don't want to see you
Scooping up the field mice,
And bopping them on the head.
I'll give you 2 chances,
And if you don't behave,
I'll turn you into a Goon!

(Sung) Little Bunny Foo-Foo,
Hopping through the forest
Scooping up the field mice,
And bopping them on the head.

(Spoken) Then down came the Good Fairy, and she said:
Little Bunny Foo-Foo,
I don't want to see you
Scooping up the field mice,
and bopping them on the head.
I'll give you 1 more chance,
and if you don't behave,
I'll turn you into a Goon!

(Sung) Little Bunny Foo-Foo,
Hopping through the forest
Scooping up the field mice,
And bopping them on the head.

(Spoken) Down came the Good Fairy, and she said:
Little Bunny Foo-Foo,
I don't want to see you
Scooping up the field mice,
And bopping them on the head.
POOF! You're a goon!

(Spoken) The moral of the story is: Hare today, Goon tomorrow!

For more motion songs, see "If You're Happy and You Know It," "Hokey-Pokey," "My Bonnie," "John Brown's Baby," and "Row, Row, Row Your Boat" on pages 196–202.

"To the Tune of..."

Kids' lyrics set to well-known melodies
(Never underestimate the inventiveness of youth.)

He Jumped from 40,000 Feet

To the tune of "The Battle Hymn of the Republic"

> He jumped from 40,000 feet and forgot to pull the cord,
> He jumped from 40,000 feet and forgot to pull the cord,
> He jumped from 40,000 feet and forgot to pull the cord,
> And he ain't gonna jump no more.

Chorus: Glory, glory, what a heck of a way to die
> Glory, glory, what a heck of a way to die
> Glory, glory, what a heck of a way to die
> And he ain't gonna fly no more.

Verse 2: He was last to leave the cockpit and the first to hit the ground,...

Verse 3: He landed on the runway like a blob of strawberry jam,...

Verse 4: They scraped him off the runway with a silver spoon,...

Verse 5: They sent him home to mother in a little wooden box,...

Verse 6: His mother didn't want him so she sent him back to us,...

Pink Pajamas

To the tune of "The Battle Hymn of the Republic"

> I wear my pink pajamas in the summer when it's hot,
> I wear my flannel nighties in the winter when it's not,
> And sometimes in the springtime, and sometimes in the fall,
> I jump between the sheets with nothing on at all.

Chorus: Glory, glory, hallelujah,
> Glory, glory, what's it to ya,
> Balmy breezes blowing through ya,
> With nothing on at all.

She Went Into the Water

To the tune of "The Battle Hymn of the Republic"

> She went into the water and she got her toes all wet,
> She went into the water and she got her toes all wet,

She went into the water and she got her toes all wet,
But she didn't get her (mmm-mmm) wet, yet.

Verse 2: She went into the water and she got her feet all wet...

Verse 3: She went into the water and she got her ankles wet...

Verse 4: She went into the water and she got her shins all wet...

Verse 5: She went into the water and she got her knees all wet...

Verse 6: She went into the water and she finally got it wet,...
Yes, she finally got her bathing suit wet!

I Know a Song That Gets on Everybody's Nerves

To the tune of "The Battle Hymn of the Republic"

I know a song that gets on everybody's nerves,
I know a song that gets on everybody's nerves,
I know a song that gets on everybody's nerves,
And this is how it goes....
(repeat ad infinitum)

On Top of Spaghetti

To the tune of "On Top of Old Smoky"

On top of spaghetti, all covered with cheese,
I lost my poor meatball, when somebody sneezed.
It rolled off the table and onto the floor,
And then my poor meatball rolled out of the door.
It rolled in the garden and under a bush,
And then my poor meatball was nothing but mush.
The mush was as tasty, as tasty could be,
And early next summer, it grew into a tree.
The tree was all covered with beautiful moss;
It grew lovely meatballs and tomato sauce.
So if you eat spaghetti, all covered with cheese,
Hold onto your meatballs, and don't ever sneeze.

Gee, Ma, I Wanna Go Home

To the tune of "They Say That in the Army," a World War II song

1. The weather at _____ Camp they say is mighty fine;
   First it's 37, then it's 99.

Chorus: Oh I don't want no more of camping life.
  Gee, ma, I wanna go, but they won't let me go,
  Gee, ma, I wanna go home.

2. The food at _____ Camp they say is mighty fine;
  Some rolled off the table and killed a friend of mine.

3. The counselors at _____ Camp they say are mighty fine.
  We get up at seven, and they get up at nine.

4. The girls (guys) at _____ Camp they say are mighty fine.
  They promised Cindy Crawford (Matt Damon) but gave us Frankenstein.

5. The swimming at _____ Camp they say is mighty fine.
  You step into the water, it freezes up your spine.

6. The nurse at _____ Camp they say is mighty fine.
  But when I broke my finger, she broke the other nine.

7. The tents at _____ Camp they say are mighty neat.
  But when you go inside them, they smell like stinky feet.

8. The toilets at _____ Camp they say are mighty fine.
  When you sit upon them, they suck in your behind.

9. The showers at _____ Camp they say are mighty fine.
  When you turn them on, they squirt out yellow slime.

My Bonnie

To the tune of "My Bonnie Lies Over the Ocean"

  Last night as I lay on my pillow,
  Last night as I lay on my bed,
  I stuck my feet out of the window,
  Next morning my neighbors were dead.

Chorus: Bring back, bring back,
  O bring back my neighbors to me, to me.
  Bring back, bring back,
  O bring back my neighbors to me.

  My Bonnie leaned over the gas tank,
  The height of its contents to see.
  I lighted a match to assist her,
  O bring back my Bonnie to me.

Chorus: Bring back, bring back,
  O bring back my Bonnie to me, to me....

My breakfast lies over the ocean,
My luncheon lies over the rail,
My supper lies in a commotion,
Won't somebody bring me a pail?

Chorus: Please bring, please bring,
O please bring a pail to me, to me....

Who knows what I had for breakfast?
Who know what I had for tea?
Who knows what I had for supper?
Just look out the window and see.

Chorus: Clams, clams, clams, clams,
Clams and ice cream don't agree with me....

My Body

To the tune of "My Bonnie Lies Over the Ocean"

My body has calamine lotion,
My body's as sore as can be,
The flowers I picked for my counselor
Turned out to be poison ivy.

Chorus: Don't touch, don't touch,
You'll get a rash from ivy, ivy,
It will itch bad
And it looks much worse than acne.

The Wrong End

To the tune of "My Bonnie Lies Over the Ocean"

Oh, rabbits have bright shiny noses.
I'm telling you now as a friend,
The reason their noses are shiny:
The powder puff's on the wrong end.

Chorus: Wrong end, wrong end,
The powder puff's on the wrong end, wrong end.
Wrong end, wrong end,
The powder puff's on the wrong end.

Ravioli

To the tune of "Alouette"

All:	Ravioli, I like ravioli,
	Ravioli, it's the best for me.
Leader:	Have I got it on my chin?
All:	Yes, you've got it on your chin.
Leader:	On my chin?
All:	On your chin. Oh-oh,
	Ravioli, I like ravioli,
	Ravioli, it's the best for me.
Leader:	Have I got it on my shirt?...

(each time substitute with pants, shoes, floor, etc.)

She'll Be Wearing Silk Pajamas When She Comes

To the tune of "She'll Be Comin' Round the Mountain"

She'll be wearing silk pajamas when she comes (yeah, yeah!)...
And we'll wear our bright red woolies when she comes (scratch, scratch!)...
Oh, we'll kill the old red rooster when she comes (hack, hack!)...
Oh, we'll all have chicken and dumplings when she comes (yum, yum!)...
Oh, we'll all have indigestion when she comes (burp, burp!)...

The Grand Old Duke of York

To the tune of "A-Hunting We Will Go"

(Each time the word "up" is sung, everyone stands up; when "down" is sung, everyone sits.)

The Grand Old Duke of York,
He had ten thousand men.
He marched them up the hill,
And then he marched them down again.
And when they're up, they're up,
And when they're down, they're down,
But when they're only halfway up,
They're neither up nor down.

Let There Be Peas

To the tune of "Let There Be Peace on Earth"

Let there be peas on earth,
And take away broccoli;
Let there be peas on earth,
For peas are what's meant to be.
Peas are delicious,
Round and firm and sweet;
Broccoli looks like a forest,
And trees were not meant to eat!
Please let there be peas on earth,
But rid it of broccoli.
I'd like all peas on earth,
But never the broccoli.
So, eat some peas,
Bring me some peas,
Peas are best for me.
Let there be peas on earth,
But take all the broccoli!

On Mules We Find

To the tune of "Auld Lang Syne"

On mules, we find two legs behind, and two we find before.
We stand behind before we find what the two behind be for.
When we're behind the two behind, we find what they be for.
So stand before the two behind, behind the two before.

Here for Fun

To the tune of "Auld Lang Syne"

We're here for fun right from the start
So drop your dignity.
Just laugh and sing with all your heart
And show your loyalty.
May all your troubles be forgot;
May this night be the best.
Join in the songs we sing tonight;
Be happy with the rest.

I Had a Little Chicken

To the tune of "Turkey in the Straw"

Verse 1: Oh, I had a little chicken, and she wouldn't lay an egg,
So I poured hot water up and down her leg.
Oh, the little chicken hollered and the little chicken begged,
And then the little chicken laid a hard-boiled egg!

Verse 2: replace hot water *with* vinegar *and* hard-boiled *with* pickled

Verse 3: gun powder — scrambled

Verse 4: mayonnaise — deviled egg

Verse 5: watercolors — Easter egg

Found a Peanut

To the tune of "Clementine"

Found a peanut, found a peanut,
Found a peanut just now.
Just now I found a peanut,
Found a peanut just now.

Verse 2: replace found a peanut *with* cracked it open

Verse 3: it was rotten

Verse 4: ate it anyway

Verse 5: got a stomach ache

Verse 6: called the doctor

Verse 7: operation

Verse 8: died anyway

Verse 9: was a dream

Verse 10: then I woke up

Verse 11: found a peanut

My Monster

To the tune of "Clementine"

Chorus: Oh my monster, Oh my monster
Oh my monster, Frankenstein,
You were built to last forever,
Dreadful, scary, Frankenstein.

Verse 1: In a dungeon, in a castle
Near the dark and murky Rhine,
Dwelt a doctor, the concocter,
And his monster Frankenstein.

Verse 2: In a graveyard near the castle,
Where the sun refused to shine,
He dug for noses and for toeses,
So he built his Frankenstein.

My Dog Rover

To the tune of "I'm Looking Over a Four-Leaf Clover"

I'm looking over my dead dog Rover
That I overran with the mower.
One leg is missing, another is gone,
One leg is scattered all over the lawn.
No need explaining, the one remaining
Is stuck in the kitchen door.
I'm looking over my dead dog Rover
That I overran with the mower.
I'm looking over my dead dog Rover
Who died on the kitchen floor.
One leg is broken, the other is lame,
The third leg is missing, the fourth needs a cane.
No need explaining, the tail remaining
Was caught in the oven door.
I'm looking over my dead dog Rover
Who died on the kitchen floor.

My Tall Silk Hat

To the tune of "Funiculi, Funicula"

One day, as I was riding on the subway
My tall silk hat, my tall silk hat
I laid it on the seat beside me
My tall silk hat, my tall silk hat
A big, a-fat-a-lady sat upon it
My tall silk hat, my tall silk hat
Christopher Columbo, now what do you think of that?
A big, a-fat-a-lady sat upon it

My tall silk hat, my tall silk hat
My hat she broke and that's no joke
My hat she broke and that's no joke
Christopher Columbo, now what do you think of that?
My hat, my hat, my hat she smashed.

My Flashlight

To the tune of "By the Light of the Silvery Moon"

By the light of my little flashlight
Wish I could see
What it was that just bit my knee.
Batteries, why did you fail me, fail me?
The chance is slim, the chance is slight
I can cast through the night
Without my little flashlight.

Oh, I Wish I Were

To the tune of "If You're Happy and You Know It"

Oh, I wish I were a little bar of soap
Oh, I wish I were a little bar of soap
I would slippy and a slidey
Over everybody's hidey.
Oh, I wish I were a little bar of soap.

Oh, I wish I were a little hunk of mud
Oh, I wish I were a little hunk of mud
I would ooey and I'd gooey
Under everybody's shoey.
Oh, I wish I were a little hunk of mud.

Oh, I wish I were a can of soda pop
Oh, I wish I were a can of soda pop.
I'd go down with a slurp,
And come up with a burp.
Oh, I wish I were a can of soda pop.

Oh, I wish I were a slippery little root
Oh, I wish I were a slippery little root.
I would sit upon the trail

And knock everyone on his tail.
Oh, I wish I were a slippery little root.

Oh, I wish I were a little bitty orange.
Oh, I wish I were a little bitty orange.
I'd go squirty, squirty, squirty
Over everybody's shirty.
Oh, I wish I were a little bitty orange.

S-M-I-L-E

To the tune of "John Brown's Body"

Verse 1: It isn't any trouble just to S-M-I-L-E *(repeat)*
There isn't any trouble but will vanish like a bubble
If you'll only take the trouble just to S-M-I-L-E.
Verse 2: It isn't any trouble just to G-R-I-N, grin...
Verse 3: It isn't any trouble just to L-A-U-G-H...

Greasy, Grimy Gopher Guts

To the tune of "The Old Grey Mare, She Ain't What She Used to Be"

Great green gobs of greasy, grimy gopher guts
Hurdy gurdy birdy feet
Percolated monkey meat
French fried eyeballs swimmin' in a bowl of pus
That's what I had for lunch!
Great green gobs of greasy, grimy gopher guts
Mutilated monkey meat
Dirty little pigeons' feet
All mixed up with a pile of poison possum pus
And me without my spoon! (We'll use a straw!)

God Bless My Underwear

To the tune of "God Bless America"

God bless my underwear, my only pair
Stand beside them, and guide them
Through the rips, through the holes, through the tears
From the washer, to the dryer, to the clothesline in the air
God bless my underwear, my only pair.

Road Kill Stew

To the tune of "Three Blind Mice"

> Road kill stew, road kill stew
> Tastes so good, just like it should
> First you go down to the interstate
> You wait for the critter to meet it's fate
> You take it home and you make it great
> Road kill stew, road kill stew.

The Twelve Days of Summer Camp

To the tune of "The Twelve Days of Christmas"

On the first day of summer camp my mother sent to me ... a box of oatmeal cookies

> Second day ... two T-shirts
> Third day ... three pairs of socks
> Fourth day ... four woolen caps
> Fifth day ... five underpants
> Sixth day ... six postage stamps
> Seventh day ... seven nose warmers
> Eighth day ... eight Batman comics
> Ninth day ... nine bars of soap
> Tenth day ... ten Band-Aids
> Eleventh day ... eleven shoestrings
> Twelfth day ... twelve bottles of insect repellent.

FURTHER SONGS FOR GROUP SINGING

More songs appropriate for campfires and other group sing-alongs may be heard on CDs available in most music stores. The following selections are perennial favorites:

Harry Belafonte. *Jamaica Farewell, Midnight Special, Michael Row the Boat Ashore, John Henry, Shenandoah, Waltzing Matilda, Banana Boat (Day-O)*
Melinda Caroll. Girl Scouts Greatest Hits comes in nine volumes of CD's and song lyric books, all loaded with popular Girl Scout and camp songs. Available at *www.gsmusic.com*.

John Denver. *Sunshine on My Shoulder, Take Me Home, Country Roads, Rocky Mountain High, Follow Me, Leaving on a Jet Plane,* and many more

Burl Ives. *Big Rock Candy Mountain, Blue Tail Fly, Git Along Little Doggie, Goober Peas, On Top of Old Smoky, Today*

The Kingston Trio. *Tom Dooley, Lemon Tree, Goober Peas, Wreck of the "John B.," Wimoweh (The Lion Sleeps Tonight), This Land Is Your Land, They Call the Wind Maria, Where Have All the Flowers Gone, This Little Light, 500 Miles, M.T.A.,* and *Blowin' in the Wind*

The New Christy Minstrels. *Today, This Land Is Your Land, Freedom, Last Farewell*

Tom Paxton. *Ramblin' Boy, Can't Help But Wonder Where I'm Bound, The Marvelous Toy, Goin' to the Zoo*

Peter, Paul, and Mary. *Puff (the Magic Dragon), Blowin' in the Wind, If I Had a Hammer, Stewball, Leaving on a Jet Plane, Day Is Done, This Land Is Your Land, Kisses Sweeter Than Wine, Where Have All the Flowers Gone, Kumbaya, Michael Row the Boat Ashore, All My Trials, Weave Me the Sunshine, The Marvelous Toy, Light One Candle, 500 Miles, Garden Song.* All of these songs, and more, are available on a single album, appropriately titled *Peter, Paul and Mary: Around the Campfire.*

Still More Songs Your Kids Probably Know

Amen; The Ants Go Marching; The Bear Went Over the Mountain; Big Blue Frog; Bingo; Boom-Di-Ada (I Love the Mountains); Born Free; Canoe Song; Day is Done; Do Lord; Dona Nobis Pacem; Dunderback; Edelweiss; Ezek'el Saw the Wheel; Funiculi, Funicula; Flicker; Fried Ham; Go Tell It on the Mountain; The Happy Wanderer (Val-de-ri Val-de-ra); Havah Nagilah; Hush Little Baby; I Believe; I'd Like to Teach the World to Sing; I've Got Shoes; John Jacob Jingleheimer Schmidt; Kookaburra; Linger; Little Brown Jug; Lord, I Want to Be a Christian; Morning Has Broken; Ninety-Nine Bottles of Beer on the Wall; One Bottle of Pop; One Dark Night; Pass It On; Rise and Shine; Seek Ye First; Simple Gifts; Sixteen Tons; Spider's Web; Study War No More; The Sun Is a Magic Fellow; Sweet Violets; There Was an Old Woman; The Teensy-Weensy Spider; They'll Know We Are Christians by Our Love; The Titanic; To Be Alive; We Shall Overcome; Whiskers; The Whistling Gypsy Rover

Chapter 9

Campfires

...So give me the light of the campfire,
warm and bright;
And give me some friends to sing with,
I'll be here all night....

Warmth and friendship — these are the feelings which a good campfire can arouse among a group of people. Unless the group is already close, however, campfire programs must be planned in advance — and planned in detail — so as not to run the risk of disaster (such as boredom). The success of the campfire program is due, in large part, to the preparation and enthusiasm of the youth leader. This in no way means that the leader should plan the entire program, rather that he or she should guide or assist the group members in the planning and implementation.

Activities always run better when the participants are involved in the planning. The youth leader should stay involved to ensure that the activities are not offensive to any individual or group.

Keep in mind:

1. Setting plays a vital role. A beautiful site should be found and cleared ahead of time (an excellent group project). The campfire site should be large enough for skits and stunts, but small enough to enhance a feeling of closeness. A major aim of the campfire is to foster group unity.
2. Other aims include fun, laughter, creativity, mystery, inspiration, and appreciation. Try to involve everyone in the spirit and activities of the campfire.

271

3. Keep your campfires interesting by varying your programs. Consider a theme for each campfire, such as story night, skit night, spook night, brainteaser night, Western night, tall tales night, song night, contest night, awards night, etc. Campfires are ideal settings for special ceremonies and rituals. Special holidays may suggest a campfire theme.

4. Campfires are ideal times for storytelling. "You cannot tell a good story unless you tell it before a fire. You cannot have a complete fire unless you have a good story teller along" (Dr. G. Stanley Hall).

5. Don't allow the evening to become monotonous. Strive for a variety of activities at a single campfire. Some activities may be funny and boisterous; others, suspenseful and scary; still others, quiet and serious.

6. Plan your program to follow the flames of the campfire: as the fire grows, build up toward a climax in your program; as the flames begin to die, gradually settle down with more quiet activities so that the evening ends with a sense of serenity.

7. The ending of a campfire can be inspirational and moving. It may include words of reflection from the youth leader. It may end with a prayer, a spiritual reading, or a poem:

> As darkness creeps into our circle of light,
> Embers that glow and sigh
> Draw our friendship circle closer,
> Whisper memories that will not die;
> God's magic dances in our fire's flames,
> And fills the gathering night
> With mystery and a wondrous peace
> That bids safe sleep 'til morning's light.

For a sparkling conclusion, pass around a bowl of sugar and ask everyone to take a small amount. At a given signal, everyone tosses the sugar on the fire, resulting in flashes of light. They may watch in silence, or you may wish to comment on flashes of memory that will make this campfire live forever.

8. Try to keep the special magic and mystery of the campfire alive, for there is indeed a certain allure to the flames which offer light and warmth in the dark of the evening. The glow of the firelight as it lights each face can also warm each heart. The circle represents an unbroken ring of friendship where no one is head. That unbroken circle around the fire can evoke feelings of equality, unity, and trust.

9. Always have an alternate plan of action in case of inclement weather.

Campfire programs can include most any activity: singing, dramatics, storytelling, games, mixers, contests, meals or snacks, discussions, debates, yells, challenges, skill training, rehearsals, tent or cabin meetings, unit or patrol reports, worship, and ceremonies. The rest of this book is filled with activities suited to the campfire setting.

Campfires need not follow a specific theme; nevertheless, themed campfires can be plenty of fun, particularly for younger kids.

CAMPFIRE THEMES

Getting-Acquainted Campfire

See Chapter One for Icebreakers and Mixers. Songs, skits, and stories should be lively, upbeat, and spirited — even noisy — where the most timid individual is drawn in. Rounds and familiar songs are especially appropriate.

Western (or Cowboy) Campfire

Cook flapjacks or hot dogs-and-beans over the open fire; sing cowboy songs (e.g.: "Home on the Range" and "Git Along, Little Dogies"); tell tall tales; perform a Western skit; learn to tie different kinds of knots.

Indian Council Campfire

Younger campers enjoy dressing in costume. Try Indian stories, songs, and dances around the campfire. Drums add a special effect. Challenges can be made and feats of skill carried out. Learn Indian lore and distinguish between the facts and myths concerning American Indian tribes. Read Chief Seattle's eloquent letter to our nation's capital.

Hobo Campfire

This is a dinner campfire in which everyone dresses in baggy, mismatched "hobo clothes." The hobos cook hot dogs on a stick over the fire and heat beans in the can. Or cook a stew (see Easy Campfire Recipes, this chapter). Elect a "King (or Queen) of the Road" to reign over the campfire program. Give awards for best-dressed hobo. Perform skits and stunts, play "Kick the

Can," and sing road/travel songs ("King of the Road," "Five Hundred Miles," "The Midnight Special," etc.).

Primitive Campfire

For more skilled campers, try a primitive campfire for which only one match is brought to light the fire. Entertainment can include use of primitive instruments, such as hitting sticks against rocks or other sticks. Other entertainment may be singing, storytelling, and dramatics.

Spook Night

Magic, spooky skits, and scary stories are the order for the evening.

Talent Campfire

Each person demonstrates, performs, or talks about some special talent or ability he or she has. Advance preparation is necessary and some kids may need your help in bringing out what special talents they have.

Closing Campfire

The closing campfire can be deeply emotional if close friendships have developed and group experiences have led to personal growth. This campfire is often a ceremony:

CLOSING CAMPFIRE SERVICE
(adapted from closing ceremony held at
Northeast Music Camp, Ware, Massachusetts)

1. Leader:

It is very fitting that we should assemble in this beautiful setting for our last night at camp. We will remember that this was the spot of the first campfire of the season. Since then, we have learned to appreciate the campsite and the campgrounds, and to see its trees and lake as nature's handiwork. This has been a wonderful camping season — a time for learning and growing, for companionship and inspiration.

The flame from this campfire serves as a symbol of the inspiration we have gained from our summer together — a beacon furnishing light. The flame has long been an important symbol of unity among all people.

Fire has always had a sort of mystery about it. It was treated with reverence because people did not know its source, though they recognized its power. As soon as man learned how to control it, it became his servant. Fire at night gave him protection from animals and the outside world. The campfire was a place where people sat and talked and gave such education as they could to their children. They sat around the fire in a circle which shut out the world and fostered a sense of community and security. Their campfire circles were much like our friendship circle here tonight — an unbroken ring of equal friendship where there is no head.

People gathered around the campfire in peace and unity. The campfire became meaningful, a place where a person could grow spiritually and attain peace of mind. The flame offered safety, radiated warmth, and shed light into the darkness. The light reminds us of that which is good in life and worth passing on to others and to generations to follow.

Light is the symbol of life, for did not God, at the beginning of the Creation, command, "Let there be light?" A Danish woman once said, "When I am lonely, I light a candle. There is so much *life* in a candle's flame." A Swedish writer has said, "The flame is the most universal of all symbols; it burns and illuminates by offering itself." Shakespeare reminds us, "How far that little light throws his beam! So shines a good deed in a naughty world." And the Bible tells us, "The spirit of man is the candle of the Lord."

Tonight we are here in friendship and common interest. We have shared many experiences and many ideas. Tonight through this campfire ceremony, we share with others what we have learned and experienced here. We pass to all we meet in the paths of life the light of our spirit which these flames represent. When the flame of our fire flickers and dims, it seems to struggle to regain brightness; so, too, when the flame of our spirit flickers and dims, we must strive to keep it burning brightly. Let us refresh our spirit by thinking back to this summer and what it has meant to us.

Edith Wharton wrote, "There are two ways of spreading light: to be the candle or the mirror that reflects it." Let us each be a light in the darkness, a lighthouse on the hill, a beacon of the good things we have come to appreciate during our time in these woods and hills.

2. Group:
Sings peaceful songs that have become favorites during the summer.

3. Leader:

Prayer of the Camper

This wood holds good things
And gives them all
For you and me.
This wood grew for many years

Fed by water and by sun,
Protecting as it grew,
Giving as it now dies.
It will give light through flames.
It will give warmth through red coals.
It will leave behind only grey ashes.
But this sacrifice will not be in vain —
For we shall take with us
The memory of this moment —
The fellowship and fun —
The song and challenge —
The story and ritual —
All to be ours forever.

[source unknown]

4. The Lighting of Candles.

The leader lights his or her candle from the campfire, then lights the candles of those sitting nearby. Each person, in turn, lights a neighbor's candle until the light from the campfire has spread to all candles. A procession is made from the campfire site to a small hillside, where the candles are placed on the ground in the shape of the camp insignia. (Alternatively, campers could be told at a given point to extinguish their candles and take them home, to be lit at Christmas or another holiday in remembrance of the friends and good times at camp.)

5. Closing.

The camp song is sung, and everyone returns silently to the cabins.

CANDLELIGHT CEREMONY

At Camp Otonka, a YMCA camp in Kentucky, the final campfire ended with a candlelight ceremony. Five candles were lit individually, each representing something learned or enjoyed at camp:

1. We light a candle for the love and enjoyment we have found in nature.
2. We light a candle for our desire to say, "I will try."
3. We light a candle for the friends who surround us and for the fellowship we have shared at camp. We came as strangers; we became friends; we leave as brothers and sisters.
4. We light a candle for the sound of singing around the campfire.
5. We light a candle for all that we have learned and shared at camp.

From those five candles, all other candles were lit and final songs were sung. Candles were then extinguished, marking the end of the season.

EASY CAMPFIRE RECIPES

Eggs in a Frame

This is an easy way to make fried eggs over a morning campfire.

Ingredients: egg, bread, butter

Using a round cookie cutter, jar top, or knife, cut and remove a 3-inch circle from the center of a slice of bread. Butter your frying pan and place the bread frame in it, heating until browned. Turn it over and break an egg into the opening. Cover pan with a lid until egg is fried.

Pancakes

For a Western theme, call them "flapjacks."

Follow directions on a Bisquick package and cook over a low flame. When using a prepared mix, measure out ahead of time the amount you need and keep in a jar or plastic container. Add liquid and eggs to the container right before cooking.

Beanie-Weenies

For this "Western Dinner," pour a can of beans into a frying pan. Add several sliced hot dogs and cook until steaming hot. Or cook hot dogs skewered on green sticks, serve the dogs on buns, and prepare beans as a side dish.

Kabobs

Ingredients: beef sirloin, onion, tomato, green pepper

Sharpen a green stick to use as a skewer. Cut meat into 1-inch pieces and cut vegetables in half. Spear the food onto the skewer, alternating meat with vegetables. Broil over hot coals, turning constantly, until meat is browned and vegetables are tender.

Campfire Stew

Ingredients: 2 ounces freeze-dried corn
1 ounce dehydrated onion flakes
1 ounce dehydrated celery flakes
1 quart water
3 ounces freeze-dried beef
2 tablespoons butter or margarine
salt, pepper, red pepper, thyme

Put corn, onion, celery and water into saucepan; bring to boil. Add remaining ingredients. Cover, cook 10–30 minutes, until tender and well-blended. Makes 4 servings.

Roast Corn on the Cob

Remove silk from corn. Place unhusked corn directly onto hot coals and roast for 20 to 30 minutes, turning frequently. Alternatively, husk and wrap corn in aluminum foil before roasting. Excellent with butter.

Doughboys

Make biscuit dough as directed on Bisquick package. Then take a small amount of dough and roll it between your hands to make a cord of dough about 6 inches long and as thick as your little finger. Heat a green stick over the fire and then wind the dough around the stick, pinching it on tightly at the ends. Toast the biscuit over the coals, usually only a few minutes before they slip off. Good with butter or jam.

Egg in a Cup

This recipe will amaze campers, because all it requires for each person is an egg, a paper cup, and water. It is essential, however, to use paper cups (not Styrofoam, plastic, or any other kind), which should be a bit larger than the egg. Place the egg in the cup and fill the cup nearly to the top with water. Then, carefully place the cup as close to the campfire as possible, right near the flames. If the upper part of the cup catches on fire, that is okay; the water will keep the rest of the cup from burning. The water will quickly heat and boil the egg. After a few minutes, carefully use metal tongs to remove the cup from the fire.

Egg in an Orange

For a unique flavor, slice an orange in half, then spoon out and eat the fruit for your daily vitamin C. Next, crack an egg into each half and place directly on the hot coals to cook the egg, perhaps 15–20 minutes. Use tongs to remove the orange from the coals before eating right out of the orange peel.

Omelet in a Bag

Here is another recipe requiring a minimum of cookware: just a zip-lock plastic bag and a pot. Crack two eggs into the plastic bag and seal it tight.

Then, squish the bag by hand — making sure not to break it — and use metal tongs to place it in a pot of boiling water. After about 5 minutes, carefully remove the bag and mix in shredded cheese, ham, onion, or other omelet ingredients, reseal, and return to the boiling water. Cook another 4 or 5 minutes until it appears done. Carefully remove the bag, open, and enjoy.

Campfire Popcorn

Loosely shape a large sheet of heavy-duty aluminum foil into a bowl and place ¼-cup of popcorn kernels and 2 tablespoons of oil into it. Seal the aluminum foil by making tight folds, making sure you leave room inside the sealed foil pot for the popcorn to expand. Poke a small hole or two in the foil to let steam escape. Place the aluminum foil pot on the hot coals and use metal tongs to shake the package until the kernels have popped.

Banana Boats

You don't need ice cream to make this campfire version of a banana split. Leaving the banana in its peel, slice it in half lengthwise like a hot dog bun, without cutting through the bottom half of the peel. Open the banana and stuff it with miniature marshmallows and semisweet chocolate chips. Wrap the banana in aluminum foil and cook over the fire or in the coals for about 5 minutes. Open the banana and eat with a spoon.

Chicken Noodle Soup

Ingredients: 1 package double noodle soup mix
Broccoli florets
1 chicken bouillon cube
1 can or package chicken meat

Boil 2½ cups of water and stir in first three ingredients. When the soup is nearly ready, add the chicken. One serving.

Hamburg Dinner in Foil

Ingredients: Hamburger patty
Potato, sliced
Carrot, sliced
Onion, sliced
Oil
Salt & pepper (optional)

Place hamburger, potato, carrot, and onion on heavy-duty aluminum foil and drizzle with a teaspoon of oil over all. Season with salt and pepper, if desired. Fold and seal the aluminum foil to create a tight package that will not leak. Place directly on hot coals with metal tongs and turn the entire package every few minutes, cooking for 8 to 10 minutes. Use tongs to remove from coals and check for doneness by making sure the meat is completely browned and potato pierces easily with a fork.

Ham Dinner in Foil

Ingredients: Thick ham slice
1 pineapple slice (from a can)
½ teaspoon mustard
½ teaspoon brown sugar

Place a thick slice of ham on heavy-duty aluminum foil, brush with mustard and brown sugar, and place the pineapple slice on top. Drizzle with some pineapple juice for more flavor, and then seal the aluminum foil to create a tight package that will not leak. Place directly on hot coals with metal tongs and cook each side of the package for 5 to 6 minutes.

Campfire Sandwich in Foil

Ingredients: Dinner roll or hamburger roll
Sliced ham
Sliced cheese
Hard boiled egg
Mayonnaise

Split the roll in half and lightly spread with mayonnaise. Then, place a slice of ham, a slice of cheese, and a slice or two of egg. Better yet, dice the ham, cheese, and egg and mix together with a little mayonnaise before spreading on the roll. Wrap sandwich in aluminum foil and heat on the grill for 10–15 minutes.

Baked Apple

Ingredients: 1 apple
2 tablespoons raisins (or other dried fruits)
½ teaspoon cinnamon sugar
½ teaspoon butter

Core the apple and place on heavy duty aluminum foil. Fill the center of the apple with raisins and sprinkle with cinnamon sugar and small dabs of butter. Wrap the apple completely and twist the top of the aluminum foil for use as a handle. Place in the hot coals for 15 minutes, turning occasionally. Cool before serving.

Other Campfire Fare

- For breakfast, convenient packages of instant oatmeal require only boiling water to make a hot, hearty, wholesome meal to start the day. Add dried fruits, like raisins or dates, for added nutrition and flavor.
- Because SPAM comes in a small can, is already cooked, and requires no refrigeration, it is convenient for a campfire. The instructions on the can indicate that SPAM can be eaten cold, but it can also be sliced like meat loaf and fried, or it can be cooked in a casserole. Dice it and mix it with a can of diced tomatoes, a can of tomato sauce, chopped onion, and a package of rice mix, then cook it in a pot for one variety of casserole. Or cook the can as is and add canned peas near the end of the cooking time.
- Bake a potato by wrapping it in aluminum foil and placing it directly in the hot coals. This may take 45 minutes to an hour, depending on the size of the potato and the heat of the coals. Pierce the potato with a fork to determine if it is tender and ready to eat.

S'mores

There's nothing like S'mores at a campfire; everyone comes back wanting some more.

Ingredients: graham crackers
milk chocolate bars
marshmallows

Spear marshmallows on a stick and brown the marshmallows over the fire. Then, make a sandwich, placing chocolate bar and marshmallow between two graham crackers. Variations: Instead of using graham crackers and chocolate, place a toasted marshmallow between two fudge striped cookies. Instead of a regular chocolate bar, use a crunch bar.

Chapter 10

Worship and Devotion

The greatest of all attitudes is reverence before the great mysteries of life. Camps and conferences can be ideal settings in which this reverence can develop and mature. Place the searching minds of a community of young people into the rawness and beauty of the great outdoors, and you have fertile ground in which the budding seeds of wonder and reverence can grow.

Worship and devotion make the most of people by directing them toward the highest spiritual powers. Not everyone comes with the same understandings. The youth leader must develop sensitivity to the differences of background and faith in the individuals he leads. Each of us can accept only what we are ready to receive: God can only be revealed in proportion to our capacity to understand. An attitude of mutual growth toward greater understanding should pervade any attempts in this great search.

In a manner of speaking, worship is recreation, a way of re-creating ourselves as we draw our attention to what is truly important. Daily devotional periods help us to focus our attention on what is sacred and meaningful, to draw ourselves up to a higher plane of thinking and living. They also allow a group of people to come together in prayer and adoration. Worship and devotions that are planned by the youth participants can have tremendous power and meaning. They need not follow any set pattern, though prayer, scripture, music, and a meditation are usually included.

Worship can take varied forms, from the clanging of cymbals to the silence of private prayer. Private meditation or devotional periods can be equally as meaningful as communal worship, especially when participants' thoughts are given focus and direction. The devotions below on being thankful are suitable to print and distribute for individual use. Encourage participants to find their own special place for a daily period of quiet time and focused meditation. Time alone to concentrate on significant thoughts is an important element of every life and offers balance, especially to the active and busy lives of young people.

DEVOTIONS ON BEING THANKFUL

If the only prayer you say in your life is thank you, that would suffice.

— Meister Eckhart

Being Thankful

Psalms: Psalm 96:11–12 and 97:22 — Let the heavens be glad, and let the earth rejoice; let the sea roar, and all that fills it; let the field exult, and everything in it! Rejoice in the Lord, O you righteous, and give thanks to his holy name!

Scripture: Philippians 4:4 — Rejoice in the Lord always; again I say, Rejoice.

Reflection: Many people live as though life is drudgery, a chore, a set of rigid rules that must be followed without joy. But this view is a serious misconception; all life is holy, and what is holy is cause for joy. In his letter to the Philippians, Paul thought joy was so important, he said so twice in the same sentence so that no one would miss his meaning: "Rejoice in the Lord always; again I say, Rejoice." The Psalmist calls the earth to rejoice, the seas to roar, and the fields to exult.

In fact, we can see the joy of God in the world he has created: in the beauty of nature — in the multi-colored flowers of the field in spring, but also in the pure driven snow of winter; in human relationships — in the cooing of little children as well as in the clasp of the hand of a friend; even in our failures, where God gently helps us to wend our way to his path; and in health, in happiness, in pleasant work to do.

The joy of God is all around to those who have a heart and mind to see it. Throughout the day, focus your heart and mind on the joy of life; seek joy in every endeavor. Try to find joy even in unpleasant tasks, and then you will.

Prayer: Thank you, God, for this day, for the opportunities it presents, for the joy it brings. Help me to see joy throughout the day and to spread my joy to other people. "This is the day the Lord has made; let us rejoice and be glad in it" (Psalm 118:24).

Thankful for the Glories of Nature

Psalms: from Psalm 104 — O Lord my God, you are very great! You make springs gush forth in the valleys; they flow between the hills; they give drink to every beast of the field; the wild donkeys quench their thirst. By them the birds of the air have their habitation; they sing among the branches. From the lofty abode you water the mountains; the earth is satisfied with the fruit of your work. You cause the grass to grow for the cattle, and plants for man to cultivate, that he may bring forth food from the earth, and wine to gladden the heart of man, oil to make his face shine, and bread to strengthen man's heart. The trees of the Lord are watered abundantly, the cedars of Lebanon which he planted. In them the birds build their nests; the stork has her home in the fir trees. The high mountains are for the wild goats; the rocks are a refuge for the badgers. O Lord, how various are your works! In wisdom you made them all; the earth is full of your creatures.

Reflection: The author of this Psalm made a list of some of the wonderful things God has created in the world of nature. He was aware that we are surrounded by beauty, that everywhere we look, we find so much to be thankful for: water, which babbles in brooks and quenches our thirst and cleanses our bodies; birds, which warble and sing and soar through the skies; animals of the land, which scamper and hunt and run free; plants, which carpet the earth and sway in the wind and provide us with food; trees, which grow mighty and tall and offer shade and protection; mountains, which rise majestically and call us to rise to higher awareness and thankfulness. The beauty is all around us, but we often are too busy to notice. From where you are sitting right now, look around you and notice how much beauty there is in nature for which you can be thankful. List in your mind all of these things, and continue this list throughout the day.

Prayer: God of the woods, teach us to be like the trees, growing tall and strong. Help us to see their beauty and usefulness, how they shelter your birds, your squirrels, and us, much like your protective hand.

God of the lake, teach us peace and patience. Grant us the serenity of this place and the strength to return to the busy world with calm and pure hearts.

God of the sun and the stars, teach us to seek the greater good and to avoid the snares of selfishness and pettiness. Help us to strive after the highest.

God of all creation, we adore you, for you made this wonderful world which surrounds us: the green grass, the singing birds, the grains of sand, the fresh air, the corn and wheat. O Divine Spirit, grant us the ability to see, to hear, to touch, to smell, and to taste what your creation offers us.

I will now, in silence and reverence, pause for a few moments to truly listen to the sounds of your creation. May the blessing of God be with me and grant me the joy of this created world. Amen.

Thankful for Goodness and Mercy

Psalm: Psalm 23 — The Lord is my shepherd; I shall not want; he makes me lie down in green pastures. He leads me beside still waters; he restores my soul. He leads me in paths of righteousness for his name's sake.

Even though I walk through the valley of the shadow of death, I fear no evil; for you are with me; your rod and thy staff, they comfort me.

You prepare a table before me in the presence of my enemies; you anoint my head with oil, my cup overflows. Surely goodness and mercy shall follow me all the days of my life; and I shall dwell in the house of the Lord for ever.

Scripture: Luke 15:11–24 — Jesus said, "There was a man who had two sons; and the younger of them said to his father, 'Father, give me the share of property that falls to me.' And he divided his living between them. Not many days later, the younger son gathered all he had and took his journey into a far country, and there he squandered his property in loose living. And when he had spent everything, a great famine arose in that country, and he began to be in want. So he went and joined himself to one of the citizens of that country, who sent him into his fields to feed swine. And he would gladly have fed on the pods that the swine ate; and no one gave him anything. But when he came to himself he said, 'How many of my father's hired servants have bread enough and to spare, but I perish here with hunger! I will arise and go to my father, and I will say to him, "Father, I have sinned against heaven and before you; I am no longer worthy to be called your son; treat me as one of your hired servants."' And he arose and came to his father. But while he was yet at a distance, his father saw him and had compassion, and ran and embraced him and kissed him. And the son said to him, 'Father, I have sinned against heaven and before you; I am no longer worthy to be called your son.' But the father said to his servants, 'Bring quickly the best robe, and put it on him; and put a ring on his hand, and shoes on his feet; and bring the fatted calf and kill it, and let us eat and make merry; for this my son was dead, and is alive again; he was lost, and is found.'"

Reflection: If you find it hard to forgive, think of the father in this story of a reckless and wasteful son. The son asked for his inheritance even before his father died; in essence, the son told his father, "I wish you were dead now so that I can receive what is due me." And then he squandered all that his father gave him. But when he returned home destitute, an amazing act of love and forgiveness occurred: without being asked, his father came running to him, embracing and kissing him. The father showed unconditional love and celebrated the return of his lost son.

For most of us, our parents are the same way. They love and care for us even when we go astray, when we do wrong, when we disappoint them. Their love is unconditional, not based on what we do in return, but a mirror of God's pure love for all his creation.

Even if our parents are not like the father in the story, God is. The footsteps of the father running to welcome his son echo the goodness and grace of God, who is always ready to welcome and accept us, to lead and restore us. The Psalmist proclaims that even though he walks "through the valley of the shadow of death," God is with him, comforting and restoring his soul.

We can be thankful for the love and guidance of our parents, our grandparents, our aunts and uncles, our teachers, and our mentors — or for anyone who is always there for us. We can be thankful to God, who out of infinite mercy and grace, accepts us, loves us, and guides us.

Prayer: I thank you, Lord. I thank you for forgiving me my waywardness. I thank you for healing me when I am ailing. I thank you for your steadfast love and mercy. I thank you for all the good with which you have blessed my life (Based on Psalm 103:1–5).

Thankful for Who We Are

Psalms: Psalm 107:1 — O give thanks to the Lord, for he is good; his steadfast love endures for ever!

Scripture: from 1 Corinthians 12:14–26 — For the body does not consist of one member but of many. If the foot should say, "Because I am not a hand, I do not belong to the body," that would not make it any less a part of the body. And if the ear should say, "Because I am not an eye, I do not belong to the body," that would not make it any less a part of the body. If the whole body were an eye, where would be the hearing? If the whole body were an ear, where would be the sense of smell? But as it is, God arranged the organs in the body, each one of them, as he chose. If all were a single organ, where would be the body? As it is, there are many parts, yet one body. If one member suffers, all suffer together; if one member is honored, all rejoice together.

Reflection: There are many differences among us, the author Paul was saying. And we are each important, each needed in this great human community of God's creation. A dull world it would be if we were all the same. We are all different, and we may be grateful for that. We may be grateful that others fill positions that must be done — that we would not want to do.

An artist who is restricted to one or two colors is limited in his ability to express himself. An orchestra comprised of all the same instrument would lack the rich and nuanced sound for conveying a meaningful theme. A sports team in which everyone possesses the same single ability would be ineffective against a team with varied abilities.

We are all different, and we need each other, Paul was saying. Each of us is important, and we must each play our part.

Once there was a doctor who was about to retire in a small French village where he had worked all his life. He had cared ceaselessly for his people, whether they were able to pay or not. A retirement party was arranged in the public square, and each citizen was to bring a pitcher of his own wine to pour into a large vat on the green. All day long people poured their wine, and at evening, the doctor, as guest of honor, took the first drink — and was shocked. It was water. Each one had said, "My little pitcher won't be missed. I have so little for myself. The others will take care of it. The little water I substitute won't be noticed."

Each person felt he was not needed, that his contribution was not important. Paul reminds us that each person is important and that we must be responsible. Responsibility is basic to any community. In a crisis, with a moral issue, on a principle, we must never look over our shoulder and ask, "What are others doing?" We must realize that we bear a responsibility to God and to others.

Every drop in the sea can say, "If it were not for me, there would be no ocean." Let us be thankful for who we are and for the part that we play. Let us be thankful for our differences.

Prayer: O God, may I be thankful for who I am and what I may become, and may we all be thankful for the different contributions that each of us makes. Guide me to see and appreciate my own strengths, as well as the strengths of others.

Thankful for Help and Guidance

Psalm: Psalm 69:1–2, 13–14 — Save me, O God! For the waters have come up to my neck. I sink in deep mire, where there is no foothold; I have come into deep waters, and the flood sweeps over me.... My prayer is to you, O Lord. At an acceptable time, O God, in the abundance of your steadfast love, answer me. With your faithful help, rescue me from sinking.

Reflection: There is a story about a sailor who fell overboard and nobody on the vessel heard the splash. Soon enough, a yacht sailed by, and a life preserver was thrown out to rescue him. "I have faith in God," the sailor called back, "so I will wait for Him to rescue me." Not much later, a cruise ship came by, and the crew offered to rescue the sailor. "I have faith in God," the sailor called back, "so I will wait for Him to rescue me." As the sailor struggled to survive, a helicopter pilot spotted the sailor and dropped a cord so that he could climb out of the water. "I have faith in God," the sailor called back, "so I will wait for Him to rescue me."

Before long, the sailor drowned.

As he entered heaven, God welcomed him. The sailor was befuddled and said to God, "Lord, I had faith in you. Why did you not prevent me from drowning?"

God replied, "I sent you a yacht, a cruise ship, and a helicopter, but for some reason you refused all the help I sent."

Human beings are the hands of God. It is through people that God does much of his work. If a person shows compassion to you, listens to you, guides you, rescues you, or befriends you, there is God in the midst of it. Human beings inspired by God are the language God uses to speak to a troubled world.

Spend some time thinking about the people who have made a difference in your life, and about those who are currently your friends and mentors. Thank God for their presence in your life, and perhaps you can also find some way to show them your appreciation, as well.

Prayer: (Bring to God the name of each person who has helped and shaped you, and offer thanks for their influence.)

Thankful for the Opportunity to Serve

Psalms: Psalm 106:1–3 — Praise the Lord! O give thanks to the Lord, for he is good; for his steadfast love endures forever! Who can utter the mighty doings of the Lord, or show forth all his praise? Blessed are they who observe justice, who do righteousness at all times!

Scripture: Matthew 9:35–38 — Jesus went about all the cities and villages, teaching in their synagogues and preaching the gospel of the kingdom, and healing every disease and every infirmity. When he saw the crowds, he had compassion for them, because they were harassed and helpless, like sheep without a shepherd. Then he said to his disciples, "The harvest is plentiful, but the laborers are few; pray therefore the Lord of the harvest to send out laborers into his harvest."

Lesson: When you read the gospels, you find that wherever there is action, there is Jesus in the midst of it. He is always there, seeking to make life better — sometimes with a parable, sometimes with the philosopher's appeal to reason, sometimes with words of reassurance to quiet the troubled heart, sometimes with physical healing. But where the action is, where trouble is, there he is.

And that's the way it must be for you and me. You'll find it won't be easy, whatever you do out of faith and love. It won't be easy, except the ease that comes in service through love. Jesus never promised his followers freedom from pain and sorrow. You aren't necessarily going to be respected for holding high moral codes or standing up for what is right and decent. But you shouldn't care.

When God sent Jesus into the world, he came all the way in, and then Jesus sent his disciples all the way in. God is where the action is: in classrooms and on playing fields, in the scientists' laboratories and the artists' studios, in the lines of the unemployed and in the homes of families in conflict, in long lines fighting for the rights of the persecuted and downtrodden, in the hospital ward, in the store or the shop.

And where do you work and play? God is there, if you are there. "The harvest is plentiful, but the laborers are few," Jesus said. We can be the laborers sent out into the harvest. We should be thankful for the opportunity to make a difference with our lives, to be co-workers with God to help those who are in need. You may say that you have nothing to give, that you are dependent upon your parents, but there is much we can all do. We can spend time with an old or infirm person. We can take food to a shut-in. We can listen with an understanding heart. Think of ways in which you can make a difference, and then do at least one of them today.

Prayer: "Teach us, good Lord, to serve you as you deserve: to give and not to count the cost; to fight and not to heed the wounds; to toil and not to seek for rest; to labor and not ask for any reward save that of knowing that we do your will" (St. Ignatius Loyola).

Thankful for Challenges

Psalm: Psalm 121:1 & 7 — I will lift up my eyes unto the hills. From where does my help come? My help comes from the Lord, who made heaven and earth.... The Lord will keep you from all evil; he will keep your life. The Lord will keep your going out and your coming in from this time forth and for evermore.

Reflection: Mountains are majestic, impassive, invincible, unmovable. They represent quiet strength. When a man is overwhelmed by the world in which he lives, he can seek sustenance for the living of each day by turning to the hills.

Mountains are also challenges. In his desperate hours, Jesus turned to the mountains for strength. When the crowds pressed too heavily upon him, he gave his Sermon on the Mount. His transfiguration was surely a mountain-top experience. It was in the mountains that he faced and conquered temptation. In the last days of his life, sensing impending doom, he went to the Mount of Olives and to Gethsemane to commune for spiritual sustenance.

Life would be drab and meaningless if we had no mountain-top experiences which moved us closer to God. As there is comfort and consolation in mountains, there is also challenge and adventure. "In mountaineering," said George Meredith, "every step is a debate between what you are and what you might become." This is true of the struggles in our lives. We need something which challenges our emotional, intellectual, and physical capacities, which exposes us to something beyond ourselves. If faith is not thought of as a challenge, it is not rightly understood. When we reach our high places, our adventure does not end there; we bring our experiences back with us to strengthen our daily lives and the lives of others.

Now, think about some trouble or challenge that confronts you and then consider how you can become a better person through facing it and working through it. If you don't know how to face it, lift up your eyes and ask for strength "from the Lord who made heaven and earth." Seek the high way to handle your struggle, and resolve to follow it.

As the Psalmist said, "I will lift up mine eyes unto the hills. From where does my help come? My help comes from the Lord, who made heaven and earth."

Prayer: I did not ask for this trouble I am facing, but I can see that I will be a better person — with greater strength and maturity — as I work through it, knowing that I can be guided by my faith in you, God. Help me to be strong and virtuous in confronting my struggles, and help me to grow from them. My help comes from you, O Lord, who made heaven and earth, and who watches over even the smallest sparrow.

DEVOTIONS FOR THE OUTDOORS

A Firm Foundation (for younger participants)

Scripture: Matthew 7:24–27 — Every one who hears these words of mine and does them will be like a wise man who built his house upon the rock; and the rain fell, and the floods came, and the winds blew and beat upon that house, but it did not fall, because it had been founded on the rock. And every one who hears these words of mine and does not do them will be like a foolish man who built his house upon the sand; and the rain fell, and the floods came, and the winds blew and beat against that house, and it fell; and great was the fall of it.

Lesson: This lesson may be illustrated with a rock and a handful of sand. Show how the sand shifts and gives way, and is therefore a weak foundation for a house. Show how the rock is strong and resilient, a solid foundation. What qualities of character can build a strong foundation for your life? What does Christ indicate to be the solid foundation upon which to build?

Group Singing: "Seek Ye First"

Prayer: Lord, help me to build my life upon the solid rock of your teachings so that when the difficult storms of life approach, I may stand firm and strong. Guide me upon the path of truth and righteousness so that I may live a full and decent life. Grant me the power to speak honestly, to live courageously, and to love others, just as Jesus taught and lived. Amen.

The Parable of the Sower (for younger participants)

Scripture: Matthew 13:3–9, 19–23 — Jesus told many things in parables, saying: "A sower went out to sow. And as he sowed, some seeds fell along the path, and the birds came and devoured them. Other seeds fell on rocky ground, where they had not much soil, and immediately they sprang up, since they had no depth of soil, but when the sun rose they were scorched; and since they had no root they withered away. Other seeds fell upon thorns, and the thorns grew up and choked them. Other seeds fell on good soil and brought forth grain, some a hundredfold, some sixty, some thirty. He who has ears, let him hear.... When any one hears the words of the kingdom and does not understand it, the evil one comes and snatches away what is sown in his heart; this is what has sown along the path. As for what was sown on rocky ground, this is he who hears the word and immediately receives it with joy; yet he has no root in himself, but endures for a while, and when tribulation or persecution arises on account of the word, immediately he falls away. As for what was sown among thorns, this is he who hears the word, but the cares of the world and the delight in riches choke the word, and it proves unfruitful. As for what was sown on good soil, this is he who hears the word and understands it; he indeed bears fruit, and yields, in one case a hundredfold, in another sixty, and in another thirty."

Reflection: This parable can be illustrated in two separate devotional sessions, the second a week after the first. On the first day, bring seeds to spread in four separate areas: (1) a busily traveled path or wayside, (2) a stony area, (3) a thorny or weedy area, and (4) good, fertile ground. Ask which seeds can be expected to develop into strong and healthy plants. On the second session, check the growth at each location. According to the parable, what is the good ground upon which we should root ourselves? How do we go about doing this?

Prayer: Thank you, Lord, for teaching us how to grow tall and strong. Help us to plant ourselves in good ground, rooted by faith in your love, so that we may bring forth good fruit. In your name we pray, Amen.

Brother Sun, Sister Moon

Psalm: Psalm 100—Make a joyful noise to the Lord, all the lands! Serve the Lord with gladness! Come into his presence with singing!

Know that the Lord is God! It is he that made us, and we are his; we are his people, and the sheep of his pasture.

Enter into his gates with thanksgiving, and his courts with praise! Give thanks to him, bless his name!

For the Lord is good; his steadfast love endures forever, and his faithfulness to all generations.

Reflection: Years ago, a young man named Francis lived in an Italian village known as Assisi. He was a remarkable man who grew to love and care for all of God's creatures. Statues of St. Francis today typically show him with a bird on his shoulder and a deer eating from his hand. Francis lived peaceably among God's creation, existing in harmony with the world and seeing the good in all beings. One of his most famous poems of praise was the "Canticle to the Sun," in which he called the sun his brother, the moon his sister, and the earth his mother.

Canticle to the Sun (by St. Francis of Assisi): O most high, almighty, good Lord God, praise, glory, honor, and all blessing belong to you!

Praised be my Lord God for all your creatures, and especially our brother, the Sun, who brings us the day and who brings us the light; fair is he, who shines with a very great splendor; he reveals you to us, O Lord.

Praised be my Lord for our sister, the Moon, and for the Stars, which you have set clear and lovely in the heavens.

Praised be my Lord for our brother, the Wind, and for Air and Cloud, calms and all weather, by which you sustain life in all creatures.

Praised be my Lord for our sister, Water, who is very serviceable to us and humble and precious and clean.

Praised be my Lord for our brother, Fire, through whom you give us light in darkness; and he is bright and pleasant and very mighty and strong.

Praised be my Lord for our mother, Earth, who sustains us and keeps us, and brings forth diverse fruits and flowers of many colors and grass.

Praised be my Lord for all those who pardon one another for love's sake, and who endure weakness and tribulation; blessed are they who peaceably shall endure, for you, O most High, shall crown them.

Praised be my Lord for our sister, Death, from which no man escapes. Blessed are they who are found walking by your most holy will.

Praise and bless the Lord, and give thanks unto him and serve him with great humility.

Prayer: The relationship which Francis of Assisi felt to God's world is similar to that which the unknown author of the following Sioux prayer experienced, when he asked God to "teach us to walk the soft earth as relatives to all that live."

Grandfather, Great Spirit, you have been always, and before you nothing has been. There is no one to pray to but you. The star nations all over the heavens are yours, and yours are the grasses of the earth. You are older than all need, older than all pain and prayer.

Grandfather, Great Spirit, all over the world the faces of living ones are alike. With tenderness they have come up out of the ground. Look upon your children, with children in their arms, that they may face the winds and walk the good road to the day of quiet.

Grandfather, Great Spirit, fill us with the light. Give us the strength to understand and the eyes to see. Teach us to walk the soft earth as relatives to all that live.

Help us, for without you we are nothing.

DEVOTIONS ON FRIENDSHIP AND LOVE

Learning to Be a Friend

This devotion involves both a skit and group participation:

The Day Before: Give each person an index card with the letters IALAC printed on it ("I Am Lovable and Capable") and offer these simple instructions: "Carry this card with you and, throughout the day, whenever someone says or does something insensitive or inconsiderate to you, rip off a portion of the card and give it to that person." (Usually, this activity is both fun and illuminating.)

Lesson: That evening, or the next morning, two or three people might begin the devotion by enacting a skit showing how easily we hurt others because of our own thoughtlessness and insensitivity. Too often, we neglect the gifts and individuality of others. Then, the scripture might be read and discussed.

Scripture: Matthew 25:31–46 — Then Jesus will say to those at his right hand, "Come O blessed of my Father, inherit the kingdom prepared for you from the foundation of the world; for I was hungry and you gave me food. I was thirsty and you gave me drink, I was a stranger and you welcomed me, I was naked and you clothed me, I was sick and you visited me, I was in prison and you came unto me." Then the righteous will answer him, "Lord, when did we see you hungry and feed you, or thirsty and give you drink? And when did we see you a stranger and welcome you, or naked and clothe you? And when did we see you sick or in prison and visit you?" And Jesus will answer them, "Truly, I say to you, as you did it to one of the least of my brothers and sisters, you did it to me."

Reflection: "Inasmuch as you did it unto the least of these, you have done it unto me." Jesus says that every action we take toward our fellow man is action toward God. We are the hands of God. We are co-partners with God in service to one another. Our faith in God is shown in how we act towards other people. A cross is not a cross when it contains a vertical line only. It becomes a cross when the horizontal is placed in position with it.

We must learn to be sympathetic and sensitive to others. Christ was asked, "When did we see you sick or hungry or in prison?" He answered, "Inasmuch as you have done it unto one of the least of these my brethren, ye have done it unto me." This is the height of sensitivity — not based on interest in oneself, but in others.

If you give of yourself to others, if you do unto others as you would be done by others, if you love and share — you are showing your love and faith in God. If you do not do these things — you are on the most certain route to an unfulfilling and empty life.

Group Singing: "They'll Know We Are Christians by Our Love"

Prayer: O God, may we appreciate one another more and more, knowing that we are like ships that pass in the night, each unaware of the rich cargo the other carries beneath its deck. May we be kind and sympathetic. May no one be afflicted but we are afflicted. May we bear one another's burdens. Amen.

Who Is My Neighbor, My Friend?

Scripture: Luke 10:25–37 — A lawyer stood up to put Jesus to the test, saying, "Teacher, what shall I do to inherit eternal life?" Jesus said to him,

"What is written in the law? How do you read?" And the lawyer answered, "You shall love the Lord your God with all your heart, and with all your soul, and with all your strength, and with all your mind; and your neighbor as yourself." And Jesus said to him, "You have answered right; do this, and you will live."

But the lawyer, desiring to justify himself, said to Jesus, "And who is my neighbor?" Jesus replied, "A man was going down from Jerusalem to Jericho, and he fell among robbers, who stripped him and beat him, and departed, leaving him half dead. Now by chance a priest was going down that road; and when he saw him he passed by on the other side. So likewise a Levite, when he came to the place and saw him, passed by on the other side. But a Samaritan, as he journeyed, came to where he was; and when he saw him, he had compassion, and went to him and bound up his wounds, pouring on oil and wine; then he set him on his own beast and brought him to an inn, and took care of him. And the next day he took out two coins and gave them to the innkeeper, saying, 'Take care of him; and whatever more you spend, I will repay you when I come back.' Which of these three, do you think, proved neighbor to the man who fell among the robbers?" The lawyer said, "The one who showed mercy on him." And Jesus said to him, "Go and do likewise." (Consider having participants act out the parable.)

Reflection: "You shall love your neighbor as yourself." Jesus expressed here the care and concern we should have for each other: just as much as we have for ourselves.

The Parable of the Good Samaritan illustrates genuine selflessness. You can imagine the priest, walking by, holding high his robes, so as not to dirty his hem in the foul mess. You can picture the Levite, so tenderhearted that he passes with his face turned away so as not to behold the bloody sight. And there is the Good Samaritan, binding the wounds of a man who was suffering.

These three figures represent pretty much all classes and conditions of people: those of us who are selfish, clinging at all costs to what is ours; those of us who suffer at the thought of the suffering of others, but only because we feel ourselves in their place; and those of us who serve because we have love to give. Which type of person are you?

Dr. Albert Schweitzer was the type who had love to give. He was a brilliant man who had made remarkable achievements in many fields — as a physician, organist, author, theologian; all this he left behind to help the sick and dying in Africa. A newspaperwoman once told him, "You have sacrificed so much to come to Africa." "No," he responded. "I have sacrificed nothing.... It is my privilege."

"Which of these three, do you think, proved neighbor to the man who fell among the robbers?" Jesus asked. The lawyer answered, "The one who showed mercy on him." And Jesus said to him, "Go and do likewise." The Kingdom of God comes, not by doing one good deed, but by truly loving and caring for our neighbors as ourselves.

Prayer: O God, show us our duty to one another. May we feel some responsibility for each other. May we see that every dark place is but the shadow cast by someone who ought to reflect your light and life and love. Help us to "go and do likewise" by showing love to our neighbors.

Love Among Friends

Scripture: John 15:9–13 — Jesus said, "As the Father has loved me, so have I loved you; abide in my love. If you keep my commandments, you will abide in my love, just as I have kept my Father's commandments and abide in his love. These things have I spoken to you, that my joy may be in you, and that your joy may be full. This is my commandment, that you love one another as I have loved you. Greater love has no man than this, that a man lay down his life for his friends."

Reflection: We will be (have been) a group for many days. We will learn (have learned) a great many things in our time together, but our greatest lesson is learning to live together as one, to care about each other, to watch over each other, and to help one another. It's all about learning to love, as though we are brothers and sisters. The message of Jesus was clear; it was not a suggestion or a proposal, but a command: love one another in the true spirit of friendship. It is the only full joy.

It is not always easy for me to love, but without love, I am nothing. The Apostle Paul wrote that, without love, I am but a "noisy gong or a clanging cymbal.... If I have prophetic powers, and understand all mysteries and all knowledge, and if I have all faith, so as to remove mountains, but have not love, I am nothing. If I give away all I have, and if I deliver my body to be burned, but have not love, I gain nothing" (I Corinthians 13:1–3).

He goes on to define love by telling us what love is and what it is not: "Love is patient and kind; love is not jealous or boastful; it is not arrogant or rude. Love does not insist on its own way; it is not irritable or resentful; it does not rejoice at wrong, but rejoices in the right. Love bears all things, believes all things, hopes all things, endures all things" (I Corinthians 13: 4–7).

By learning to be patient and kind in our dealings with each other, by avoiding jealousy and boastfulness — which are merely forms of self-love — by rejoicing in each other's accomplishments, we are not only working together as a unit, we are also understanding the nature of love.

[If the group has already grown close together, personal words at this point would be appropriate. Likewise, if a group has had conflict, personal words may be poignant.]

This is what we hopefully will learn (have learned) during our time together. Take note of the words of I John 4:20–21: If any one says, "I love God," and hates his brother, he is a liar; for he who does not love his brother whom he has seen, cannot love God whom he has not seen. And this commandment we have from him, that he who loves God should love his brother also.

Prayer of St. Francis: Lord, make me an instrument of your peace. Where there is hatred, let me sow love; where there is injury, pardon; where there is doubt, faith;

Where there is despair, hope; where there is darkness, light; and where there is sadness, joy.

O divine Master, grant that I may not so much seek to be consoled as to console, to be understood as to understand, to be loved as to love.

For it is in giving that we receive, it is in pardoning that we are pardoned, and it is in dying that we are born to eternal life.

Amen.

Chapter 11

Inspiration for Leaders

What Makes a Good Leader?

There is no formula for the effective youth leader, but all good leaders share common traits.

Good leaders are positive people. They offer encouragement and support. They realize that sometimes even a simple smile or kind word can make a difference.

Good leaders listen. They realize that often what others need most is an attentive ear, and they are not so egotistical to think that they cannot learn something from others.

Good leaders involve the team in both planning and implementation. They work as part of the team, guiding rather than dictating.

Good leaders challenge others. If people are not pushed beyond where they already are, they will not grow. The mind, like the body, must be stretched and challenged or it will stagnate.

Good leaders take people places they might otherwise not go — to new insights, skills, joys, and spiritual heights.

Good leaders realize that what they do has influence. Abraham Lincoln and Mother Teresa were both influenced by others; so was Adolf Hitler. They, in turn, shaped history, for good or for ill.

Good leaders persist. They encounter obstacles and conflicts but persevere to work through them.

Good leaders maintain a sense of humor. Humor lightens us and allows us to put things in perspective. Laughter is good for the soul.

Good leaders possess vision. They look forward and imagine possibilities.

Good leaders dare to be different, to be creative, to follow the less-traveled path of truth and goodness.

Good leaders care about the environment, about the world, about living things, and especially about people.

Good leaders convey a passion for life and for work. They see beauty in simple things. They enjoy people, and they express that joy.

Good leaders are worthy to be emulated. They strive to be what they hope to nurture in others. They themselves are curious, respectful, disciplined, open, joyful, and enthusiastic.

— Roger E. Barrows

SECRETS OF LEADERSHIP

- Keep one step ahead.
- Take care of the little jobs and the big jobs will take care of themselves.
- Be proud of what you are doing.
- Make a project seem profitable, fun, and easy.
- Never say, "I can't."
- Be persistent; never give up.
- Have a positive attitude.
- Do a good job so you won't have to do it again.
- Help the followers to lead; show that leaders can follow.
- Follow through.
- Be serious and put forth your greatest effort.
- Be patient with people.
- Set a goal and work toward it.
- Be sincere.
- Plan ahead.
- Be enthusiastic.
- Patience and humility lead the way.
- Keep your team inspired.
- If you treat people kindly, they will treat you kindly.
- Listen to others' ideas.

- Plan thoroughly; follow through.
- Make people feel wanted.
- If your mind can conceive it and believe it, you can achieve it.
- Care for everyone and work as a whole.
- Reach out to everyone.
- Believe in yourself.
- Every human being wants desperately to be a part of something bigger than SELF.
- All phonies are eventually found out.
- Never shut out the ideas of another person just because you are a leader.
- Know that, for every human action, there is a motivation behind it.
- Nothing is impossible.
- Everyone is an individual who deserves to be recognized for just being alive.
- Know God as a friend and advisor.
- Everyone needs to feel needed, wanted, accepted. Give each person this and you have a worker.
- People tend to support those things they helped to create.
- Expect more from yourself than from others.
- Respect everyone for what he or she is.
- Be a dreamer.
- Stand up for what you believe in.
- Be open-minded.
- Use your sense of humor.
- Respect other people; keep their respect in you.
- Love and understanding can solve the problems of the world.

> — Compiled from students'
> secrets of leadership at
> Florida Association of
> Student Council Summer
> Workshops

IF

by Rudyard Kipling

If you can keep your head when all about you
Are losing theirs and blaming it on you;

If you can trust yourself when all men doubt you,
But make allowance for their doubting too;
If you can wait and not be tired by waiting,
Or being lied about, don't deal in lies,
Or being hated don't give way to hating,
And yet don't look too good, nor talk too wise:

If you can dream — and not make dreams your master;
If you can think — and not make thoughts your aim,
If you can meet with Triumph and Disaster
And treat those two impostors just the same;
If you can bear to hear the truth you've spoken
Twisted by knaves to make a trap for fools,
Or watch the things you gave your life to, broken,
And stoop and build 'em up with worn-out tools:

If you can make one heap of all your winnings
And risk it on one turn of pitch-and-toss,
And lose, and start again at your beginnings
And never breathe a word about your loss;
If you can force your heart and nerve and sinew
To serve your turn long after they are gone,
And so hold on when there is nothing in you
Except the Will which says to them: "Hold on!"

If you can talk with crowds and keep your virtue,
Or walk with Kings — nor lose the common touch,
If neither foes nor loving friends can hurt you,
If all men count with you, but none too much;
If you can fill the unforgiving minute
With sixty seconds' worth of distance run,
Yours is the Earth and everything that's in it,
And — which is more — you'll be a Man, my son!

QUOTATIONS FOR LEADERS

On Encouragement...

There is a story — whether true or myth, it is characteristic of him — that when Thomas Edison was working on improving his first light bulb, he handed a finished bulb to a young helper, who nervously carried it upstairs, step by step. At the last moment, the boy dropped it. The whole team had to work another 24 hours to make another bulb. Edison looked around, then handed it to the same boy. The gesture probably changed the boy's life. Edison knew that more than the bulb was at stake.

— James D. Newton,
Uncommon Friends

Though no one can go back and make a brand new start, anyone can start from now and make a brand new ending.

— Anonymous

On Valuing Others...

If you do not find God in the very next person you meet, it is a waste of time looking further.

— Gandhi

You are not your brother's keeper; you are your brother.

— Hindu belief

There are two types of people — those who come into a room and say, "Well, here I am!" and those who come in and say, "Ah, there you are."

— Frederick L. Collins

On Example...

Example is not the main thing in influencing others. It is the only thing.

— Albert Schweitzer

"One preaches well who lives well," said Sancho, "and that's all the divinity I can understand."

— Cervantes

On Making a Difference...

Die when I may, I want it said of me by those who knew me best, that I always plucked a thistle and planted a flower where I thought a flower would grow.

— Abraham Lincoln

Even if I knew certainly the world would end tomorrow, I would plant an apple tree today.

> — Martin Luther

The greatest use of life is to spend it for something that will outlast it.

> — William James

There are two ways of spreading light: to be the candle or the mirror that reflects it.

> — Edith Wharton

Let no one ever come to you without leaving better and happier.

> — Mother Teresa

Be the change you want to see in the world.

> — Gandhi

My doctrine is this, that if we see cruelty or wrong that we have the power to stop, and do nothing, we make ourselves sharers in the guilt.

> — Anna Sewell

He who governed the world before I was born shall take care of it likewise when I am dead. My part is to improve the present moment.

> — John Wesley

On Service...

We make a living by what we get.
We make a life by what we give.

> — Winston Churchill

I don't know what your destiny will be, but one thing I know: the only ones among you who will be really happy are those who will have sought and found how to serve.

> — Albert Schweitzer

What do we live for, if it is not to make life less difficult for each other.

— George Eliot

Service to others is the rent you pay for your room here on earth.

— Muhammad Ali

Give, and it shall be given unto you; good measure, pressed down, and shaken together, and running over, shall men give into your bosom. For with the same measure that you mete withal it shall be measured to you again.

— Luke 6:38

It is one of the most beautiful compensations in life, that no man can sincerely try to help another without helping himself.

— Ralph Waldo Emerson

Never look down on anybody, unless you plan to help them up.

— Jesse Jackson

On Love...

But I say unto you who hear, love your enemies, do good to them who hate you, bless them that curse you, and pray for them which spitefully use you.... And as you would that men should do to you, do also to them likewise.

— Luke 6:27–28, 31

You get so much more out of yourself if you forget about yourself and care about other people.

— Maya Angelou

It is not what you keep but what you give that makes you happy.

— Benjamin Mays

Those who bring sunshine to the lives of others cannot keep it from themselves.

— James Barrie,
A Window in Thrums

The best way to cheer yourself up is to try to cheer somebody else up.

— Mark Twain

The man who foolishly does me wrong, I will return to him the protection of my most ungrudging love; and the more evil comes from him, the more good shall go from me.

— Buddha

Love, and you will be loved.

— Ralph Waldo Emerson

The means to gain happiness is to throw out from oneself like a spider in all directions an adhesive web of love, and to catch in it all that comes.

— Leo Tolstoy

People need loving the most when they deserve it the least.

— John Harrigan

A part of kindness consists in loving people more than they deserve.

— Joseph Joubert

The salvation of man is through love and in love.

— Victor Frankl, *Man's Search for Meaning*

Love thy neighbor is a command, not a piece of advice.

— Bono

On Friendship...

The only reward of virtue is virtue; the only way to have a friend is to be one.

— Ralph Waldo Emerson, "Friendship"

Show me your friends, and I'll show you your future.

— Anon.

All that we send into the lives of others comes back into our own.

— Edwin Markham

On Conscience...

The only tyrant I accept in this world is the "still small voice" within me.

— Mahatma Gandhi

Cowardice asks the question, Is it safe? Expediency asks the question, Is it polite? Vanity asks the question, Is it popular? But conscience asks the question, Is it right? And there comes a time when one must take a position that is neither safe, nor polite, nor popular — but one must take it because it's right.

— Martin Luther King, Jr.

On Difficulties...

Let me not pray to be sheltered from dangers, but to be fearless in facing them.

— Rabindranath Tagore

It is not the critic who counts; not the man who points out how the strong man stumbled, or where the doer of deed could have done better. The credit belongs to the man who is actually in the arena, whose face is marred by dust and sweat and blood; who strives valiantly; who errs and comes short again and again; who knows the great enthusiasms, the great devotions; who spends himself in a worthy cause; who, at the best, knows in the end the triumph of high achievement and who at the worst, if he fails, at least fails while daring greatly, so that his place shall never be with those timid souls who know neither victory or defeat.

— Theodore Roosevelt

The best way out is always through.

— Robert Frost

On Courage...

You have to accept whatever comes, and the only important thing is that you meet it with courage and with the best that you have to give.

— Eleanor Roosevelt

On Excellence...

Excellence— The quality of a person's life is in direct proportion to their commitment to excellence, regardless of their chosen field of endeavor.

— Vince Lombardi

On Failure...

To fail is not unworthy, since it implies that one had attempted something.

— George Clemenceau

Failure is only the opportunity to begin again, more intelligently.

— Henry Ford

The men who try to do something and fail are infinitely better than those who try to do nothing and succeed.

— Lloyd Jones

Many of life's failures are people who did not realize how close they were to success when they gave up.

— Thomas Edison

I don't know the key to success, but the key to failure is trying to please everybody.

— Bill Cosby

On Success...

I like to see a man proud of the place in which he lives. I like to see a man who lives in it so that his place will be proud of him.

— Abraham Lincoln

Life is not a matter of holding good cards, but of playing poor ones well.

— Robert Louis Stevenson

That man is a success who has lived well, laughed often and loved much; who has gained the respect of intelligent men and the love of children;

who has filled his niche and accomplished his task;
who leaves the world better than he found it...
who never lacked appreciation of earth's beauty or failed to express it;
who looked at the best in others and gave the best he had.

— Robert Louis Stevenson

Success comes in cans; failure comes in can'ts.

— Anon.

On Humility...

I believe the first test of a truly great man is his humility.

— John Ruskin

We have to acquire a peace and balance of mind such that we can give every word of criticism its due weight, and humble ourselves before every word of praise.

— Dag Hammarskjold,
Markings

On Taking Action...

All that is necessary for the triumph of evil is that good men do nothing.

— Edmund Burke

The man who moves a mountain begins by carrying away small stones.

— Chinese proverb

The wind of God is always blowing; but I must hoist my sail.

— Anon.

Never let the fear of striking out get in your way.

— Babe Ruth

A journey of a thousand miles begins with a single step.

— old Chinese proverb

He has half the deed done, who has made a beginning.

— Horace

On Patience and Persistence...

Nothing in this world can take the place of persistence. Talent will not; nothing is more common than unsuccessful people with talent. Genius will not; unrewarded genius is almost a proverb. Education will not; the world is full of educated derelicts. Persistence and determination alone are omnipotent. The slogan "press on" has solved and always will solve the problems of the human race.

— Calvin Coolidge

In any contest between power and patience, bet on patience.

— W.B. Prescott

On Joy and Happiness...

Joy is a net of love by which you can catch souls.

— Mother Teresa

Many persons have a wrong idea of what constitutes true happiness. It is not attained through self-gratification but through fidelity to a worthy purpose.

— Helen Keller

Happiness is when what you think, what you say and what you do are in harmony.

— Mahatma Gandhi

The human race has one really effective weapon, and that is laughter.

— Mark Twain

If you want others to be happy, practice compassion; if you want to be happy, practice compassion.

— Dalai Lama

Sharing joy brings double joy; sharing sorrow brings half-sorrow.

— Anonymous

On Believing in Yourself...

Argue for your limitations, and sure enough, they're yours.

— Richard Bach, *Illusions*

Whether you think you can or think you can't — you are right.

— Henry Ford

There is a time in every man's education when he arrives at the conviction that envy is ignorance; that imitation is suicide.... Trust thyself: every heart vibrates to that iron string.

— Ralph Waldo Emerson,
"Self-Reliance"

It is easy in the world to live after the world's opinions; it is easy in solitude to live after our own; but the Great Man is he who in the midst of the crowd keeps with perfect sweetness the independence of solitude.

— Ralph Waldo Emerson

The answer to the last appeal of what is right lies within a man's own breast. Trust thyself.

— Aristotle

On Dreams and Aspirations...

Ideals are like stars; you will not succeed in touching them with your hands, but like the seafaring man on the desert of waters, you choose them as your guides, and, following them, you reach your destination.

— Carl Schurz

Far away there in the sunshine are my highest aspirations. I may not reach them, but I can look up and see their beauty, believe in them, and try to follow where they lead.

— L.M. Alcott

Only he who attempts the absurd is capable of achieving the impossible.

— Miguel de Unamuno

If one advances confidently in the direction of his dreams, and endeavors to live the life which he has imagined, he will meet with a success unexpected in common hours.

> — Henry David Thoreau,
> *Walden*

Love not what you are but only what you may become.

> — Cervantes, *Don Quixote*

A man's reach should exceed his grasp or what's a heaven for?

> — Robert Browning

One ship drives east and another drives west
    with the selfsame winds that blow.
'Tis the set of the sails and not the gales
    which tells us the way to go.
Like the winds of the sea are the ways of fate,
    as we voyage along through life;
'Tis the set of a soul that decides its goals,
    and not the calm or strife.

> — Anon.

On Appreciating and Nurturing the World...

This we know, the earth does not belong to man, man belongs to the earth. All things are connected, like the blood which unites one family. Whatever befalls the earth befalls the sons of the earth. Man did not weave the web of life, he is merely a strand in it. Whatever he does to the web he does to himself.

> — Chief Seattle

Most people live on the world, not in it.

> — John Muir

To be whole and harmonious, man must also know the music of the beaches and the woods. He must find the thing of which he is only an infinitesimal part and nurture it and love it, if he is to live.

> — William O. Douglas

The most beautiful thing we can experience is the mysterious. It is the source of all true art and science. One to whom this emotion is a stranger, who can no longer pause to wonder and stand rapt in awe, is as good as dead; his eyes are closed.

— Albert Einstein

I believe that a leaf of grass is no less than the journey-work of the stars.

— Walt Whitman,
Song of Myself

Climb the mountains and get their good tidings.... The winds will blow their own freshness into you, and the storms their energy, while cares will drop off like Autumn leaves.

— John Muir

There are no passengers on spaceship Earth — only crew.

— Buckminster Fuller

On Living Fully...

May you live all the days of your life.

— Jonathan Swift

The glory of God is in man fully alive.

— St. Iraneus
(2nd century)

I always take life seriously; that's why I find it so funny.

— Debra Barra

On Character...

Better keep yourself clean and bright; you are the window through which you must see the world.

— George Bernard Shaw

We often pray for purity, unselfishness, for the highest qualities of character and forget that these things must be earned.

— Lyman Abbott

The highest reward for man's toil is not what he gets for it but what he becomes by it.

— John Ruskin

Though we travel the world over to find the beautiful, we must carry it with us or we will find it not.

— Ralph Waldo Emerson

What lies behind us and what lies before us are tiny matters compared to what lies within us.

— William Morrow

First keep the peace within yourself;
then you can also bring peace to others.

— Thomas a Kempis

Do not pray for easy lives. Pray to be stronger men! Do not pray for tasks equal to your powers. Pray for powers equal to your tasks.

— Phillips Brooks

On Perceptions...

Change your thoughts and you change your world.

— Norman Vincent Peale

A pessimist sees the difficulty in every opportunity; an optimist sees the opportunity in every difficulty.

— Winston Churchill

Never measure the height of a mountain until you have reached the top. Then you will see how low it was.

— Dag Hammarskjold

One does not discover new lands without consenting to lose sight of the shore.

— Andre Gide

Never lose a holy curiosity.

— Albert Einstein

Nothing here below is profane for those who know how to see. On the contrary, everything is sacred.

— Teilhard de Chardin

I see each person who comes into my life as an opportunity to learn something about human nature, and myself. Each person has a lesson to teach me. I try to learn.

— Holly Archer

I will permit no man to narrow and degrade my soul by making me hate him.

— Booker T. Washington

Life is 10% what happens to me, and 90% how I react to it. And so it is with you. We are in charge of our attitudes.

— Charles Swindell

If we live good lives, the times are good. As we are, so are the times.

— St. Augustine

On Learning...

I hear and I forget. I see and I understand. I do and I remember.

— Chinese proverb

To educate a man in mind, and not in morals, is to educate a menace to society.

— Theodore Roosevelt

Nothing in life is to be feared. It is only to be understood.

— Marie Curie

Index